The Play of Light

SUNY SERIES
LITERATURE...IN THEORY

SERIES EDITORS

David E Johnson *Comparative Literature, University at Buffalo*
Scott Michaelsen *English, Michigan State University*

SERIES ADVISORY BOARD

Nahum D. Chandler *African American Studies, University of California, Irvine*
Rebecca Comay *Philosophy and Comparative Literature, University of Toronto*
Marc Crépon *Philosophy, École Normale Supérieure, Paris*
Jonathan Culler *Comparative Literature, Cornell University*
Johanna Drucker *Design Media Arts and Information Studies, University of California, Los Angeles*
Christopher Fynsk *Modern Thought, Aberdeen University*
Rodolphe Gasché *Comparative Literature, University at Buffalo*
Martin Hägglund *Comparative Literature, Yale University*
Carol Jacobs *German and Comparative Literature, Yale University*
Peggy Kamuf *French and Comparative Literature, University of Southern California*
David Marriott *History of Consciousness, University of California, Santa Cruz*
Steven Miller *English, University at Buffalo*
Alberto Moreiras *Hispanic Studies, Texas A&M University*
Patrick O'Donnell *English, Michigan State University*
Pablo Oyarzún *Teoría del Arte, Universidad de Chile*
Scott Cutler Shershow *English, University of California, Davis*
Henry Sussman *German and Comparative Literature, Yale University*
Samuel Weber *Comparative Literature, Northwestern University*
Ewa Ziarek *Comparative Literature, University at Buffalo*

The Play of Light

Jacques Roubaud, Emmanuel Hocquard, and Friends

Ann Smock

Cover illustration: Félix Vallotton woodcut, *la Mer*, 1893, courtesy of the Bibliothèque Nationale de France.

Published by State University of New York Press, Albany
© 2021 State University of New York
All rights reserved

Printed in the United States of America

No part of this book may be used or reproduced in any manner whatsoever without written permission. No part of this book may be stored in a retrieval system or transmitted in any form or by any means including electronic, electrostatic, magnetic tape, mechanical, photocopying, recording, or otherwise without the prior permission in writing of the publisher.

For information, contact State University of New York Press, Albany, NY
www.sunypress.edu

Library of Congress Cataloging-in-Publication Data

Names: Smock, Ann, author
Title: The play of light : Jacques Roubaud, Emmanuel Hocquard, and friends
Description: Albany : State University of New York Press, [2021] | Series: SUNY series SUNY series, literature . . . in theory | Includes bibliographical references and index.
Identifiers: ISBN 9781438481494 (hardcover : alk. paper) | 9781438481500 (paperback : alk. paper) | ISBN 9781438481517 (e-book)
Further information is available at the Library of Congress.

CONTENTS

ACKNOWLEDGMENTS vii

Introduction: Varieties of Light 1
1 "Thy blackness is a spark" 17
2 "Birth was the death of him" 49
3 Palindromes 71
4 Beware of Enigmas 83
5 Is This a Dream? 109
6 Interlude: All and Nothing 119
7 Fin' Amors 133
8 Diaphanous 163
9 Entre Deux 175

NOTES 185
BIBLIOGRAPHY 223
INDEX 229

ACKNOWLEDGMENTS

The author wants to thank Éditions du Seuil for permission to reproduce poems from *Le Grand incendie de Londres. Récit, avec incises et bifurcations (1985-87)* and *Poésie: (Récit)*, by Jacques Roubaud; Éditions Gallimard for permission to reproduce poems and parts of poems from *Quelque chose noir, La pluralité des mondes de Lewis, La forme d'une ville change, hélas, plus vite que le coeur des humains,* and *Churchill 40* by Roubaud; Bénédicte Vilgram and Bernard Rival, of Théatre Typographique, for permission to reproduce parts of "Mont Cicada" from Roubaud's *La fenêtre veuve*; Catherine deléobardy, of Éditions A. M. Métailié, for permission to reproduce material from Roubaud's *Echanges de la lumière*; Patrizia Atzei of Éditions NOUS, for permission to reproduce poems from *Tridents* by Roubaud; Vibeke Madsen, of P.O.L, for permission to reproduce poems and parts of poems by Emmanuel Hocquard from *Un privé à Tanger, Théorie des tables, Un test de solitude, Conditions de lumière, L'Invention du verre* and *Méditations photographiqus sur l'idée simple de nudité*; also poems and poem fragments from Anne Portugal's *Le plus simple appareil, De quoi faire un mur* and *et comment nous voilà moins épais*; materials from Volume I of Danielle Collobert's *Oeuvres*; and from *Poèmes de métro* by Jacques Jouet.

The author is also very grateful for permission granted to reproduce poems and parts of poems in translation. I thank Anne Portugal for permission to cite material from *Nude*; Joshua Edwards, of Carnarium Books, for permission to cite parts of Hocquard's *The Invention of Glass*; Michael Palmer and Peter Gizzi, of o-blek editions, for permission to cite poems and poem fragments from Hocquard's *Theory of Tables*; Cole Swensen, of La Presse, for permission to reproduce material from *Exchanges on Light* and *Sleep Preceded by Saying Poetry* by Roubaud, and from *Conditions of Light* by Hocquard; Rosmarie Waldrop, of Burning Deck, for permission to cite from Hocquard's *A Test of Solitude* and from *Crosscut Universe* by Norma Cole. Finally, I thank John O'Brien, of Dalkey Archive Press, for permission to reproduce material from *Some Thing Black*, *The Plurality of Worlds of Lewis*, *The Form of a City Changes Faster, Alas, Than the Human Heart*, and *The Great Fire of London*, all by Roubaud.

Small portions of reworked material from four previously published articles appear in this book: "Cloudy Roubaud," *Representations* 86 (Spring 2004): 141-74; "Everyday," *l'esprit créateur* 49, no. 2 (Summer 2009): 62-76; "Jacques Roubaud's 'Sonnetomanie,'" *Literary Imagination* 12, no. 3 (2010): 344-54; and "Geranium Logic," *Qui Parle* 21, no. 2 (2013): 27-59.

I am especially grateful for the friendly encouragement offered me as I was finishing this book by Pierre Alferi, Norma Cole, Peter Gizzi, Robert Kaufman, Michael Palmer, Anne Portugal, Jean-Jacques Poucel, Cole Swensen, and Rosmarie Waldrop.

I've been lucky to have had the sure and generous guidance of Rebecca Colesworthy at SUNY Press.

Michael Sheringham was a unique champion of twentieth- and twenty-first-century French poetry. I had the great good fortune to know him and to participate in two stimulating and festive poetry events he organized. I wish I could show *The Play of Light* to him. I hope that Priscilla Sheringham will find some pages to like in it.

And I will be extremely glad if my Berkeley friends and acquaintances—teachers, students, and allies past and present—will sense in my book a spirited salute to them.

The Play of Light is dedicated to one among them: Carol Dolcini.

Introduction
Varieties of Light

Emmanuel Hocquard, one of the poets to whom this book responds, takes a great interest in a particular kind of question: the kind that, as he puts it, has no object. For its ostensible object is the reply.

> Si la réponse est *ceci*
> qu'est-ce que ceci? est une question sans objet
>
> If the reply is *this*
> what is this? is a question with no object. (*Theory of Tables*, 34)[1]

In these lines you may sense the tremor or blink that frequently occurs in Hocquard's pages—it can bring you up short—when something opaque suddenly turns transparent, or vice versa: clarity abruptly blackens. Dark/light. Bright/dim. For the question whose object is instead its answer seems by turns so obvious there is no point asking it *and* utterly inscrutable. Thus, the blackness of a fish's back glimpsed by the protagonist of Hocquard's novel (*Aerea in the Forests of Manhattan*), alternates swiftly in sea water with the white flash of the fish's belly. Curved surfaces of fallen leaves underfoot in Manhattan's Riverside Park cast shadows on each other, while their thin edges catch the pale winter sunlight and gleam. "Alternation of shimmering and fading, of brilliance and matte" (*Aerea in the forests*, 104/*Aerea dans les forêts*, 102).[2]

"Toutes les évidences lui sont mystère," Anne-Marie Albiach wrote, and Hocquard cites her, as though the observation applied to him.³ Everything obvious is for him an enigma. Each clue is a mystery, everything clear obscure. Sometimes in the blink between the light and the dark something seems to come unfastened just for an instant.

> Une fraction de seconde
> un trou de lumière grand
> comme une pointe d'aiguille (*Théorie des tables*, 29)

> A fraction of a second
> a light-hole as large
> as the point of a needle (*Theory of Tables*, 29)

Something opens and snaps shut, like a camera's shutter, and in the interval (as large as it is tiny) you see—what you do not. A "nonvisible" is suddenly exposed.

Jacques Roubaud, the other protagonist in this book, places his own variety of odd question at the heart of his life's work. I believe he calls it "l'auto-énigme" because it bears solely upon itself. The question is: What is it? Or you might say, the question asks, What am I? Dominic Di Bernardi's translation of "auto-énigme" is "self-riddle."

Roubaud sometimes calls it "mute question"—when he is thinking of the young knight Percival, dumbstruck in the palace of the Fisher King. Had Percival known what question to ask when he saw the mysterious objects passing before him, shining lance and gleaming cup, he might have cured the ailing king and redeemed his wasted land. But no: "question sans question," "question muette."⁴

The questionless question, inasmuch as it is the answer that nothing can provide, resembles light, which nothing illuminates. According to Pseudo Dionysius, an early sixth-century Christian Neoplatonist who inhabits Roubaud's universe, light makes all things visible, but is not itself among these things. It does not itself figure among the visible things of this world. Light itself is black. At the heart of Roubaud's work there is "some thing black," an enigma. It is the black beauty of light.

So, darkness and light, dark tones and pale, blindness and sight contribute a good deal to this book. Their contrasts and paradoxical interchanges play a big part. Their reversals, too, as in silver halide photography, where black is also light, as Hocquard observes. Roubaud cites Faraday remarking that in Talbot's early negatives "all the lights are black and all the shadows luminous."[5] Roubaud's black sun, the awful, closed countenance of light when it withdraws into itself, leaving the world derelict, is doubled by a snow-white sun, the star of melancholy and memory. There is "some thing black"[6] in Roubaud, and then too "the light, there // the light // there, there // in the street // lapped up light / the light, there."

> La lumière, là
>
> la lumière
>
> là, là
> dans la rue
>
> la lumière bue,
> la lumière, là
>
> la lumière,
>
> là   (*Poésie*, 13)[7]

I count on such dark/light, black/white juxtapositions to provide this book with an unobtrusive underlying order: a pattern that can surface from time to time, but also recede, modestly.

For several different qualities and colors of light, and also varying degrees of obscurity—fog and cloudiness—pass through this book as well. The light of dawn that slowly encroaches on the circle of electric light that has shone since long before daybreak on Roubaud's desk. The weakened light late in the evening hesitating over the uneven surface of a wall, suggesting to him a quivering fountain with nymphs all around it. The agitated clouds reflected in a puddle of rainwater, seen from a streaming window. The rainbow hues of darkness, thanks to Hocquard. "For in darkness too are rainbow colors," he writes, citing Lucretius.[8] The gleam of ceramic shards, laid out on an archeologist's table on the Mediterranean coast where Hocquard grew up, or the sparkle of glass strewn in pieces on another table—this one set up one morning at a garage sale, I gather (on the banks of the Delaware, where he visited)—to display old bric-a-brac. Among the jumbled items were several made of "Depression Glass." Dinner plates, ashtrays, bud vases shone with a singular brilliance in the morning sun. He lists them, and names their colors.

Green, pink, amber, white, black amethyst; more rarely blue.

(*Ce qui n'advient pas* [unpaginated; my translation])[9]

He called one of his poetry books *L'Invention du verre* (*The Invention of Glass*)[10] and another *Conditions de lumière*.[11] There he pictured language as a trove of radiant fragments: one has but to gather some up, he said, and place them, gleaming among themselves, in a clear glass bowl. Roubaud contemplates pale honey spreading across a white plate, and also urges, "Watch how yellow penetrates fields and leaves, how blue gains the cedars, watch the violet petals of the sun."[12]

The Play of Light will follow an uneven path, with one train of thought often sidetracking to another. My aim is not to offer a complete account of the work of any of the writers I consider, or to construct, based on analyses of their texts, an argument about the condition of poetry in France from the 1970s to the present. I do not see a consistent theory made of concepts or preoccupations common to them all. Instead, I propose to move about among the books of Roubaud and of Hocquard, of Danielle Collobert, of Jacques Jouet and Anne Portugal, drawing some of these books into a juxtaposition that shows each one to great advantage (I hope), while providing at the same time a milieu suitable for brief appearances by a few philosophical hypotheses, bearing on identity, for example, on not-being and being, on communication, and secrets. These will just pass through like the colored lights that Anne Portugal evokes when she describes people and poems passing through public gardens. "They have the fugitive state of leaves, of fountains," she observes: "the dazzle of lights, or of winter's extreme nudity. They are among others. They are the others" ("The Garden," 40).[13]

They—the hypotheses, that is, that pass through this book—owe a good deal to certain philosophers: to Ludwig Wittgenstein, for one, because both Roubaud and Hocquard refer to him explicitly. Hocquard adopts one of his statements practically as a motto: "A poetic work"—a *philosophical* one, actually, in Wittgenstein's words—"consists essentially of elucidations."[14] Hocquard liked to take the stance of a private eye, and I don't doubt he had *Philosophical Investigations* in mind when referring, in a voice like Philip Marlowe's, to the murky affairs in language that he has to clear up. Various propositions from the *Tractatus* are like touchstones for him: "The world is all that is the case," for example. Or, "The subject does not belong to the world: rather, it is a limit of the world." Hocquard's insular side, his "tests of solitude" continually recall the solipcism in Wittgenstein which, "when its implications are followed out strictly, coincides with pure realism. The self of solipcism shrinks to a point without extension, and there remains the reality co-ordinated with it."[15]

Roubaud, too, keeps a collection of Wittgenstein concepts, such as "language games," and "forms of life," for use in various connections. He practically always indicates that it's a Wittgenstein of his own that he evokes: "a pseudo-Wittgenstein." The distinction in the *Tractatus* between "saying" and "showing" underlies the relation he describes between his own poetry and his prose, and it informs the "biipsism" (not solipsism, now, but "biipsism") that he and Alix Cléo Roubaud lived together—he, a poet, "saying," and she, a photographer (avid reader of Wittgenstein, too), "showing."

> In this world her images;   my words. The biipsism of the images and language. to show, to tell.[16]

Such Wittgenstein topics, adapted for his own purposes, coexist in Roubaud's mind with other key ideas, and key riddles and intriguing formulae that have caught his attention in a number of philosophers from the Middle Ages to the present (Nicholas of Cusa's "Li non Aliud," for example, or Alexius Meinong's "stateless beings," or David Lewis' "ersatz worlds"). Wittgenstein's conviction that there is no such thing as private language comes into play in the present book because I want to listen for a private, intransmissible language in Roubaud, one that says, but not anything. I want to follow Roubaud along one in particular of his various paths: the path of the impossible, "la voie de l'impossible."

Giorgio Agamben is another philosopher on whom *The Play of Light* draws, and this is partly because he and Roubaud are, in a way, colleagues: both remarkable readers of medieval literature and thought, who develop similar interpretations of *fin' amor*. The Middle Ages saw early on, they seem to agree, how unnatural love is. The procession of ghosts through Roubaud's writing, the dim forms shedding all their attributes at dusk, the images swimming into sight in the darkroom recall Agamben's "phantoms of eros."[17] Nothing to win, or possess.

More significant, though, for *The Play of Light*, is no doubt the fact that in one of his poetry books Roubaud borrows a number of passages straight from Agamben's *Coming Community*.[18] They bear on "whatever being" and on "potentiality." Roubaud borrows these passages and "twists" them, as he states. He thinks Agamben may not recognize them. They allay for him though, I think, the dread in poetry, and the dread of it.

As far as I know Hocquard never mentions Agamben, but I suspect that he tacitly alludes to his "potentialities" in one poem at least, which I will discuss, and where—on account of this silent allusion—Hocquard passes for a while into Roubaud's neighborhood. (This drift happens from time to time, for various reasons.)

Let me emphasize that Agamben and Wittgenstein are present in this book only via a small number of particular concepts that Hocquard and/or Roubaud draw attention to, puzzle over, or mobilize. I do not aspire here to confront more than a few facets of Agamben's or of Wittgenstein's work—the ones that surface in Roubaud's twists, or Hocquard's adaptations, and that illuminate, in turn, certain riddles in the poems. It might be said though, that Agamben leaves a more conspicuous mark on the present book. Whereas I might have dwelt on *potential* as it is celebrated in the activities of the *Ouvroir de Littérature Potentielle* (the *Oulipo*—that long-lived literary group of which Roubaud has been a pillar since 1968), instead, I speak of Agamben's potentialities, and of the potential for impotence that he brings out, in particular. In fact, this might be considered a somewhat distinctive characteristic of *The Play of Light*: not to dwell, that is—at least, not very much—on the Oulipo, and to favor, instead, over the wealth of potential, the impotence in Roubaud.

Because of this propensity for underachievement, my readings in this book might claim a kinship with a certain nonproductive current in contemporary literary theory. Instead of pursuing meanings that can and even must be affirmed and developed, it bends toward language's nonrealizing dimension. I think of the distinction Werner Hamacher makes in his *95 Theses on Philology* between propositional language, "the medium and object of ontology as well as of all the epistemic disciplines under its direction," and "meaningful but nonpropositional language," which "knows no 'is' and no 'must', but only a 'be' and a 'would be' that withdraw themselves from every determining and every determined cognition." Hamacher allies reading and thinking with this withdrawal, which is to say with poetry, and not with any "object." The philology to which he is devoted "only turns to that which is for no one and nothing."[19] Such indifference (being for no one and for nothing) inspires an aimless love—longing, but not for anything that could ever be an object or a goal.

If distraction like this presents a problem—I allude to Paul North's book, *The Problem of Distraction*—this is in part at least because it is not an experience that anyone can, properly speaking, have. "I am distracted" is not something anyone can really say. "No one is distracted," North writes.[20] No one's grammar, which does without subjects as well as objects, informs the language I try to hear in *The Play of Light*. And no one's life is what I want to share, in a vacant patch of oblivion, just between us, where no one can encounter anyone, the way a cat can look at a king.[21]

Indeterminate, featureless life is a secret message my book hopes to confide—"anonymous life," to borrow the title of a different book, by Jacques Khalip.[22] This life, though "ravishing" for Hocquard at least, does not animate or brighten anything up. It is one with the "indifference of being." And yet one of my principal emphases in this book is the paradoxical *singularity* of the nondescript—the distinction of life so common it belongs to none, solely to none. This particular stress comes mainly in my readings of Hocquard, and it is what links *The Play of Light* to Jean-Luc Nancy. But just as I claim to welcome in this book only a fraction of Wittgenstein, and only the Agamben of "whatever being" and the potential for impotence—just as I hesitate (and really cannot presume) to locate my work within the world of Hamacher and his students—so I wish to greet here, warmly, for reasons of friendship as well as on account of theory, only a handful of French words that Nancy changed for good: *singulier* and *pluriel, partage, commun, communauté*. These terms, the thoughts they carry, the ethical demands they bring to bear as well as their political implications have been pondered and tried by Nancy himself and many others.[23] I am only glad that my book has a chance to send back to Nancy, and to the scholars working from various perspectives on ideas about commons and communities, a response from out in left field, as it were: from an Emmanuel Hocquard often at pains to say how much he prefers detective fiction to philosophy, and who never, as far as I am aware, refers to *The Inoperative Community*,[24] or the *Unavowable Community*,[25] and who would not, I suspect, be especially pleased to have these ideas "applied" to his pages.

No doubt it is via indifference and "the neutral" that *The Play of Light* reflects Maurice Blanchot. A wish of mine to depart from Blanchot, and the writers in his orbit who for so long preoccupied me, was one of the impulses at the origin of this book. Its second chapter treats a similar, more pronounced impulse on the part of Hocquard, especially. But I place in the foreground of that chapter a question of "intonation," and suggest that reading Hocquard helps one to hear the sound of Blanchot's voice differently.[26]

Speaking of voice—Hocquard once wrote an "Ode against a Nightingale."[27] He'd been kept awake all night by a real one—a terrible squawker, nothing like the warbler in poetry composed by people who, he concludes, might never have actually heard a nightingale. He would have preferred a pneumatic drill, he writes, or "a contemporary poet." His indignant vituperations against the obstinate nightingale are funny and intended as a relief from Romantic odes, with their imagery and their music, and their Nature. The real nightingale sounded like a mechanical noise box: "Fabrique de bruit, / mécanique stridente."

Hocquard's complaint, I mean to say, is less about his loss of sleep than about lyric poetry—about the song in language that, according to him, puts one to sleep. And he is quick—in many other texts—to assimilate that song (that expressive subjectivity) with "everything we're used to": with language that holds no surprises. Sometimes he describes it as a tick lodged in the ear, sometimes as a rumor. All that matters to Hocquard is the interruption of this soporific tune. He writes to provoke a surprise one can't recover from. I am simplifying his perspective here, to be sure, exaggerating a somewhat dogmatic vein in his thought: his impatient dismissal of expressive language, as though there were never anything to hear in odes, ballads, elegies but a reassuring hum (or as though Literature were necessarily a mere affectation), and his rather unsparing austerity (grammar is my affair, he often declares—grammar, "the skeleton of language." No music, then, just the bare bones). I put things baldly here in order to acknowledge that Hocquard is a writer with a distinct stance: it is not a foregone conclusion that the startling perceptions to which his writing exposes a serious reader—the ravishing ontological surprises I've placed at the center of this book—are of an entirely different order from that stance, that attitude, that circumscribed position.

Roubaud is, if anything, an even more opinionated individual than Hocquard. More contrary. Against practically everyone who has ever longed to throw out the artificial strictures of traditional verse, he defends a concept of tradition and of rules, which he considers the rebels too coarse to appreciate. He is an experimental practitioner of "fixed forms" old and new, who scorns avant-garde theatrics. His first book of poetry was a sonnet book; it was the initial outcome of the decision he made, in 1961, to live. He was close to floundering and wanted something firm to hold onto. The fact that two great contributors to the history of the sonnet (the Sicilian master known as il Notaro, the Notary, whom Dante acknowledges in the *Purgatorio*, and his heir, Cino da Pistoia) were accustomed to juridical language—to the rigor, that is, that informs "the iron language of law"—contributed not a little to the appeal the sonnet had initially for Roubaud.[28]

World War II was the broader scene of his childhood, and the war was still quite recent at the beginning of the 1960s. Roubaud's family had been in the Resistance. He had a lot of sympathy for poems of that period, which he knew had been written under the threat of death at the hands of the Nazis. And those poems were sonnets: the thirty-three composed by Jean Cassou while in solitary confinement, without pencil or paper, in his head, and *Les Sonnets de Moabit*, written with his own blood by Albrecht Haushofer, one of the conspirators in the plot to assassinate Hitler in 1944. Those two poets were not like each other in any way except their turn to sonnets when faced with brutal death, and Roubaud thought this brought out something essential about the sonnet form: being so very compact, it lends itself extra well to concentration; it focuses all one's mental powers. It's a discipline, good for the memory.

Notwithstanding, though, his strong association of sonnets with the Resistance and with anti-Nazi heroism, another of Roubaud's main reasons for choosing the sonnet form in 1961 was to express in this way his *opposition* to "engaged poetry" and to political freight in poetry (poetry can perfectly well convey meanings of all kinds, including political meaning, he holds, but this is not what it does essentially, as poetry).

This specific gesture of opposition to engaged poetry was part of a whole program of contrariness: Roubaud chose sonnets against the surrealists and their hostility to form; against avant-gardism in general and its conception of poetry as rupture; against the predominance of free verse in France. The contempt widely felt for traditional versification from the *crise de vers* on, fell likewise on traditional forms like the sonnet, and Roubaud chose sonnets in cheerful defiance of writers like Claudel who described them as little music boxes, "tabatières à musique."[29] Finally he chose sonnets in 1961 against the idea of a national poetry—a poetry of France, "mère des arts, des armes et des lois" (You must be joking, he writes, in effect, in *Poésie*: we were deep in the Algerian War).[30]

I will come back briefly, around the middle of this book—in the Interlude—to the formalist character of Roubaud's work and to his first book of sonnets. At this point, I will just note speedily, as if on a poster or a banner, a few more of the opinions he characteristically maintains (preferring Jane Austen to Balzac, for example, Zukofsky to the Beats, Queneau to Breton), not so much because they are especially important to *The Play of Light*, but to signal, as I did for Hocquard, the *posture* that is Roubaud's, impossible to isolate completely from his poems and prose—lest I appear in this book to present Roubaud's writing and the thought in it as a sort of oracle.

Joyce **NO**, Stein **SI!**
Philippe Sollers and *Tel Quel* **NO**, Jean-Pierre Faye and *Change* **SI!**
Denis Roche, David Antin **SI! SI!**
Helen Vendler, Rita Dove **NO! y NO!**

I will indicate too, among the signatures he affixes from time to time to one or another of his declarations (e.g., "Jacques Roubaud, poète"; or "Jacques Roubaud, compositeur de mathématique et de poésie"), this one: "Jacques Roubaud, poète provençal"—because, for one thing, since he is actually a "poète parisien," it suggests that exile is an element of his condition, and for another thing, because it indicates his alliance with a lost language, a ruined world, a scattered company of "compositeurs de poésie," the troubaours.

As I have said, I adopt in this book a discontinuous or mildly distracted mode, and in this regard I am imitating Roubaud's and Hocquard's two styles of thinking and of writing. (R. and H. are the two principal figures in this book; the others hover around them, Jouet with his determination to banish the word *impossible* from the French language, Portugal splashing a bright swath toward the end, to answer Collobert's very dark one at the start. I will introduce Jouet and Portugal later, when they join the gathering; Collobert will enter shortly.) Roubaud, especially in his prose, is unapologetically digressive. I have enjoyed pursuing one or another of his many subjects (how to make jam from cherries that grow only among the perfumed scrub and umbrella pines of Languedoc; recent developments in logic by Lawvere and Heyting or the pre-Adamism of Isaac La Peyrère), only to discover that it has veered off into some other volume, or has dived into an underpass and will eventually return via the upper route. Diverging, ramifying, and doubling back to intertwine are cardinal characteristics of Roubaud's work.

He also likes to open parentheses within parentheses, and he stashes "bifurcations" and "incisions"—detours in his reasoning, or his remembering; or patches of additional material too big to fit in his prose where they first occur to him—in separate sections of his prose works. He provides a numbering system allowing you to flip to these addenda right away or postpone, hoping to fit them back into the "whole" you will eventually have read. (See *Le grand incendie de Londres* for examples of this arrangement.)[31]

The "thought in speaking" stutters and starts over all the time, he says in the prologue to a volume of poetry intended to be spoken aloud. But it returns to its initial subject along routes that proliferate and intersect to form a kind of braid.[32] In a similar way the various distinct components of Roubaud's entire oeuvre communicate with each other—the prose layer with the poetry, the poetry with the mathematics—the parts belonging to the end of night (which he labors over in the very early morning), with the parts belonging to the end of day (to which he systematically devotes the evening hours). A reader's attention is apt to rove from region to region of this capacious oeuvre, and it is sometimes only a step to a corner that by another route is still weeks away.[33]

As for Hocquard, not only does he fight smooth transitions and the seamless continuities they are supposed to guarantee; not only does he stake everything on cuts, interruptions, gaps, holes, favoring disjointed forms like the chronicle, the list, the recipe (patches of words, scrappy voices); not only does he emphasize segmented worlds, splintered space, broken-up languages foreign to each other and untranslatable; he also takes a great interest in a particular kind of unorthodox path he sometimes calls a "chemin de traverse." That means a path cutting across some terrain, perhaps a shortcut. "Interior margin" is another name he has for it. "Le chemin de Wittgenstein," winding through Trinity College, Cambridge, is an example he has sometimes given; also the path of the rhinoceros across the room where Wittgenstein once refused to concede to Bertrand Russell that there *was* no rhino.

So much, then, for my critical approach. It reflects, in its mild way, the writing whose challenge I wish to accept. It may give *The Play of Light* a kind of usefulness different from that of other current books on poetry, in that this one is relatively light on poetics and heavier on poems. I hope I have not weighed them down. In a last comment about my methodology, let me add that for better or worse I remain attached to an idea I expressed long ago in the first book I wrote: there is a form of literary criticism—one among many—which is more or less equivalent to playing a piece of music: an interpretation on the trumpet, say. To play the notes that are written is the way I characterized long ago the literary critical ambition that to this day is my biggest one.

In the lively manifesto called *Poetry, etcetera: Cleaning House*, Roubaud states that poetry says,[34] "Elle dit." That is all. It doesn't say something, it doesn't say anything. For saying something, anything with any meaning, requires that there be something else to say, by way of clarification, in answer to someone who, not quite understanding, would ask, "What?" And poetry says nothing that any other words could clear up. It just says what it says by saying. "Elle dit ce qu'elle dit en disant." If there were an answer to the person asking of a poem, "What? What do you say?" it would simply be the poem, which that person doesn't understand. Poetry hides nothing, shows nothing. There is no solution, one might say, where this enigma is concerned—no solution save the riddle itself, which is therefore as impossible to ask as to answer.

Roubaud's conviction about poetry's saying, but not anything, develops as follows: if something—anything at all—is to be said, the thing cannot just be the utterance itself, it must be something else. Poetry, however, doesn't say anything else. "Elle dit ce qu'elle dit en disant" (*Poésie, etcetera*, 76/*Poetry etcetera*, 77). Again, in *The Plurality of Worlds of Lewis*, 72, alluding to Bartleby, "[Poetry] does not say anything. It ' would prefer not to '." Or again: "It does not say except by saying." ("Elle ne dit rien; elle ' préférerait ne pas '. Elle ne dit qu'en disant.")[35]

Of course, Roubaud does not want to insist that poetry really never says a single thing that any other words could explain. It does, he willingly acknowledges, because it is a game that is played in language, where words laid end to end, no matter how perplexing, always end up having meaning, or at least bits and snatches of meaning. But this meaning, transmissible via other words, is something different from what a poem says by being a poem. It accompanies, combines, or collides with what a poem says essentially, but *that* is unparaphrasable, intransmissible—not, in short, anything that can be said, or that ever is (*Poetry, etcetera* 86/*Poésie, etcetera* 86). By being a poem a poem says something that cannot be said, and is not.

In this book I will collide repeatedly with impossibility ("cannot," "is not"), coming at it from a few different directions, with different writers. I plan some detours, and lighter moments (Jouet!). But here I enter Danielle Collobert's statement, remembered by Roubaud when she died: "Je ne peux pas la poésie." (I am incapable of poetry.)

Her longest work is titled *Say*; *Dire* in the original (with two parts, *Dire I*, *Dire II*). Say, just say; use up the few words remaining or let them rot; just say. As in *Be, just be*. Or *Live*.

> arriver à être
> essai — essai   (*Dire II*)[36]
>
> manage to be
> try — try   (My translation)

After her suicide in 1978, when she was thirty-eight, Roubaud composed a text in her honor, and recalled her saying, "Je ne peux pas la poésie. Je ne sais pas ce que c'est que la poésie."

"Tu ne m'en voudras pas de te le dire. Je ne sais pas la poésie." [37]

"You won't hold it against me if I tell you. I don't know poetry."

She wrote in prose, "la prose du récit," Roubaud said: narrative prose born of poetry's impossibility, its death. Raymond Queneau saw to her first book's publication by Gallimard in 1964.[38] It is a series of short narratives, composed in the first person more often than in the third; brief scenes, tiny stories, sometimes dreams, one suspects; descriptions of a small town with a port, and of stones and plants in the town's environs. The title of this book is *Meurtre. Murder*.[39]

Eventually, when narrative ran down and died too, poetry came back for Collobert, Roubaud said in 1979; it came back but just as exhaustion: for want of the strength to keep writing all the way across the page. Roubaud called the poetry of *Dire I* and *II* nonverse: "cette forme non-vers." Jean-Pierre Faye published it in the collection *Change* in 1972; four years later he published *Il donc (It then)*,[40] as well. The broken-up lines resulted from asphyxia, Roubaud thought; it reflected no particular formal plan. Or, it served an inclination not to occupy the page but instead to lodge in blanks, silences, in what remains when nothing is any use anymore, not punctuation, sequencing, or progression.

Bit by bit this nonverse, Roubaud writes, became indistinguishable from "la parole d'identité voulue abolie." It amounted to the same, I believe, as the answer to the riddle "What am I? Who?" "Parole d'identité." This is a word sought for, even hunted, like a snark ("parole voulue"), and annulled ("abolie"), like the kind of snark called Boojum, which, if ever captured, disappears right away, along with its captor.[41] "L'Enigme reste énigme, jusque dans les yeux troués du cadavre," Roubaud writes, somewhere along one of the many twisting paths of his autobiography.[42] "The enigma remains an enigma, all the way into the eye sockets of the corpse."

Danielle Collobert persisted, slower and slower, Roubaud thought, detour by detour, only to end up at the bottom of the circular trap where the sameness of the truth and its extinction awaits. "Elle retrouva après tout détour le même du piège circulaire . . ."[43]

Roubaud is acquainted with this "*même*," this "same," and sometimes calls it "la mort même. identitique à elle même même." In Rosmarie Waldrop's translation, "Death itself-self. identical with itself-self."[44] He considered that the six short poems comprising Collobert's last work, completed just before her death and called *Survie* (*Survival*), give their title the lie at the last moment, "because nothing returned from any 'elsewhere' except 'what's the use' applied to everything."

je parole s'ouvrir bouche ouverte dire je vis à qui

I speech opening mouth open to say I live to whom[45]

Emmanuel Hocquard published *Survie* the year Collobert finished it (1978), in the collection *Figurae*, put out by Orange Export Ltd.—the press Hocquard directed with Raquel Levy between 1969 and 1986. In the anthology of contemporary poetry that he published later, in 1995, he introduced Collobert by comparing her to a pianist of the sort he admires: she does without pathos. He refers to her "touch," and says she brought off that tour de force which consists in detaching notes, with dashes, impassively, at the edge of what can be written. "Au bord de l'écrit."[46]

Born in 1940, only a bit after Roubaud and the same year as Hocquard, Collobert differs from them quite strikingly, not only because she lived so much shorter a life (Roubaud is still writing in the summer of 2019; Hocquard died at the very beginning of that year), but also because she published relatively little during her lifetime (just the four works I've mentioned, published all together by P.O.L, in 2004).[47] She traveled—by herself, without any stipends or residencies or invitations to readings—far and wide, notably in North Africa (during the Algerian War) and Indonesia, but also in Italy, Germany, Greece, Holland, the United States (whence all the "ailleurs" mentioned by Roubaud), leaving behind here and there one more volume's worth of notebooks, outtakes, fragments, two radio plays. She never bothered to construct any stable dwelling place for herself in the world of French letters, as both Roubaud and Hocquard did, in their two different, eccentric ways.

Hocquard founded, with Raquel Levy, the press Orange Export Ltd., which brought together a small group of friendly writers, including Claude Royet-Journoud and Anne-Marie Albiach, and which published many American poets little known in France at the time, such as Robert Duncan, Keith and Rosmarie Waldrop, Cid Corman, Larry Eigner, and Paul Auster. As director, from 1977 to 1991, of *les lectures de l'ARC*, a long-standing program of poetry readings at the Museum of Modern Art in Paris, Hocquard invited and published many American writers, as well as French ones. As director, with Juliette Valéry, of Le Bureau sur l'Atlantique, a center for exchanges of all kinds between French and American poets, which lasted from the end of the 1980s well into the twenty-first century, Hocquard was one of the main animating figures in the small, unconventional, international world of poets that formed during the 1970s on two shores of the Atlantic and that Norma Cole calls a "crosscut universe."[48] Roubaud—fabulously prolific, a great formal experimenter and inventor—has been prominent for a long time. His prose and poetry have appeared steadily since 1967, when Raymond Queneau oversaw the publication of his first volume of poetry at Gallimard, and recruited him for the Oulipo. He was the founder of Le Cercle Polivanov (a center for research in comparative poetics); cofounder of *Change*; and a regular contributor to other important reviews of the time, *Action Poétique* and *Po&sie*—as well as to the Cercle Polivanov's highly specialized journal *Mezura*.[49]

"je ne marcherai jamais dans leur jeu," Collobert wrote. I'll never play their game:

se défendre contre tous

fatigue

fatigue [50]

defend against all

tired

tired

1

"Thy blackness is a spark"

— Edward, Lord Herbert of Cherbury, *Sonnet of Black Beauty*

Identity

Now poetry, Roubaud suggests—poetry, inasmuch as it never, in its essential poetry mode, says anything but the sheer saying, which nothing *else* can explain or clear up—is like light, as defined by one of the six learned participants in the six-evening colloquium on light whose proceedings Roubaud published in *Exchanges on Light*.[1] A Mr. Goodman seems to have been the convener of this colloquium; he invites the participants to imagine, each evening as they gather, that they are looking out through windows open to the west, onto an English park, and beyond that toward "low hills in the soft English distance." We will meet Mr. Goodman again in the pages of Roubaud's books, at different stages of his life.[2] The six contributors to his six-evening seminar on light include, in addition to Goodman himself, Pseudo-Dionysius the Areopagite, Basil of Caesarea, John Herschel, David Lewis, and Edward Herbert.[3] It is Pseudo-Dionysius, going modestly by the alias Dennis Ps. (all the seminar participants modestly adopt pseudonyms), who states, "But light is essentially present to itself; it is the revelation of the self to the self. It has no need, no way of knowing itself outside itself" (*Exchanges*, 51/*Echanges*, 51). Poetry likewise is identical to itself, its own sole disclosure, "revelation of the self to the self"; there are no *other* means to know it or for it to know itself (but it needs no other ways).

More than one of the specialists in *Exchanges on Light* stress that no brighter light exists to make light visible the way light itself makes objects visible in the world. If there were some brighter light to shine on light and make it show, then the light it would reveal would not be light itself, but some lit-up thing among all the visible things around us. And light, light itself, is not some illuminated thing, it is illumination. It is not among the colorful *other* things that it makes visible. Nothing reveals it, save its just being what it is, light. Which is to say, it is not visible. It is black. "Light itself," or "the beauty of light," is "the beauty of the dark" (*Exchanges*, 23/*Echanges*, 24). "Nuit, c'est cela," Roubaud writes, in a poem called "Beauté du noir," after two sonnets by Edward Herbert. William H. recites the opening lines of this poem during the fifth session of *Exchanges on Light* (69/60).

> Nuit, c'est cela
> chevelure
>   de noir révérend la lumière n'est
>   que pour le définir[4]   (*Echanges*, 69)

> Night, that
> reverend black
>   shock of hair light is just
>   there to define it   (*Exchanges*, 60)

Daylight, with all its brilliance, and all the lovely hues it illuminates each morning really only exists, the poem says (I paraphrase shamelessly), to indicate the outer edges of the venerable black, light's "influx." When, as only it can do, light reveals itself, it "blacks":[5] withdraws into itself and leaves the world. For "Identity only exists in invisibility. The beauty of light must leave this world [. . .] to give itself over to invisibility" (*Exchanges*, 29/*Echanges*, 30).

"Some thing," as Roubaud puts it elsewhere—"some thing" bearing no relation to anything else, utterly unlike—surges up just where suddenly the whole world is brought up short: it is some thing drawn back into itself, totally aloof, locked, and black.

> Tout se suspend au point où surgit un dissemblable. et
> de là quelque chose, mais quelque chose noir.
> [. . .]
>
> Quelque chose noir qui se referme. et se boucle. une
> déposition pure, inaccomplie.   (*Quelque chose noir*, 76)

> Everything depends on the point when the unlike appears.
> and thence something, but some thing black.
> [...]
>
> Some thing black which closes in. locks shut. pure, un-
> accomplished deposition.   (*Some Thing Black*, 73-74)

With this black retreat the whole world leaves the world, draws back into itself, emitting a pitch-black radiance. Roubaud seems to have an awful propensity for this: for night. Not so much for the kind of night that eventually comes to an end, "qui va disparaître au jour," but for "the other night," the one that is coming, "celle qui vient." In that dark—when it comes, should it come—I would see, in the black, the hidden, blacker black.

> nuit tu
> viendrais
>
> ce serait
> nuit je verrais
>
> dans le noir le
> noir le
>
> noir plus épais
>
> que tu caches   (*Le grand incendie*, 408)
>
> night
> you would come
>
> it would
> be night I would see
>
> in the blackness the
> black the
>
> black most dense
>
> that you hide   (*The Great Fire*, 318)

If on very black nights we do not discern, or barely even suspect an extraordinary light (a still denser black hidden in the dark, a "spark / of light inaccessible"), perhaps it is because we are blinded by lesser suns than this black one. "N'est-ce pas," Roubaud writes, after Edward Herbert,

> que nous sommes aveugles à ce qui vient
> d'en haut
> à cause des soleils bas?   (*Le grand incendie*, 406)

Is it not the case that all would find that "shining light in darkness,"

> Were they not upward blind
> With the sunbeams below.   (*The Great Fire*, 316)

I do not especially like moonlit nights, Roubaud writes in *La Boucle*, or starry nights or glimmery or greyish nights. I prefer nights that are night through and through, "nuits entières."

> Above all there are entire nights, compact, impenetrable, opposing the yellow light of lamps with something akin to their own black radiation. This "beauty of black," which renders the world incomprehensible and inexplicable, and which assures me that the world is and will remain incomprehensible and inexplicable, this "blackness unvarying to the eye" (which is the world, the world withdrawing into itself in disdain) attracts me, it keeps me pressed against the window, unmoving, watching. (*The Loop*, 26/*La Boucle*, 27)

In *Exchanges on light* this blackout is associated with the disappearance of identity (for "l'identité n'existe que dans l'invisibilité"), and with the pain of this loss, "la douleur," which is said to be the condition for beauty among us (*Echanges*, 30/*Exchanges*, 29). It is the sorrow just behind all joys, and these, the joys, are like lamps that come on at nightfall. Each session of the seminar on light starts at day's end, when the natural light recedes and the lamps start coming on in the parks outside, and on the streets.

Dusk

Hocquard describes the twilight during Ramadan in Fez (he grew up in Morocco).

> Every evening the women go up on the roof terraces of the medina to watch for nightfall. As the light gradually withdraws, a particular silence settles in.

> The daily fast comes to an end at the moment when it is no longer possible to distinguish "a white thread from a black one." Then a joyful clamor arises from the roofs and the streets of the entire city.
> And everyone goes home.
> ("Deux Leçons des ténèbres," in *Un privé à Tanger*, 201; my translation)

Speaking of his friend Raquel Levy's canvasses, Hocquard says that they show painting "à l'approche des ténèbres," as darkness nears, when a white thread is practically indistinguishable from a black one.

The electrician for the apartment building where she had her studio asked once, Hocquard recounts, if he might see her paintings. She invited him in, and turned the spotlights on her somber, almost monochrome diptychs. The electrician looked at them for a while in silence and then, rather surprised, turned to her, asking, "Where are the paintings?" ("Deux Leçons," in *Un privé*, 201).

It seems they came as close as possible to showing what we do not see: indifferentiation, "le neutre." A bluish red, I imagine, for example, on one panel, as close as possible to a reddish blue on the same diptych's other leaf: the shadowy separation between, where their separateness practically disappears. "The neutral is not visible. [...] We don't see indifferentiation" ("Deux Leçons," in *Un privé*, 203).

Raquel said, Hocquard reports, that her blues and reds are not colors, but an attempt to show light itself, which we do not see.

Light itself, ever so close to neutral. I think she meant that with her blues and reds she tried to show light when it does not serve to distinguish one thing from another: does not allow us to appreciate the contrasts among bright objects or between pale and dark surfaces. Her reds, her blues, if I am right—her purples and violets—would not be distinctive features of anything; they would not be proper to anything or properties at all.

They would not be the colors of anything, but rather, just colors. The colors of nothing.

Or maybe the various shades of colorlessness. Indistinction's rainbow.[6]

I suspect Raquel's paintings bear a relation to the red cube which Hocquard suggests elsewhere we consider not to be a cube that is red, but rather a red that happens to have taken the form of a cube.[7] A red brick would be a brick of red. Perhaps Raquel's colors are, so to speak, baked like clay into bricks, *cooked into* the forms whose outer attributes they might have been, in someone else's paintings. For Hocquard observes that her work shows "something like the inside of a brick." "The inside of a brick has no color" ("Deux Leçons," in *Un privé*, 205).

In the garden that he describes in his book of sonnets, *Un test de solitude*,[8] there is a "souche brûlée," a tree stump burned according to an ancient Roman method, by letting it "consume itself from the inside." Soon after the flames attacked the top of the stump, we read, a crater formed into which the embers slowly sank deeper and deeper until after three weeks they reached the roots, and on their slow way down they cooked the gray clay enveloping the roots into a hard, rose brick (*Un test*, IX/*A Test*, IX).

In Hocquard's novel there is a volcanic island whose name sounds a little like *la cécité*, blindness: it is called "la Cecilia." Its "scorched landscape" seems to have been formed in the same way as the hard, rose brick in Hocquard's garden, for the volcanoes on it are its "very substance." Every particle of it has "baked in the inner ovens of the planet." Burning lava, in successive eruptions, has soldered "the great mummified body of the island to its sarcophagus." La Cecilia resists every influence from outside that might soften its "savagery" (*Aerea in the forests*, 116-17/*Aerea dans les forêts*, 155-56).

"L'attribut incorpore le sujet," Hocquard writes in a poem. The attribute incorporates the subject. It is as if he were imagining some feature or quality like the color red—some attribute—sinking deep into whatever subject it might otherwise have qualified, and combining with it so thoroughly as to form with it a single, featureless substance. But I should say also that Hocquard must be imagining some predicate—say, *blue*—fusing with the subject of the sentence it is in—say, *sky*, (*the sky*)—and thereby forming a tautology where, in someone else's writing, there might indeed have been a sentence complete with subject, verb, and predicate. For in another poem, he writes,

> [...] Si *jolie* n'est pas
> un attribut de Maylis
> *Maylis est jolie* est une
> tautologie, un cas sans sujets
> qui annule les personnes.   [*L'Invention du verre*, 54]

> [...] If *pretty* is not
> an attribute of Maylis
> Maylis is pretty is a
> tautology; there are no subjects;
> people don't count.   (*The Invention of Glass*, 54)

When loveliness is not among Maylis's attributes, then *Maylis est jolie* says *Maylis est Maylis*. It says prettiness is not a feature proper to Maylis, it is just she, simply her being the one she is. Her colorless being.

As a tautology *Maylis est jolie* says that being is lovely, but no one's, nothing's ("Beauté n'appartient pas," Hocquard writes, in a different poem: Beauty does not belong[9]). *Maylis est jolie*, perceived—by accident, perhaps, when your ear suddenly pops or your reading gets stalled for a second at the turn of a page—*Maylis est jolie* perceived, then, unpredictably as a tautology says that loveliness, the special feature of no one, has happened, like color taking the form of a cube or a brick, to take the shape of Maylis. Suddenly the sight of her reveals nothing. Suddenly, to see her is to see the being of no one. "Quelle rencontre ineffable!" (as Hocquard wrote in a similar context. "What an ineffable encounter" [*Aerea in the forests*, 19/*Area dans les forêts*, 30]).

For Hocquard, who would like, I gather, to write in such a way as to favor the sudden perception of tautologies in what are ordinarily taken for propositions stating something about something else—for Hocquard, then, the whole point of poetry, like the whole point of painting for Raquel Levy, is to see what you do not. Beauty. Indifference. *Le neutre*.

If one reads these lines "... une / tautologie, un cas sans sujets / qui annule les personnes," a little stupidly, word-for-word (not as well as Swensen and Smith do in their translation), then one gathers that a tautology is a *case*, which annuls persons. One thinks of grammar (and begins to feel the a-grammatical current in Hocquard), but also of Wittgenstein's axiom, "The world is all that is the case."[10] For this famous statement comes up in a conversation between Hocquard and his friend Claude Royet-Journoud:[11] Royet-Journoud's version of Wittgenstein's axiom is "The world is everything that happens [tout ce qui arrive]," and it is linked in his mind to something he calls the accident, "ce tranchant de l'accident." I expect he has in mind the etymology of case (*cas*), which is *cadere*, to fall (or he might be thinking of the German word, *Fall*, for case). So, among the various meanings of the word *case*, I imagine he means to stress this one: a thing that befalls. An occurrence, event, chance (*Oxford English Dictionary*). For Hocquard, who also emphasizes accidents from time to time in his writing, I expect that the *cas* in "tautologie, un cas sans sujets," is the fact, but more precisely the unforeseeable *event* of something's, anything's, anyone's being. The one it is. The total surprise. The sudden exposure of colorless, faceless being. Its dazzling, incomparable indifference.

Nightfall

Each of Mr. Goodman's seminars on light begins with the fall of darkness ("à l'approche des ténèbres"), and on and off, from one meeting of the erudite group to another, one of the participants (William H.) recites snatches, like this one, of a poem called "Night" (which indeed drifts through a good deal of Roubaud's oeuvre, with slight variations):

> Nuit
>
> tu
> es venue
>
> les
> lumières
> ont poussé
> sur
>
> les herbes, les pentes
> vidées
> de
>
> lumière, les
> lumières sont
>
> venues dans l'absence
> de la lumière
>
> sombres
> de la lumière perdue
>
> de la lumière qui fut
> belle   (*Echanges*, 10, 13, 31. See also, for example, *Le grand incendie* [408-9], and *Dors* [practically every other page])

> Night
>
> you
> came
>
> the
> lights

have grown
over

the grass, the slopes
emptied
of

light, the
lights have

arrived in the absence
of light

dark
of light lost

of light that was
beautiful   (*Exchanges*, 30)

Roubaud associates poetry—at least, this is my understanding—with the lost light, "the light that was / beautiful;" with light itself in whose absence lamps and lanterns, candles, torches appear and shine, dark with loss. Poetry departs, I mean, like daylight after sunset, giving itself to the unsaid. Roubaud often calls it "l'absente de tous bouquets," remembering Mallarmé, and "l'absente de tous poèmes" (e.g., *Poetry, etcetera*, 86, 87/*Poésie, etcetera*, 87, 88). I expect that for him poetry tinges all poems with sorrow, like the absence of light itself darkening, even as it allows there to be, light in this world.

Or again poetry is associated with a certain doubtfulness, delight's accompaniment, its somber double—the hunched and clouded Vesuvius, for example, brother to sunlit, verdant Mount Cicada.

Doubles

In *la fenêtre veuve*, Roubaud reports a memory of Giordano Bruno's: "I remember your light, Mount Cicada,"

>   et qu'enfant je
> grimpais entre les touffes et duvet de ton ventre .

>   and how as a child I
> would clamber among the tufts of down on your belly .

He recalls the olive trees and laurel, the chestnuts, oaks, poplars, and elms on Mount Cicada

                                                                 et la
vigne aux bourses noires où   comme je tendais la main vers la grappe éparpillée   sur la nappe tendre de lumière .
   . j'entendis que ta voix me disait :
    : regarde vers le sud regarde ce frère mien de ce côté là Vésuve .

                                         and the
vine hung with black purses where   when I held out my hand
                                                toward
the bunch scattered   upon the tender cloth of light .
    .   I heard your voice telling me :
      :look toward the south   look   my own brother on that side there Vesuvius .

Do you see him, my brother-mountain to the south, Vesuvius? bright Cicada asked. If I send you there, will you go? But when Bruno looked south, he saw only a heavy gray shoulder covered with clouds, and asked, Why go there?

                il n'y a   rien là-bas
ni jardins ni raisins ni figues pennèques .
[…]

rien l'obscur l'éteint le triste le
tremblant le médiocre l'avare .

             there is nothing   over there
neither gardens nor grapes nor *penneque* figs .
[…]
                  nothing the dark the extinguished the sad the trembling the mediocre the meagre .

                                   (My rough translation)

But Cicada, laughing, said it was his brother, and to go. So Bruno did, and saw Vesuvius all bright, with poplars and olive trees and laurel; its vines had bunches of black grapes that fell into his hand in the sunlight, "chemise propre de la journée à venir" (fresh shirt of the day to come). Turning back joyfully to the other brother, he perceived Mount Cicada as a poor gray shoulder, coughing fog, "obscur éteint triste." So he concludes his recollection saying, "On that day I learned doubt, from those two hermetic twins my parents, and all my life, whenever I stretch my hand up toward the grapes hanging on the vine, whenever I hold it out to take up the bright new shirt of the day to come, your voice Mount Cicada, will intervene saying 'Go toward my grey, clouded twin, toward memory.'"

va va vers
mon frère gris   mon jumeau ennuagé   la mémoire   .¹²

One thinks of the evening lamps in *Exchanges on Light*, clouded a little, darkened by the loss of light that was, beautiful. Harboring its memory.

One recalls the "inverse flower," too, that Roubaud came upon long ago, at the beginning of his study of troubadour poetry, in a canso by Raimbaut d'Orange: an ice flower with dagger-sharp petals, the reverse of springtime. The cold petals struck him as something like the harsh bloom of the flower's absence. Or as the presence, in a poem, of poetry's disappearance.

> Er resplan la flors enversa
> Pels trencans rancx et pels tertres.
> Quals flors neus gels e conglapis
> Que cotz e destrenh e trenca.
>
> Alors brille la fleur inverse
> entre falaises tranchantes et collines
> quelle fleur? neige gel et glace
> qui coupe et tourmente et tranche.
>   (Roubaud's translation from the Provençal)
>
> Then shines the inverse flower
> among sharp cliffs and hills.
> Which flower? snow frost and ice
> that cuts and torments and slices.   (*La Boucle*, 21/*The Loop*, 20)

The ice negates the flower, the spring, sweet season of love. In the snow, nightingale and thrush are silent. The "poétique négative" characteristic of Raimbaut d'Orange and Arnaut Daniel—their severe love poetry called obscure and hermetic—never forgets the frost just behind love's greatest joy. Their style of trobar, called *clu* (closed, secret), as distinct from the trobar *leu* (light, clear), remembers, behind song's loveliness, the "ferocity," as Roubaud puts it, "of reality mixed with death." In this "via negativa" he recognized his own path, he says. In the frigid silence he perceived a strange dissonance, glad music together with its hopeless absence. Both poetry's radiance and its black. Its all and its nothing (*La Boucle*, 21-24/*The Loop*, 20-23).

"I learned doubt," Bruno says, in Roubaud's text: "I learned doubt from those hermetic twins," Mount Cicada and Mount Vesuvius, on the day I saw the bright one gray and the cloudy one bright. And ever since, when he reaches out to greet the sunshine on a new day he remembers Cicada's advice: go to my gray brother, my cloudy twin, "la mémoire." Thus memory and doubt are associated, and I suspect it is because memory, poetry's "inner shadow caught in poems,"[13] is a shadow of doubt: doubt about poetry's "all," but also about its "nothing." Memory dreams a world that was, beautiful. A world that is, lost. It preserves this phantom world—poplars and laurels, vines heavy with fruit, a world for love—despite the harshest evidence: the world's perfectly plain, indubitable pitch black. Poetry *itself* would entertain no doubt at all, or even any make-believe belief (in love), for it belongs to the absolutely certain incomprehensibility of the world when it withdraws disdainfully into itself. *On Certainty* is the first text Roubaud cites in the first lines he could write after he saw the corpse of his wife.

> L'ayant vue, ayant reconnu la mort, que non seulement
> il semblait en être ainsi, mais qu'il en était ainsi certai-
> nement, mais qu'il n'y avait aucun sens à en douter.
> (*Quelque chose noir*, 13)

> Having seen, having recognized death, that it didn't just
> seem, but was, there was, certainly, no sense doubting it.
> (*Some Thing Black*, 11)

Memory, poetry's "shadow caught in poems," persists doubting. Whereas poetry itself, "l'absente de tout poème," accords with the black that "assures" the everlasting inexplicability of the world. Its only mode is that of vanished beings—cypress trees, laurels and poplars, stone walls, clouds, gone. I mean, poetry, as distinct from poems, lies in things' being utterly themselves—undeniably withdrawn, blacked. Roubaud considers their absence in a prose poem called "formes" (*La pluralité des mondes*, 94/*The Plurality of Worlds*, 94), where he seems bent on getting closer and closer to the *infallible* night that swallows them: "Chercher à éteindre sa pensée, se rapprocher de l'absence une et infaillible qui absorbe toute chose . . ." ("If we try to leave off thinking, try to approach the one, infallible absence that absorbs all things ...). Again, in a nearby poem called "nuages" (*La pluralité*, 98; "clouds," in *The Plurality*, 98), he seems intent on reaching the absences of the clouds (the clouds of the Provençal sky, which he has watched on and off all his life, while stretched out on the rocky ground with its scrub and thyme): "Cherchant à éteindre ma pensée, à me rapprocher de leurs absences, je m'allongeai, la tête sur les touffes de thym..." (*La pluralité* 98). ("Trying to leave off thinking, to approach their absence, I lay down, my head on tufts of thyme ... [*The Plurality*, 98]).

Impossible

These phrases, and the brief poems they belong in, with their suggestion of an annihilation pursued, are part of a longer text, called "Fin des nuages" ("The End of Clouds"), which appears in *La pluralité des mondes de Lewis*. The title of this volume is borrowed from the logician David Lewis, author of *On the Plurality of Worlds*, and in the same volume, in a poem called "Voie de l'impossible" ("The Way of the Impossible"), Roubaud writes, citing a premise of Lewis's, that while for everything that can possibly exist, there is a world where it does, there is no world for what cannot. In no world does the impossible obtain. Poetry must be worldless, then, absent from all possible worlds, for it says the impossible.[14] No impossible can be said except the way poetry says, for poetry says, but not anything. *Elle ne dit qu'en disant.*

>   aucun impossible ne peut être dit
>   autrement, ailleurs
>   qu'en disant.   je ne tais rien
>   disant : ' toi '.
>   je ne montre rien non plus.   (*La pluralité*, 29)

>   nothing impossible can be said
>   otherwise elsewhere
>   except by saying.   I hold nothing back
>   by saying : ' you '.
>   and I show nothing either.   (*The Plurality*, 30)

"The Path of the Impossible" is but one among Roubaud's various paths—which include a Via Negativa, and a Path of Double Negation, and winding itineraries all over the map of Paris, and the dark, twisted paths of the Forêt de Brocéliande ... It is along the "Voie de l'impossible" that we are following him now, though, learning a mode of poetry that does not show rather than say what can't be said, as language does in Wittgenstein's world, or keep silent about what can't be spoken of, as Wittgenstein advised (see the *Tractatus*, 4.1212; 7), but *says*. It says *you*. You utterly you, object of absolute love; the unmistakably-you you, gone from this world, alive in none. On many pages, Roubaud's wife Alix.

> Gouffre pur de l'amour.
> [...]
> Je t'aime jusque là.   (*Quelque chose noir*, 15)

> Sheer abyss of love.
> [...]
> I love you to this point.   (*Some Thing Black*, 13)

Poetry addresses this nothing, this no one anywhere, you.

> Devenue identique.
> [...]
> Disparue.   (*Quelque chose noir*, 68)

> Become identical.
> [...]
> Gone.   (*Some Thing Black*, 66)

> Dire de toi : dire tout rien.   (68)

> To say of you : to say absolutely nothing.   (66)

To say absolutely. To say *all* and, exactly the same, *nothing*. "L'absolu vide de l'amour."[15] To say of you. I love you to that extreme.

Here is the poem, in *La pluralité des mondes de Lewis*, called

> *Voie de l'impossible*
>
> l'impossible, en aucun monde, n'est le cas.
> et dans un monde tout, toujours, n'est que possibles.
> aucun impossible ne peut être dit
> autrement, ailleurs
> qu'en disant.   je ne tais rien
> disant ' toi.'
> je ne montre rien non plus.   (*La pluralité des mondes*, 29)[16]

The Way of the Impossible

the impossible is not the case in any world.
in any world everything, always, can only be possible.
nothing impossible can be said
otherwise, elsewhere
except by saying.   I hold nothing back
by saying : ' you'.
and I show nothing either.   (*The Plurality of Worlds*, 30)

Identity, Continued

Poetry, saying, but nothing, says you, I claim. You utterly you ("devenue identique;" "disparue"). "Viviane est Viviane," say the fifty-seven sonnets in Emmanuel Hocquard's *Test de solitude*.

Viviane est Viviane, seule, évidente.
                    (*Un test* II. The phrase is repeated many times.)

This sentence has no author, one sonnet says (XX)—it is too obvious to be attributed to anybody (XX, Book II). One might describe Hocquard's ambition as a poet by observing that he wishes to write things so clear they practically white themselves out. "La lumière prend toute la place" (*Méditations photographiques*, 15). "Light takes up all the room." He has a special affection for the blank letters, the brilliant white bits of paper that appear passing from hand to hand in several Vermeer paintings.[17]

Viviane est Viviane—an expression to be taken *à la lettre*—has no author, and the *is* in it is not a verb, we learn, of which the first Viviane would be the subject and the second a predicate, because there is but a single Viviane. *Seule, évidente*. And being she is not—as we came to understand when thinking of indistinction and being—a property of hers, or an attribute.

She is she is not a sentence, really, because sentences are never alone, Hocquard believes; they always link up together (*Un test*, XXI/*A Test*, XXI). *Viviane est Viviane* is a tautology, which is to say the solitary type of statement that nothing leads up to and that nothing follows from. Sheer disconnect.

Rien ne l'explique. Elle n'explique rien. Elle se
suffit. Rien ne l'amène, rien ne la suit. Elle est

elle-même, seule, évidente.
"Comme notre vie." (*Un test*, XXI)

Nothing explains it. It explains nothing. It is
sufficient unto itself. Nothing leads up to it,
nothing follows it. It is itself, *alone, evident.*
"Like our lives." (*A Test*, XXI)

The *is* in a tautology is not a verb, or even, as it turns out, exactly a word. But rather it's the term of which another poem of Hocquard's says that it is *is not*.

[…]
Un pont est fait de trois
l'élément central n'est pas énonçable

Ce troisième est *n'est pas*
[…] (*Théorie des tables*, 22)

[…]
A bridge is made of three
the central element is inexpressible

This third is *is not*
[…] (*Theory*, 22)

Sometimes he calls this central, inexpressible element "the tautology's empty middle." Or again, "the word that lacks"—by which I believe we must understand: the word whose lack is *it*. We will return to these puzzles, but for the moment I wish only to enter, next to Roubaud's preoccupation with impossible identity, these Hocquard-induced premonitions of a hole in language where *is* is—I mean, where it is not, but *is not* is: in short, where you cannot tell *is* from *is not*. A white thread from a black one.

Hocquard and Roubaud knew each other, read each other's books, sometimes collaborated, and shared an interest in Wittgenstein, as you will have guessed from Hocquard's quoting *On Certitude*—"There, like our life."

Rien ne l'explique. Elle n'explique rien. Elle se
suffit. Rien ne l'amène, rien ne la suit. Elle est
elle-même, seule, *évidente.*
"Comme notre vie."

Private Language

Now one of the implications of Roubaud's axiom, *la poésie ne dit qu'en disant* (poetry says, but not anything), is that poetry does not conform to the "publicity of meaning rule." It says nothing transmissible, interpersonal. When it occurs, it occurs for someone in particular. *In* someone. In private.

It occurs as the effect of a memory, Roubaud declares, in *Poetry, etcetera*. It happens as a memory-effect in a specific person. "It's your memory and no other," he states. "Non-interpersonal" (*Poetry, etcetera*, 105/*Poésie, etcetera*, 103).

"Poetry in your language is the memory of your language in you," he goes on. I expect he means that the formal demands to which a poet subjects his language animate its hidden joints, its colors, and shadows—all the various dissonances and jolts that (apart from everything words can be understood by everyone to mean) matter privately in different ways to different speakers. Poetry lights up in individual readers their own incommunicable memory of their language (poetry is, as Roubaud often states, "amour de la langue"). I suspect, though, that he suggests something further. The "memory of your language in you" that he speaks of does not seem to be remembrance, exactly, or recollection, in any ordinary sense, for Roubaud writes that "[p]oetry, for someone, is the *being* of his language" (*Poetry, etcetera*, 106/*Poésie* etcetera, 104; my emphasis). Poetry, I daresay, is, in some particular person, his or her own language's presence to itself. Its identicalness, in that person—its self-revelation. For I suppose a person's own language has no way be known save by itself—in him or her. Nor does it need any other way.

If a person welcomes and recognizes it, poetry makes the language she or he happens to speak *her* language, Roubaud asserts; it makes them the possessor of their tongue. "My language is mine through poetry" (*Poetry, etcetera*, 106/*Poésie, etcetera*, 104).

Yet poetry is the *memory* of a person's language, in him or her, as we saw. So one suspects that in Roubaud's view poetry occurs as the memory of a "revelation-of-the-self-to-the-self language. The memory of a private language that no language is.

Wittgenstein ruled private language impossible (see *Philosophical Investigations*, 95-111). Wittgenstein mattered to Roubaud, largely because of Alix Cléo Roubaud, to whom he was married from 1979 till 1983, when she died. Wittgenstein and photography were her two passions (see *Le grand incendie*, 404/*The Great Fire*, 315).[18]

Poetry is its *own* memory, Roubaud insists (*Poetry, etcetera,* 119/*Poésie, etcetera,* 117). I understand him to mean poetry is self-memory in us (in each one separately, privately).

But not the memory *of* anything (or anyone), not even *of* itself. Poetry does not seem to be, in Roubaud's thinking, any *thing* that is remembered (any more than light ["essentially present to itself"] could be any thing that is illuminated). Poetry is not an object of memory or an object at all, especially not its own (the idea that literature takes itself for its own object is what Roubaud describes testily as a "*contresens barthésien*"). Poetry is *now,* he regularly stresses. It *happens* inside us (differently in each one), and *now* cannot be an object of memory. "Memory does not take poetry as its object. Poetry *is* its own memory" (*Poetry, etcetera,* 119/*Poésie, etcetera,* 117; Roubaud's emphasis). Poetry is the memory of nothing ... else.

Strange self-memory.

The light of poetry memory is black: "Memory of poetry: black light of memory: diaphanous of the darkness, in us" (*Poetry, etcetera,* 108/*Poésie, etcetera,* 106).

Emmanuel Hocquard would call such immediate memory, of nothing (else)—a *souvenir sans objet*: a reminiscence that cannot be connected to any past. It surges up, by surprise, in the present. Now.[19]

Like Roubaud, Hocquard has an attachment to private language.

Intonation

He observes that while everybody uses the same words—the all-purpose ones that fill the dictionary (and he sees no need for any other, special words for poetry; the ordinary ones will do)—still, nobody's words are really at all the same as anyone else's (see, for example, *ma haie* 232-33). Poetry, or, as Hocquard usually prefers to say, writing, starts from this interruption in communication, this disconnect.

Everyone knows the meaning of the word *table,* he concedes, and in the unlikely event of a disagreement, anyone can look it up. But nobody learned to speak from the dictionary; we all learned somewhere in particular, at a particular time, among particular people, and the household that happens to have been ours, the family members we shared our meals with, the stuff that would appear on the table at lunch and breakfast and so on, color differently the words, such as *table,* that each one of us uses. The particular tables we happen to have sat at, or stood before, or studied—the circumstances of our having done so, our particular sensibility—give table different *intonations* in each one of us, as Hocquard often puts it.[20] Different registers, timbres, tone colors. We all use the same word and understand each other—"tout le monde se ressemble"[21]—but it's not the same: "Ma table n'est pas ta table." My table is not your table. I speak as you do, and you as I; on either side of a glass partition, we mouth each other's words.

Thus, no language that is in general use convinces Hocquard. He hates the uniform grammar that regulates us (with its persons and their properties, its subjects and objects)—the standard vocabulary not stained by any specific set of circumstances, not stuck to any particular speaker—he detests the all-purpose lingo, the choral idiom we chant in unison, which bears on distant objects and general topics, and ensures the generalized, third-person knowledge shared by people who have never met. In short, he takes the dimmest possible view of the "community" we are led to evoke and the belief that we share a common world. For he considers what we really share to be the interruption of that continuum. What connects people, and things, is what does not. "Ils ont en commun ce qui les sépare: un bord d'ombre," he observes.[22] They have in common what separates them: a shaded edge.

And

> Ils ont en commun ce qui
> ne communique pas   (*Conditions de lumière*, 70).

> What they have in common
> does not communicate   (*Conditions of Light*, 70)

An incommunicable commonplace: this is Hocquard's paradoxical preoccupation. A divisive bond, or a partition of sameness.

So, he isn't interested in being an author, with a public. He can do without literature, that cultural institution—apparatus for producing authors, readers (critics, influences, exchanges, round tables: in short, more literature, which is the same in this regard as TV: every night, on every channel, all that's showing is TV[23]).

I should say that nothing in Jacques Roubaud's outlook really corresponds to this aversion to literature, though Hocquard is not alone among his contemporaries in feeling it. It isn't exactly that Roubaud loves literature; rather, he recognizes as his own the lyric tradition launched by the troubadours in the thirteenth century in Provence, which he sums up as follows: *l'amour le chant la poésie*. Love Song Poetry. He explains that you must understand *l'amour la poésie* as *l'amour de la poésie* (just as *La mort Artu* means *la mort du roi Arthur*); that all possible permutations of the three terms are significant (*la poésie de l'amour, l'amour du chant*, etc.), and that on every level, in every sense, by every means, the trobar affirms the unity of song and poetry and love. "Le chant chante que le chant est d'amour devenant poésie."[24] Song sings that song is of love becoming poetry.

Among the troubadours, though, those with whom he feels the closest kinship are the severe, hermetic ones, like Raimbaut d'Orange and Arnaut Daniel, as we saw; and we saw, too, that their songs tend to "black." Roubaud named his book about troubadour poetry *La Fleur inverse* after the ice flower—the cold, knife-like bloom of poetry's absence (inverse flower)—in the canso by Raimbaut d'Orange that so impressed him when first he encountered it. And *La Fleur inverse* begins with an analysis of the famous song by Guillaume d'Aquitaine called "vers de dreit nien": poem on absolutely nothing. Love, absolute love, absolutely nothing. "Gouffre pur." Of course I am speaking recklessly. I will come back later to Guillaume d'Aquitaine, more soberly, but here I only mean to stress, while reporting Hocquard's aversion to Literature, Roubaud's "éloge inverse": his harsh, inverse praise, of poetry.

Private Language, Continued

Hocquard, for his part, not caring to be a literary author, undertakes to be a letter writer: to write in the first person, that is, and to someone. To someone he knows, and who knows him. Dear Norma, Dear Pierre, Dear Olivier, we often read on his pages—which he frequently signs, Emmanuel. For example, in *ma haie* (416-42), one can read a dozen issues of a newsletter, *Les Dernières Nouvelles de la cabane* (Latest News from the Cabin), which he put out each week toward the end of the 1990s ("on Fridays, time permitting"): he addressed each issue, bearing on various thoughts and projects of his, to one or two particular friends and mailed it to them.

To write in the first person—to write to someone, for someone—means, in Hocquard, at any rate, to write not *about* anything, certainly not about oneself, but *from* some*place*. For example, from the *cabin*. He refers in an interview to a film Godard was once commissioned to make about Lausanne, and which he lifted out of the dismal travel-writing genre by composing it *from* Lausanne, instead of *on* or *about* the city, and by addressing it to a friend, Freddy Buache. The film was called *La Lettre à Freddy Buache*. (See "Comment en suis-je arrivé là?," in *ma haie* 443 ff).

This is to say that Hocquard does not wish to *represent* anything when he writes. The point of writing for him is rather to convey, to someone, what *cannot* be represented and *about* which there is nothing to say. It is not an object, in the world, that you could point to, discuss, and so on. Rather, it is a particular gaze, *on* a world. A specific lookout or vantage point, by definition singular, impossible to communicate or share. The point of writing for Hocquard is to write from there. From his own island observation station, as it were, trained on whatever happens to lie right in front of it, right now.

> Octobre. Le retour des rouges-gorges. Ce que j'ai
> sous les yeux (*Un test de solitude*, II)

> October. Return of the robins. What's in front of
> my eyes. (*A Test of Solitude*, II)

or

> Si je *vous* écrivais au passé j'aurais l'impression
> de mentir. (*Un test*, I, Livre II)

> If I wrote to *you* in the past tense I would feel I
> was lying. (*A Test*, I, Book II)

or again

> *Vous* décrire d'où je *vous* écris en tournant le dos
> à mes livres. Face à l'ordinateur.
> La table d'écriture. La table de lecture sous la
> fenêtre. Deux table. Lampe sept. (*Un test*, IV, Livre II)

> To describe where I write to *you*, turning my
> back on my books, facing the computer.
> My writing table. My reading table under the
> window. Two table. Lamp seven. (*A Test*, IV, Book II)

The computer, the lamps, the returning robins—the things lying in a particular field of vision at a particular moment, now—are just hints suggesting something about the gaze under which they fall. They are "indications of my solitude," Hocquard writes elsewhere.[25] Signs or symptoms of a singular *regard*'s particular character. "quelqu'un = un regard / Pas quelqu'un," he writes. "someone = his gaze / Not someone" (*Theory of Tables*, 43)

So in this respect Hocquard thinks like Wittgenstein: the world is my world; its limits are those of my language. It is the reality coordinated with a specific point, of view, a specific outlook.[26] This is not the world of a self, with a past, a personality, a psychology, about which a lot could be said (the self is just a point, a vantage point), but neither is it the world as generally construed and administered, with many features bearing names everybody knows how to use. It is rather the world where some particular stray list of errands (Meet R. at 4; pick up the cleaning) means something, or where there is a lot to be made of this reminder (which concludes a poem of Hocquard's): "Ce soir pour le diner / un demi-lapin aux carrottes" (*Cette histoire est la mienne* in *ma haie* 479-80).

> this evening for dinner
> half a rabbit with carrots[27]

He opposes to monopoly—to the rule of one, one whole, one standard system of circuits and connections guaranteeing the dependable correspondence of anybody with everybody—a bunch of discontinuous individual lives and segmented worlds, splintered space, broken-up languages . . .

> Trois points de vue
> trois pronoms
>
> Tu es le monde
>
> Personne ne passe
> d'une à un autre une
>
> Les objets défilent
> tu et je ne se touchent pas
>
> Quelqu'un est immobile
>
> Regarde   (*Théorie des tables*, 45)

> Three points of view
> three pronouns
>
> You are the world
>
> No one passes
> from a one to another one
>
> The objects file by

> *you* and *I* don't touch
>
> Someone is motionless
>
> Looks   (*Theory of Tables*, 45)

Nonetheless, Hocquard's is a confidential language. It entails no representation, only a present—which is nothing without a receiver: without someone to be *for*. Whence the great importance of the addressee. Let us say, Norma. Writing, in Hocquard's letter-writing mode, is necessarily between two. Strictly *entre nous*.

> Je n'ai jamais écrit à quelqu'un
> qui ne sait de quoi
> je vis et j'ai vécu   (*Théorie*, 23)
>
> I have never written anyone
> who doesn't know how
> I live and have lived   (*Theory*, 23)

Correspondence

"Dear V.," we read in *Theory of Tables*, "take what you have at hand / sort what there is on a table..."[28] I understand this to mean, "Dear V., write me back"; and to suggest that writing a letter to someone—writing in the first person, that is—amounts to surveying a scattering of language bits, motley pieces of a common language, and picking out those one likes, for whatever reason. The words that appeal to Hocquard are not at all unusual, but they look to him, he says, as if by chance they'd fallen out of common usage and were just lying around like tesserae that no one has been able to piece back together into a larger mosaic they might once have been part of. And they strike him as a likely present for someone. Someone specific. Just meant for her, or him, you might say. So, having copied, or printed them out, he signs, and puts them in the mail. To Oscarine. Whatever they might convey to somebody else—a member of the general public, say, a Reader of Literature—to their *destinataire* the words in them will say that they are for her, from Emmanuel. They will mean that in his eyes they are meant for her. She will see in them the color or sheen of his hand, the particular cast of his gaze. That is, she will see how he sees, and writes. Not *what* he sees, by any means, or even *what* he writes, but *how*—from his solitary outpost, his island. Writing, as I understand Hocquard's, just bears an intonation. It isn't about anything, anything representable; it simply has an accent. "What I write says nothing but how I say what / I say here," we read, in one of the sonnets in *A Test of Solitude* (the twenty-second).

Robinson

Hocquard is a serious copier—all solitaries are, he says. All islanders. His favorite islander is Robinson Crusoe, after whom he names a method: "la Méthode Robinson" (*Cette histoire est la mienne*, in *ma haie*, 484-85). Stranded on his island, and using only the materials he found at his disposal, Robinson made copies, Hocquard observes, of various things that had furnished his world before the shipwreck. And these new things, the same as their original models, nonetheless had, as you might say, a slight accent. "Robinson, on his island, acts like Crusoe before the shipwreck," Hocquard writes, "but makes the same thing resound differently."[29]

Hocquard claims that all of his books are copies of themselves. As if the point were always to hear the ordinary words in them sounding a little different. This could serve as a definition of *literality*, a term Hocquard stresses, and which many of his readers employ to characterize his writing in general. When, slipping out of your habitual ways of hearing or reading, you abruptly take a sentence literally (see it all of a sudden as if it had been copied out for you as, say, a grammatical example or as a little present), it sounds the same as usual but also not quite. Likewise, should you unexpectedly (perhaps by accident) perceive an ordinary statement such as *Maylis est jolie* as a tautology. It doesn't sound quite the same.

Here is an interesting example: the thirty-first sonnet in *Un test de solitude*. Hocquard asks there what name to give a certain space: the apparently impassable, immeasurable span between the water feature and the burnt stump in his garden. Or rather, he states that *What name shall we give . . .* is a question. And then, he writes that *the word that lacks is that name* is an answer. Finally, he proposes to consider *the word that lacks is that name* as a tautology. When *I* do that, I think, all of a sudden with surprise: Oh! *That's* the missing word. I found it. It's the missing one!

Hocquard observes elsewhere that sometimes an intractable problem will suddenly, effortlessly solve itself. A problem, notably, such as what to call, how to measure, how to cross, how to *get out of* an aporetic space (for example, a deep woods, or a dismal story, or a hole). Often, just by chance, such a problem will provide its own solution. You could say that chez Hocquard, all the mysteries are clues.[30]

In what I myself have written earlier here about, for example, "the colors of nothing," I have been counting on effects of *intonation* similar to the ones I have just been trying to bring out in Hocquard's pages. Further along in this book, as I keep stressing "the feature that distinguishes no one," and other similar "properties," I will be hoping to provoke a slightly odd sensation of the kind that comes over one when, unpredictably, one stumbles upon a lacking name, a missing word, a nonexistent answer right in its place: just where *is not* is.

Blue Nash, Angry Chicken, Foxgloves, Geraniums . . .

Now when the world opened, as Hocquard puts it, onto writing for him, it let a certain number of things fall out of it. These dropouts included bits of the garden beside the house in Tangiers where he grew up, a few cranes from the port, plus a blue Nash, a dead titmouse, and some fragments of the domestic language spoken in his home when he was small (it was a sparse, concrete tongue, low on adjectives and metaphors, whose every word served to name some specific, existing thing or person: the seamstress who did the family's mending, the well in their garden, foxgloves, geraniums). These items have shaken loose from the world as it is generally recognized and engineered; their names have fallen out through some holes in the standard French he learned in school (that trove of words that people who have never met each other can confidently exchange, even if they've never seen the thing they're discussing). The blue Nash, two or three cranes, an angry chicken have dropped out, among other shards, in no particular order, washed of context; they are of no use for anything but to Hocquard's eyes all the better for that: marvelously distinct and gleaming. They have fallen onto the pages of his books, and lie there scattered like pieces of ceramic on an archeologist's table.

He contemplates them, and it seems to him that he is seeing them for the first time. He calls each indubitable one an "instant de conviction."[31] I am inclined to think they are little pieces of a language that is his alone, as opposed to the one in general circulation—little odds and ends of a first language, the one that still names *his* chicken, his and no one else's garden gate, and so on. Fragments of a private language, then. Or no. Rather, I suspect the conviction that they inspire in him stems from their striking him unexpectedly as bits of a language he has never heard before, yet recognizes—a language that would be his own were there such a thing as a person's own language or, better: a language that would belong, exclusively, to someone, maybe to him, if there were a person—he?—to whom nothing at all belongs, to whom nothing whatsoever is proper.

Personne

Hocquard wrote a poem once in honor of such a person, the poet named No one, Pessoa.[32] The part of it that I wish to dwell on here bears on Fernando Pessoa's uniqueness.

> Fernando Pessoa est unique,
> c'est-à dire comme un géranium
> au milieu d'autres géraniums,
> c'est-à-dire comme tout le monde.
>
> Fernando Pessoa is unique,
> which is to say like a geranium
> in the middle of other geraniums,
> which is to say like everyone.   (My translation)

Pessoa is unique, as I understand it, not in the sense that we are all special, as we all so like to say (each of us with our very own perceptions, opinions, tastes), but in the way a geranium in the middle of a geranium bed is that geranium, the one no other one is. All geraniums being the same in that respect means that being the one no other is is by no means a distinction. Or rather, it is that which distinguishes no one. It was Pessoa's distinction.

It does not attach to Pessoa, however, or to anyone, it is no one's particular attribute, simply anyone's at all, *indifféremment—everyone's*, for that matter. So, it offers nothing to see, but is rather what you do not see: the radiance Hocquard in a later book calls nakedness, suffusing a body it by no means belongs to and with which it cannot be identified, a body whose face it erases.[33] Let me stress this apparent paradox, then, which pervades all Hocquard's writing: the trait most properly mine is not attributable to me (or to anyone) and is not a trait (not an attribute).

Fausse propriété

"Fausse propriété" (false property) is a useful expression for designating this most proper of all properties, which consists in not being one. "Fausse propriété" can serve to name the distinction, between any one of us and any other, that we share (it *belongs* to no one). "Fausse propriété" is Hocquard's French translation of the title of a book by Gordon Matta-Clark, *Fake Estates*. Fake estates are tiny parcels of land *in between* big-city buildings, thin strips left empty by architects and urban planners that nobody can make any use of because they are so narrow. They aren't anyone's estate, they are the property of no one. Hocquard shares with Matta-Clark an affection for these slender stripes of inactivity here and there in an animated, busy metropolis. They are like blanks. Vacant intervals. Hocquard adopts the expression fake estate or *fausse propriété* in *L'Invention du verre*,[34] and on his pages it suggests a blank or empty spot, a hole opening up just where you'd expect to find the unique character, the special attribute belonging to anything that simply is what it is. The property of being—the property that consists for any being in its state of being—is, for Hocquard, a property that, like Matta-Clark's fake estate, doesn't belong. Its loss, you might say, or its lack, is it.

Private Language, Encore

To anyone—any one—who simply is that one, the one no other is, not even being that one (all alone, perfectly plain) belongs. Nothing belongs to him. Hocquard said once that his ambition is poverty (see "Ma vie privée," in *ma haie*, 272). The Nash, the foxgloves and the geraniums are scraps of *his* tongue, then, without attribution. They are scraps of no one's language, or just anyone's, without distinction.

So you see that my reflection on his *intonations*—on the tone color of words, specific to each separate speaker, impossible to represent or introduce into general circulation—you see that my reflection on all this keeps veering away from common assumptions about the general and the particular, the public and the private (the singular and the commonplace, the unique and the ordinary). For this reason I do not want to overdo the garden gate, the titmouse corpse (first sights, first words, the vivid, palpable vocabulary of early childhood, or its pared down, "literal" character—even though Hocquard does state at one point that when both the "petite langue" of his childhood and the child he was were past and gone, poetry seemed to him "a kind of diminutive domestic language within language in general"[35]—even so, I won't dwell on it, because for one thing, *literal*, for Hocquard, means the *letter*, and all he cares about is what happens in books (as he says, exaggerating a little, no doubt); moreover, "there is no beginning." No first things.

And yet, I won't forego here the occasion to think of Collobert (for whom there is no beginning either): of the struggle that a reader of her pages feels to *say*, to bring forth a word, a few, and of a hope, invested briefly in "a different language." It wouldn't be a language exactly, but sounds, the sounds of a language not understood, or simply noises—not just any noises but noises that have been chosen and used and loved by lips that are loved—smoothed by use like stones worn by water; sounds with meaning, having faces the way stones long washed in the sea do; transfigured sounds, the repeated ones heard by the crib, as I imagine, and at the high chair ... Nothing much comes of it, in Collobert's texts, but still ...

                       —non pas des bruits
quelconques—des sons déjà tout faits—déjà usés par des
lèvres—aimés—roulés longtemps—des sons signifiants
aussi—choisis pour quelque chose—aimés—transfigurés

visages de mots—de sons lourds—essayer—ouvrir à peine
les lèvres—coller la langue au palais—faire passer l'air
lentement—en soufflant—ça pour la tendresse
                                      (*Dire II*, in *Oeuvres I*, 244-45)

                       —not just any noise
—sounds already formed—already worn away by
lips—beloved—smoothed over time—meaningful sounds
too—chosen for something—loved—transfigured

faces of words—of heavy sounds—try—just barely open
the lips—place the tongue against the palate—make air pass
through slowly—by breathing—do that for tenderness   (My translation)

Accident

Once Hocquard composed a poem—right in the letterpress printer's form, composing stick in hand, he says—whose words, sparsely arrayed across facing pages appear to mirror each other on either side of the split or fold running down the middle.[36] We might consider associating this break or crease with the divisive commonplace we have so far just barely met up with in his thinking, or with the central section of a bridge made of three—the inexpressible, the silent part. Or, possibly, with the hole we've thought we could locate in language wherever *is* is (I mean, is not).

    In any case, in "une" (the name of the poem I am describing), replicating patterns—each something like the inverse of the other—reflect or mime each other from side to side of a central divide. "Une surface. A côté une autre surface qui lui ressemble," Hocquard notes, elsewhere—in a fragment called

"Diptyque" (*Un privé*, 17). "Entre les deux une fente d'ombre." (One surface. Next to it another surface resembling it. Between the two a shadowy cleft [my translation].) So, we could also consider associating the seam running down the middle of the book, and of the poem, "une," with the hinge between two panels of a diptych by Raquel Levy, where two different shades become indistinguishable, where the painter comes as close as she can to painting light itself, *le neutre*, almost.

It seems the two facing surfaces form the subject of a narrative. "In the succession of pages, two by two, the juxtaposition of the scenes is the subject of the narrative" (*Un privé*, 17). Two like pages, or panels—two similar scenes or stories—face each other across a dark crack. Or again, two shores, you might think (remembering Hocquard's lookout as a child in Tangiers on the Strait of Gibraltar) double each other on either side of a tight passage. Nothing passes, though, from shore to shore. The two scenes don't communicate. "Two narratives cannot coincide. They have in common what separates them: a shaded edge" (*Un privé*, 17)

Here is a "récit" based on a few particular words that drift through Hocquard's writing, reappearing fairly often, but never really linking up to form a story. I linked them up on my own, in the little narrative I am about to present. I more or less made it up, thinking it would help me begin to understand Hocquard's world, with its interior edge, its "bord d'ombre." Echo—daughter of the earth and the air ("terre et air")—annoyed Juno and was punished by being silenced. She lost her voice. The narrows between shores, the dark groove between doubled, mirroring pages are not unlike her constricted throat. "Tu avances dans le détroit, ni terre ni air. C'est le lieu où la voix s'étrangle," we read in a poem called "Un jour, le détroit" (*Un privé*, 15). (You advance in the strait, neither earth nor air. It is the place where the voice is stifled.) The doubled scene, "le récit des bords," folds a throttled voice into the central divide.

And the bright language bits that fetch up unexpectedly in Hocquard's mind or on his tables, so brilliant—each so solitary, so contextless he feels he is seeing them for the first time (and which command his "conviction," startling him with the sound of a familiar tongue never heard before)—bring to his ears the sound of the voice that Echo lost. There was no voice at all till there was not hers. Ever since—ever since the "accident"—there have been many, echoing each other. There was no world till space broke up and there were many, all incommunicable; and there is no *one*, till life divides or makes itself into separation—till "la vie se fait division" (*Un test*, XVI, Livre II). Thereupon there are three, at least, impersonations, masks. And this as soon as ever life is life. *Is* hollows out an impassable channel through the middle, of being. "*V* [*V* for *Viviane* and for *vie*] *est V.* [...] *Fold in*" (*Un test*, XXVIII).

More than one story like this—about loss, long ago, before anything had even begun—make dim, fleeting appearances in Hocquard's writing, but I suspect they may actually prove to be ways out of such stories: and out of stories in general: out of the language where sentences link up and one thing leads to another ("Aucune autre histoire, Viviane, que comment se / libérer des histoires." "No stories, Viviane, save how to / get free of stories" [*Un test*, XXIV]). I suspect the story I want to introduce now—it comes from Hocquard's novel *Aerea*—is really a way out of the Book of Genesis. Adam is the name of its main character, and "I'll have no descendants" are his words on page one. But that is not what I will emphasize right away.

Around the middle of this story Adam spends a quiet morning playing a board game. At one point he throws the dice and lands on square 42, the labyrinth. Ah, too bad! his friendly opponent says. You must pay the standard price and return to square 30. Adam observes that the square he is on should really be called not labyrinth, but forest. His friend's response to this comment—it must be strange, he says, for a person as cautious as you to get lost in the woods—suggests that it isn't only on the game board that Adam has, unexpectedly, got lost. Adam merely points out to his friend that when speaking of getting lost in the woods one shouldn't say, as the friend had, "se perdre en forêt," but rather "s'y être perdu." The distinction, as I understand it, is between someone who would be going along more or less well but then, unfortunately, would lose his way, and, on the other hand, someone who would get lost without ever having been anywhere at all yet. Such a person would *come to be*, lost. He would, if you like, come into the world a missing person. The forest would be that world; it would be the place—the person's birthplace—where all at once, before he knew it, he'd be, no place. Adam explains: "S'y être perdu [c'est] être en même temps quelque part et nulle part. Dans la forêt et hors de tout" (52). "To 'be lost there' [is] to be at the same time somewhere and nowhere. Inside a forest and outside of everything" (37).

I dare say it would be frightful, in that forest world, to see that a thing, or a person is born. It would be awful just to see that he is there. Or that anything is—that anything just is, what it is, it alone, perfectly clear. For you would also see that it is not.

So much light, so much dark, both at once.

A flash of darkness in broad day, a tiny fracture in the relentless continuity of things—all my writing, Hocquard has stated, bears on "*l'écart*," the split.

I think it must be an "*accroc noir dans le jour*"—flash of *nothing* "*soudain là*," right under your nose—that Adam has in mind when he tells his friend, during the continuation of their board game in *Aerea*, that the forest is "engendered in fear." The forest, a bad square to land on in the game—a trap far worse than a labyrinth in Adam's account—must be something like a world engendered by the fear of finding oneself lost in it: a world brought forth by the dread of being born, that is; the dread of being, at all. Once—not in *Aerea*; in another text—Hocquard described this dread by evoking the "*peur sans nom*," which everyone must feel at least once in his or her life on encountering all of a sudden the utter opacity of some ordinary word. Some word like *table*, which for you has a specific intonation (it is *your* table), but which you also share with everybody else and which, as commonplace, is for you utterly impenetrable, "*pure énigme*." It is a matter, I believe, of suddenly seeing, in what is properly one's own, something that belongs to nobody—but to absolutely anybody, without distinction. It would be like seeing one's own face abruptly erased. Or, like not seeing anyone, in a mirror. "*C'est comme être brusquement devenu aveugle*," Hocquard writes, "*ou se trouver quelque part et soudain ne pas du tout savoir où l'on est. Etre perdu*" ("*Tout le monde se ressemble*," in *ma haie*, 233). (It is like having abruptly gone blind, or finding oneself somewhere and suddenly having no idea where one is. Being lost.)

The horror of such perdition engenders the forest world of *Aerea*, I expect; likewise women give birth in pain.

The forest is a genre, a genre engendered in fear, and elegy is the name that Hocquard assigns to it. Here is its pattern, as he briskly sums it up: "*Ah! everything was great but time passed, and Alas! now all is lost*" (*Cette histoire est la mienne*, in *ma haie*, 467/"Ah!→Alas!" in *This Story Is Mine*).

So elegy appears to be informed by the idea (comforting?) that, contrary to what Adam explains to his friend, getting lost in the forest is something that happens *after* everything has been going well. In other words, loss is the loss *of* something that was present before; loss has an *object*.

An object toward which there is a tendency to turn back, longingly (or regretfully, as from square 47, the forest, to square 30, after paying the price).

I expect the elegiac genre—the turning-back (the chastised) mode (the mode, if you will, of representation and remembering, where a representation always represents *something* (else, prior), and memories always have objects)—I expect the elegiac genre is engendered by the fear of loss without any object: loss, but not *of*; loss but not of anything *else*. Startled by something that *is* its lack, or whose loss is *it*, one turns away, retreating in fear.

Probably loss with no object bears a relation to questions that also have none—whose ostensible object, I mean (*this*, for example, when the question is *What's this*?), answers them. The startling, swift easiness of such questions bars your way, you can't face it, you turn back.

And such a question might well come to you, in a flash, when you surprise something right before your eyes whose obscurity bursts out all sparkles. What is this thing whose blatant clarity falls suddenly over your eyes like the final curtain? "Toutes les évidences lui sont énigme," Anne-Marie Albiach wrote. So much light, so much dark, both at once. So much black, and white, but which is which?

2

"Birth was the death of him"

— Beckett, *A Piece of Monologue*

Uteri terrae

There is a boy in Hocquard's pages who is frightened by the sheer weirdness of things being there, cropping up in front of him. This child is terrified by their unaccountable materialization. In an essay called "Uteri terrae," "Womb of the Earth" (*Un privé*, 123-26), Hocquard recounts coming upon a cricket once when he was small and trying to capture it. He describes the terror he felt when he couldn't detach it from the dusty ground to which it seemed riveted. Probably it was laying its eggs, but this explanation did not occur to the boy. He had thought crickets belonged in the airy domain of leaves and branches, whereas this one was planted in the ground, rooted like a vegetable. Too strange.

This cricket reappears occasionally in Hocquard's writing; there is also a terrible dog that regularly barred his approach to a favorite playmate's house, and a scorpion that stops Adam in his tracks in *Aerea*. It seems this spider was itself terrified, for we read that its own fright worked its way into the boy as surely as its venom would have done. Adam backed up and returned the way he'd come. "Yes, I turned back, for the first time, that day" (*Aerea in the Forests*, 4/*Area dans les forêts*, 9).

In "Womb of the Earth," after the cricket anecdote, Hocquard evokes Lucretius's description of an aged, sterile planet, unable to engender any but mutant creatures with distorted features and missing parts, and he observes

49

that however strange they were, nature has ever since, via haphazard combinations, produced more and more like them. So the disquiet they provoke in us cannot be attributed simply to their forms or circumstances; it lies in their just existing, in the unaccountable, incontestable fact of their birth. "Their strangeness is entirely due to one thing only: their existence. Their enigma stems from the unjustifiable and singular necessity of their birth" (*Un privé*, 126). I expect it is the staggering *nowhere*, flaring up black as night with anything that *is, right there*—anything that suddenly materializes and stands there radiantly, right before your eyes—I expect it is *that* that makes birth so weird and dreadful.

Generally people cast a blind eye on what happens to appear in their field of vision, or falls, as Hocquard sometimes says, under their gaze. Habitually they look away the better to ward off the fear of things' perplexing strangeness—the better not to notice the "unjustifiable necessity of their birth." But the whole point of poetry is to see something. This is a motto that Hocquard adopted from Louis Zukofsky (*ma haie*, 16). And he adds: The point is suddenly to see what you do not see. What you are in the habit of overlooking. The point is to become unaccustomed. Stripped of habits. Surprised.

This means, among other things, that the point of reading a poem is to look straight at what is written, instead of seeking, as usual, what lies *behind* the letter (the point is to read literally). This is hard, as Wittgenstein exclaimed. Hocquard quotes him in French: "Comme il m'est difficile de voir ce que j'ai sous les yeux!" (*ma haie*, 236). How hard it is to see what's staring me in the face.

But what you see all of a sudden, right before your eyes thanks to poetry, is what you do not see: at least, it is what you and just about everybody else are in the habit of overlooking, because you are afraid. The whole point of poetry, then, must be suddenly to see the "accroc noir dans le jour"—the flash of *nothing* "soudain là"—and not be frightened, not turn back. The point of poetry must be not to let terror turn you around.

And not to recoil in shame when you are discovered: I mean, when, stripped of habits, you see that you are naked.

Guilty!

Figures that bar the way, in Hocquard's pages, and make a person turn back—the scorpion which I've mentioned; the dog—suggest the angel with flaming sword at the gates of Eden, turning the biblical Adam and Eve out of paradise.

There is even a little kid, whom I haven't mentioned, who springs up more than once in *Aerea*, right in the middle of the adult Adam's path, yelling inexplicably, "Go away! Go away!" (*Aerea in the Forests*, 9/*Aerea dans les forêts*, 18). "Guilty," Adam thinks. "But of what?" (58/80).

Of nakedness, perhaps—of being, naked, or of being, period. Of being quite like what Hocquard calls elsewhere a "naked lie" ("mensonge nu"). This is a representation, with no prior presence to refer back to—no object faithfully to imitate. Or to fake, either. A naked lie is a fiction that neither reproduces nor falsifies any reality. It is a role, you might say—a theatrical role—but no one's. A shadow that nothing casts.

Indeed, Adam sometimes refers to himself as a specter. By this he seems to mean both ghost and spectrum: both the person who comes into the world lost (arrives nowhere), but also the whole breakout, so to speak—the entire gamut—of *personae* that grammar provides, *plus* the colorful spectrum of light, and of life when, as soon as it is life, "se fait division": shatters into countless reflective splinters glittering and gleaming among themselves.

There is this phrase that appears somewhere in Hocquard's pages, which at first makes one think of Hamlet's father: "They poisoned me in the garden in order to take over my state." But in our current context, it could be attributed just as well to the Biblical Adam, and suggest that a state, of being (no one's state, or again the kaleidoscope condition, the rainbow state) has—in some garden such as Eden—been infected with remorse and terror.

So we might think that the whole point of poetry is to resist the takeover. Not to plead guilty or give in to shame or fear.

"With you I'll never be afraid," Adam, in *Aerea*, recalls saying as a child to a grownup friend named Médé, "old mountain warrior turned gardener, basket weaver, watchman," who showed him how to grill locusts over a charcoal fire, helped him plant lentils and gather pears and walked with him once on a holiday evening just at nightfall through the Square of the Great Sokko, drenched in light from hundreds of acetylene lamps hanging over the market stalls. So bright and raw was that white light that it all but silenced the loud, festive hubbub—it "reduced almost to silence the din of voices and shouts that mingled with the nocturnal sounds of the drums and little nasal flutes" (*Aerea in the* Forests, 73/*Aerea dans les forêts*, 99). This brilliant, muted place reminds me of other silent, luminous spots in the world of Hocquard—for example, the central part of a bridge made of three: the "inexpressible part," that is, "la plus lumineuse, la plus silencieuse," where *is not* is, and being cannot be distinguished from not. The scariest part, then. You could even say "le lieu de perdition." Where one comes to be, lost. Under the acetylene lamps at the Great Sokko on the holiday night he walked there with his old friend Médé, it seems Adam practically passed out from happiness. At the middle of the suspension bridge in San Francisco, though, on a trip he took to the West Coast of the US as an adult and not accompanied by Médé, he turned back.

So I am inclined to locate Hocquard in, or perhaps just at the outskirts of, a constellation of twentieth-century writers that I imagine taking its knobby shape around Beckett's bleak joke, "Birth was the death of him." Or, I'd place Hocquard in a serious relation, at least, to this group that I picture converging around Maddy Rooney's recollection (in *All That Fall*) of some remarks she once heard the Regius Professor make: there was a girl who had something wrong with her that no one could diagnose, until it turned out she had never been properly born. I expect she was "gone from the word go," as Beckett puts the same problem elsewhere. In Maurice Blanchot's version, being is the outcome of a disaster which, before there was anything caused it all to disappear, and then made this disappearance come forth into the light of day. "This appearance is only that of disappearance…" (*The Space of Literature*, 43/45).[1] "'I' die before being born," Blanchot characteristically writes. "To live without a lifetime—likewise to die forsaken by death. Writing elicits such enigmatic propositions" (*The Writing of the Disaster*, 101/*L'écriture du désastre*, 157; The Writing, 136/*L'écriture*, 206).[2]

"Nous autres, mort-nés," Philippe Lacoue-Labarthe writes. "We stillborns." Lacoue-Labarthe was for a while a close friend and ally of Hocquard's; they were, I believe, fellow readers of Blanchot, and both shaken by his books.[3] "Mourir nous a fait naître" (Lacoue-Labarthe); "nés sans naissance." "Dying is what made us be born […] all born without birthright."[4]

Accident is Hocquard's word for being, for the fact of being, born: "se trouver quelque part et soudain ne pas du tout savoir où l'on est. Etre perdu." Before there is anything, anyone, an accident obliterates it all, breaks it up, rescinds everything in advance. All of a sudden, before you know it, you are in the forest, nowhere ("Fait accompli," Hocquard sometimes adds). *Voilà la naissance*. Terrifying. "TERROR," Pascal Quignard wrote, in Latin, in 1977, in a poem ("Inter Aerias Fagos") that Hocquard, a close friend, published the following year, and published again in 1979 along with his own French translation, "Dans l'air entre les branches des hêtres." "Il est tombé à terre le naissant," Quignard wrote later, commenting on his own poem. "Terre qui terrifie celui qui naît. […] Corps natal, atterré, terrifié."[5] "The one being born has fallen to earth.

[...] The earth terrifies whoever is born. [...] Natal body, fallen to earth, terrified" (my translation).

"On ne sait pas ce que c'est d'être né..." "No one knows what it is to be born." This is Jean-Marie Gleize, in *Le livre des cabanes*. "Je dis être né sans rien savoir, et je continue de courir / entre les tombes, en apnée, être né ici, peut-être."[6] "I say I was born without knowing anything, and I keep running / among the tombs, breathless, having been born here, perhaps" (my translation).

As for Roubaud, his books often suggest that life is from the start an aftermath, a sort of survival. Its loss, in other words, instigates it; its end launches it as a memory, or a dream, of before.

It is common for characters in his prose to be living a second life, which began when the first one, very early on, was over, because their entire world was destroyed by World War II. Their parents were deported and murdered, their safe hiding places ripped up. I think of Mr. Goodman, for example: of the whole second family he acquired after he was abruptly left alone, an orphan in 1944; I think of the second family that sustains him in his second life, with its complicated network of aunts and cousins (some of whom are also survivors), its overlapping names, the kinship mix-ups caused by the grafting of different genealogies. Characters like Mr. Goodman don't know exactly who they are, what their right name is, where they are from. Their path in life is an odd sort of quest: to discover the life of which the quest itself is a patchy memory, a dim, fitful dream.

Roubaud was eight in 1940. If his books are pervaded by the sense that to start living is to embark on an expended life, which you are in search of perhaps this reflects his childhood's having coincided with the war. It may well also be related to his "choice" of twelfth-century Provence and the poetry of the troubadours as his model for writing poems and thinking about poetry. One has to be obstinate, he says, in *La Fleur inverse* (16), to compose poetry at the present time, and for him, persisting implies the choice of a model and of a favorite period, when poetry flourished. He decided, for his part, on the troubadours and their world. He sees in them the first example of an idea of poetry which informs, he says, much of the writing he prefers in the European tradition right up to the present (the idea of poetry as art, as artisanship, passion and play, as violence, as knowledge, as an autonomous activity and a form of life). The world of the troubadours is all but lost, and, without dwelling on this excessively, one might observe that it has this in common with the world of Roubaud's childhood in Provence, which he left behind when his family moved to Paris at the end of the war, and which he reimagines, in texts such as *Parc Sauvage* (to which we will return), as a sanctuary shared briefly by children who did not survive.

In *La Boucle*, he describes the strong effect that one of the first troubadour poems he learned as an adult had on him. He came upon it in the course of his poetry apprenticeship. It seems to have given him a new kind of access to a particular, frequently recurring memory—a memory of the type that "resembles nothing so much as itself" (*The Loop*, 19/*La Boucle*, 20). "It is one of the most significant visions of my childhood [...] an image from the beginning of time" (20/19). It is a memory of black. More precisely, it is a vision of a windowpane on a winter night, covered with flowers of frost. Behind the voice in the poem by Raimbaut d'Orange that Roubaud discovered as a grownup—*and* behind the frost on the window he remembered from earliest childhood—lies "the nocturnal nothingness of things past and gone" (*The Loop*, 22/*La Boucle*, 23). It seems Roubaud recognized in Raimbaut d'Orange's lines—"spontaneously and emotionally"—his own way in poetry.

At the risk of obtrusiveness, one might associate, with these beginnings (an image from "the beginning of time," a poem from the beginning of Roubaud's life in poetry which is itself a poem from the childhood of European lyric poetry in vernacular languages), the suicide of Roubaud's youngest brother, Jean-René, which happened just before Roubaud undertook *Le Grand Incendie de Londres*, his own alternative to voluntary death. When Roubaud suggests that writing has to do with a dream of "before"—before one's birth—one might consider he means the dream of a life that would have been, was going to be, but was not. And that the self-riddle at the heart of his work—the "auto-énigme" which we will puzzle over again later in this book, bears a relation to this life that is past and gone when still it lies in the future. For the riddle (Who am I?) is answered so fast (immediately laid to rest), it has ever yet still to be asked (let alone resolved).

At any rate, in certain of Roubaud's poems, especially in some of those called *rue* or *une rue* or *la rue*, one is apt to come upon a random creature, or some stray object—a dog, say, or a bike parked against a wall—that look a little like signs or symbols, or reminders of something. But what? And one gathers that a person, stumbling along an overgrown path, might half-grasp, from such opaque signals, that *this will have been life*. Three yellow dogs, a bicycle, a bakery in one poem; a leaning tree, a bicycle, and a dog in another.[7] These inscrutable signs are reminiscent of Merlin's "paroles obscures," prophesies encountered along the twisted forest paths of Arthurian legend, which never make sense until too late, when what they predict has already happened, and which say, to the stumbling knights who wonder at them, *this is what will have been revealed* (see *The Loop*, 218/*La Boucle*, 235).

I consider Roubaud an occasional visitor to the "gone from the word go" convergence. I doubt that Blanchot or Beckett ever had much of a hold on his thoughts; I think of him as a passerby who has his own particular reasons for being in the neighborhood. We will return to these reasons in chapter 4. With Hocquard—whose serious relation to the "mourir nous fait naître" obsession involves a determined resistance to it—*intonation* is crucial, I believe. It is a matter of how different the same thing can sound.

"Flexit oculos"

"Il est tombé à terre le naissant," Pascal Quignard observes. "Perdue est la perdue." "The newborn has fallen on the ground. Lost is the lost one."

(Terror) FLEXIT OCULOS   ("Inter Aerias Fagos," in *Inter*)

"Il tourne les yeux," we read in the long commentary Quignard offers of his Latin poem in *Inter*. The newborn looks back, like Orpheus to see Eurydice. "C'est la flexion des yeux. C'est Orphée dans Ovide. Il est tombé à terre le naissant. Perdue est la perdue" (*Inter*, 23).

So the newborn is the backward-looking one, who turns his eyes toward the lost one lost again. "Il tourne les yeux dans la détresse . . ."

My life is this backward look, Quignard continues: the twisted neck, the shoulders rotated—an impasse embodied. "Aporia in person. A hesitation to be born. The retrospection that can annihilate everything. *Natus* ou *regressus*" (*Inter*, 29; my translation).

The whole forest in Hocquard's *Aerea* could have grown out of this initial contorted posture (twisted shoulders and neck); the forest is like a nightmare induced by a terrorized retrospection. It is an "aporia," an impassable expanse. And the "accident" that lands one in it is called "un accident très feutré du sens"—"a noiseless irregularity of direction," in Lydia Davis's translation (*Aerea in the Forests*, 38/*Area dans les forêts*, 72). A disruption affecting forward and back. *On perd le fil*, as they say. Indeed, Adam remarks that a thread or "fil" is of no use to the forest's captives (the forest is precisely not a labyrinth). It is futile to drop crumbs or pebbles behind you as you go. There is no point in retracing your steps back toward the starting point. For though everything in the forest is a sort of imprint in Adam's description—the mark of something now gone—no past can be attached to any of it. Everything came second, but without precedent. That is how disorienting the forest is, how serious the "accident du sens." Since everything is familiar *and* has yet to be encountered, memories and premonitions are each other's inverted image; predictions and recollections mirror each other; past and future turn round, each after the other in a circle with no beginning or end, front or back. All this secondariness secondary to nothing suggests the world of a child without attachment, filial ties—without a thread, or "fil," in life. Adam fits this description. He seems to inhabit a world where a birth, far from linking one generation to the next, effecting the transmission of a name, an inheritance, cuts life. "La vie se fait division." And having once turned back in fear, you yourself turn around in circles for good like a moron, never getting anywhere. "The forest is engendered in fear."

"*Comment passer?*" This is a crucial question in Hocquard, How to *get out?* as a fish *passe à travers le filet*. Escapes the net. Also, how to *cross* the forest—instead of turning around in circles? And then too, no doubt, how to pass from one one to another one? How to bridge the separation (which they have in common) between one solitude and another?

Quignard's texts—many of them, Quignard says himself—stay caught in the impasse (forward or back, "natus ou regressus"), halted between air for a first breath and the impalpable form of "la perdue," naught but air.

> On parle, on écrit, on crie
> on n'étreint que l'air impalpable
> l'adieu se dissout dans le souffle qu'on découvre
> dans l'air
> et on retombe à chaque instant dans l'abîme d'où
> on sort sans fin.   (*Inter*, 50)

> You speak, you write, you cry out
> and clasp only the impalpable air
> the farewell dissolves in the breath you discover
> in the air
> and you fall back at every instant into the abyss from which
> you issue without end.   (My translation)

"Without end." "Avec l'art, on n'en finit jamais," Lacoue-Labarthe observes.[8] There is no finishing with art ("You talk, you write, you cry out..." [Quignard]). One is never too old to get pressed once more into the service of a fable—even if one's aim is to escape ("In speaking or writing or reading or translating one seeks the exit" [Hocquard]).⁹ Even if one is tired to death of it all. I know the song by heart, Lacoue-Labarthe says, in *Phrase* (48/trans., 31).

Lacoue-Labarthe must have known by heart the fragment Maurice Blanchot wrote, and rewrote and called *Scène*, or *Une scène primitive* or *Une scene primitive?*, or *("Une scène primitive?")*. As far as I can see, Lacoue-Labarthe never did get over it. His initial response to it, a piece called "L'Émoi"—"Dismay"—was published by Hocquard in 1977.¹⁰

Here is Blanchot's "scène." A child—is he seven years old, or eight perhaps?—stands by a window, draws the curtain, and looks through the pane. He sees the garden, wintry trees, the wall of a house—in short, his play space. And then, idly, he looks up toward the sky, the ordinary sky, a little cloudy, "pallid daylight without depth," which suddenly opens,

> absolutely black and absolutely empty, revealing (as though the pane had broken) such an absence that all has since always and forevermore been lost therein—so lost that therein is affirmed and dissolved the vertiginous knowledge that nothing is what there is—rien est ce qu'il y a—and first of all nothing beyond.¹¹

A scene appears to open from time to time in Lacoue-Labarthe's own *Phrase*, the book of his poems that was published in 2000 and where "L'Émoi" also reappears. Sometimes this scene seems to accompany the welling, or seeping up in him of a "phrase," the words of which he never makes out; he doubts he has ever quite taken it in, and certainly it is nothing he himself has composed; he expects it dates back to some ancient story, beyond remembering, "old indistinct murmur / counting out the generations." "This abortive utterance, this sense of being haunted, this decidedly I call literature," he says (*Phrase*, 12/trans., 7, 8).

If a scene opens along with this forgotten rumor's surging up in him (draining away, miscarried), it isn't that there is anything to represent—any drama at all, any image to speak of; no visual or plastic figure stands forth, no emblem of the origin, no model; no: nothing. "Rien est ce qu'il y a."

Maybe you could call it a primal scene, or the scene of a birth that Lacoue-Labarthe describes paradoxically as "innée (dégénérée)"—with "innée" suggesting both inborn and unborn. The scene, if it is one, tends to feature a grieving mother, or three women stationed together, perhaps at a grave perhaps not, and a child.

In any case nothing happens. "Il ne s'est évidemment rien passé," Lacoue-Labarthe wrote, in "L'Émoi," "but I knew that it had already happened to me; I knew this, not knowing it . . ." I could, he grants, say all this in another way. With expression. "In my mythic, deadly style." He could, I imagine, resurrect the deadened murmur that passes rhythmically from generation to generation ("vieux murmur indistinct"); he could resuscitate the draining-away thing, "aborted utterance," literature. He could declaim it, sing. "However poignant King Marke's or Golaud's pain, it's sung. Declaimed. And I know those moments off by heart: the declamation I could do over and over. But the pain, which touches worse than the heart, makes it impossible (48/trans., 31)." "No music!" we read, elsewhere in *Phrase* (106/trans., 75). "Pas de musique! Pas maintenant."

Hocquard, incidentally, claims not to like music and often states his intention to relieve poetry of song (*le chant*). Down with enchantment.[12] There is one "vieux murmure" in particular, though—"counting out the generations"—about a young gaze hauled back toward our first home, the land of nothingness. It seems that practically no wisdom, disillusionment, or self-respect withstands the mix of horror and delight, the enchantment it stirs up when it comes mercilessly back to mind. "Avec la littérature, on n'en finit jamais," one might say. "Ach, die Kunst!" Lacoue-Labarthe wrote once, in *Poetry as Experience*, quoting Celan. The small volume in which he published a text by Hocquard (touching on childhood) was called *La Misère de la littérature*. Literature's misery. It came out the year after Hocquard published "L'Émoi."

Maybe no disenchantment is deep enough—no weariness of art and literature sufficiently profound—to forego an occasion to intone the old backward-looking song once more. *Der Erlkönig*, *Death and the Maiden* (Schubert's sounds in Beckett's *All That Fall*), or again the narrative poem about twenty-five pages long, which is all that Louis-René des Forêts preserved of an aborted novel—*Les Mégères de la mer* (1962). Quignard, as it happens, devoted one of his first books to des Forêts.[13]

Les Mégères is the story of a young boy's submission to the low melody of a witch's blue gaze singing to him in a strange language "avec toutes les manières de la mort." With all the artfulness of death.

She reeled him in by promising death. Not the death said to end our life and rumored to free us from care, for that death is no different from this life. "Etre et n'être plus sont pareille malédiction"—as though birth already had caused us no longer to be. "We stillborns . . ."

The hoarse voice in the gorgon's eyes promised the young boy another death: restitution to "la patrie néante," the land of nonbeing, whence we were unduly wrenched by birth and hung like spoiled fruit on a funeral stele. The hag crowned with seashells standing under the vault of a cave at the sea's edge and beckoning to the child with her blue gaze sang to him in a mother's voice of the first hibernation, "le premier hivernage."[14] And she so charmed him that ever since he has been condemned to sing his own enchantment by her song—to assume once more his charge as cantor, ritual celebrant of his own surrender to a mirage (he, once so unbending—"I who was of old so proud, so intransigent a boy").

Les yeux dans les yeux

In Hocquard, the woman dwelling at the ocean's edge, who smiles the smile of her rocky island realm itself, is no mother. Her smile is not a mother's smile, nor is her voice a mother's voice, and her island (called Cecilia) is all darkening and decline. It has no history, "apart from the long degeneration of its inhabitants." She is the island's last clear form, but she belongs to it "body and soul": she belongs, I should say, to "l'approche des ténèbres."

Her name is Remedios—Remedy—and I expect this must be because her eyes, Adam says, can soothe the wound, "la déchirure," that we suffer "when our gaze meets another one" (*Aerea in the Forests*, 97/*Aerea dans les forêts*, 129). When our gaze meets that of another person, presumably, or for that matter, we read, the gaze of a fish, or of the extinct volcanoes looming above.

There is, in another part of *Aerea*, a memorable description of two gazes meeting, and it is called birth. "What an ineffable meeting! Born of a gaze as if from a thunderbolt!" Perhaps the "déchirure" that Remedios's own eyes can heal corresponds to this "coup de foudre"—a birth that is itself the sheer astonishment of love at first sight.

Here is the description of birth offered to Adam in *Aerea* by an ornithologist called David, who recognizes in Adam a fellow hunter-gatherer and evokes a scene he must know, when one of them suddenly notices something, right in front of him, to pick, or collect, or just look at. "Quelle rencontre ineffable!" David exclaims. What an inexpressible, *unutterable* encounter.

When your attentive gaze happens to fall abruptly on a bronzed boletus at the foot of a stump or in a patch of dead leaves, though obviously nothing was hiding it, what an ineffable encounter, Adam! [...] It is as though this object, suddenly there at your feet in its unblemished necessity and its tender sexual compactness, had come into being through the aleatory virtue of one of your fleeting looks. Born of a look, as of a lightning bolt! (*Aerea in the Forests*, 19/*Aerea dans les forêts*, 30)

It isn't that the bronze-colored mushroom is there initially (next to a stump or among dead leaves) and *then* by a stroke of luck seen. No, the mushroom comes into being solely because, accidentally, it is glimpsed: there it is, "dans son intacte nécessité," born of the gaze it surprises and that surprises it. The normal sequence of before and after is brusquely eliminated. What about the filial relation, between forebears and descendants? Maybe love's thunderbolt ("coup de foudre") suddenly suspends the whole engendering process. In favor of an abrupt, inexplicable connection. Or "rencontre." Which is also an interruption in the course of things, a cut. *Déchirure*.

Language is abruptly condensed here, short-circuiting the standard relation between verb and object (seeing and what is seen), as well as between object and subject (the thing seen and the one who sees it). These familiar grammatical relations get so squeezed down here that one cannot distinguish among perceiver, perceived and perception; it is as though language all of a sudden just clammed up. "Quelle rencontre *ineffable*." "Une aussi abrupte naissance, un si violent silence inaugural." Instead of the familiar flow of sentences from the start of one on to the next, and the development of a story, a life, a genealogy—instead of all that, a sudden clap of silence. "Eclipse au lieu de la fable," Hoquard writes elsewhere. "Eclipse instead of fable" (*Conditions of Light*, 78/ *Conditions de la* lumière, 78).

So it seems that birth, for him—it seems that being born, or *being*—is a gaze, a sudden, surprising one, and that seeing what is—seeing whatever happens to crop up right in front of you—means all of a sudden to *be seen*. You see yourself seen, then, on the occasion of this abrupt and unforeseeable *rencontre*, which is to say you see yourself surprised, exposed, laid bare. You see, in the mirror that reflects your own look, that what is there is not. Its not being there flares up before your eyes, a flash of night in broad day, and this sudden black hole, this *déchirure*, is you. *Voilà la naissance*. A swift cut (you might think of the midwife who knows just the right instant to intervene, briskly cutting the umbilical cord)—a swift cut in all the vectors pointing from subject toward the object via a verb, from here across to there, from before to after. "Achrone" is an Hocquard word for birth, and "instantanné." In his language "inaugural space" names the place where one suddenly finds oneself, lost: it is impassable, directionless, a place that snaps like a trap around you at the instant of the accident, "l'accident du sens." Place of birth: *une aporie. Lieu de perdition.* This sounds dire. But in darkness, too, there are rainbow colors, and in a life suddenly no one's, a whole range of tonalities.

> Beauté n'appartient pas
> plus que sommeil ou faim
> C'est pareil Quand tu parles ou
> quand tu dors
> Rouge mineur (*Conditions de lumière*, 87)

> Beauty does not belong any
> more than sleep or hunger
> It's the same When you speak
> or when you sleep
> In red minor (*Conditions of Light*, 87)

Hocquard likes to point out, citing Wittgenstein, that one can say "I am afraid" in a cheerful tone, too, and "I am in pain" in a smiling voice (*ma haie*, 488). Furthermore (as he sometimes adds, quoting Aristotle), one can compose a tragedy *or* a comedy with the same words. So, the ornithologist in *Aerea* exclaims that birth (sudden clap of silence, eclipse) can only set off a great peal of laughter. "Le rire de Dieu," he says.

> Such an abrupt birth, such a violent initial silence can only result in a great burst of laughter. God's laughter when he sees Adam for the first time, the divine laughter, unexampled, endless, whose crystalline echoes reverberate their perpetual harmony through the Universe (*Aerea in the Forests*, 19/ *Aerea dans les forêts*, 30).

Médé's Smile, and Remedios's

Médé, with whom Adam would never have been scared—and who might have helped him not turn back, when confronted with the scorpion, for example, or the suspension bridge across San Francisco Bay—seems to have reserved a smile especially for his young friend Adam. I suspect it is this smile, dispelling fear, that floats in and out of *Aerea* and of other books, too, by Hocquard. It is not a smile that says Everything will be fine, after all. If I bring it up here in an attempt to suggest the color or intonation of Hocquard's "état," which is not exactly des Forêts' or Quignard's or Lacoue-Labarthe's—though not exactly not, either—I do not mean to suggest that where *they* are somber he is jocund. Granted, he himself, in a related context, does emphasize his own cheerfulness as opposed to the melancholy mood of traditional elegists (you will recall that elegy is the backward-looking genre engendered in fear).

> Contrary to the nostalgic elegist who proclaims his longing for the golden age, innocence and paradise lost, the reverse elegist, who loves to laugh, study, and play, makes a deal, trading ennui and a serious spirit for play, work for study, and sadness for delight. (*Cette histoire est la mienne*, in *ma haie*, 475-76).[15]

I expect, though, that Médé's smile is related to the "smiling tone" in which Wittgenstein observed that one can say "I am afraid," or "I am in pain." It does not say "Everything will be all right," but rather "All is well" *and* "All is lost" in such a way that no one can tell the difference, any more than at nightfall ("à l'approche des ténèbres") anyone can distinguish between a white thread and a black. If it made any sense to attribute a smile, or an expression of any kind to indifference (to indifferentiation, to what one does not see), then I would say the smile that dissolves fear is the smile of neutrality.

It is the particular character of the featureless, I mean; the distinctive trait of the completely undistinguished. Pessoa's uniqueness. No one's incomparable grace. The look of what one does not see, neutrality—the look of light itself, we might think, remembering Raquel Levy's paintings.

"Some people," we read in *Aerea*, "may have seen this smile in a dream; upon awakening all that survives of it is an incommunicable but tenacious disturbance, dissipating slowly like a perfume or a pain" (*Aerea in the Forests*, 102/*Aerea dans les forêts*, 136).

Remedios has this smile in *Aerea*—Remedios, so closely related to her island, Cecilia; to its dark sterility, its decline; Remedios belongs completely to the approach of darkness. "If it made any sense to attribute a smile to a chaos of sterile lava," Adam remarks, he would say Remedios had "the smile of Cecilia itself" (*Aerea in the Forests*, 102/*Aerea dans les forêts*, 136). If you recall the description of the island, "la Cecilia," in *Aerea* (the description I evoked earlier, when speaking of the "incorporation" of a subject by an attribute)—if you remember Cecilia, then, as a mummified island welded by continual volcanic eruptions into itself as into its own sarcophagus—then you will have to understand the island's smile as the expression of a rocky protuberance whose every outer feature, whose very character, has been baked completely into it, so as to form with it a single, characterless mass—a brick.

I associate Cecilia's smile with the "unhabitual beauty that certain people secrete, at times," as Hocquard writes at the end of *Aerea*. It is nothing of theirs, exactly; they are its "ephemeral depositaries." It is as if nature were lending them "this very disturbing increase in charm that indifferently diffuses around it consolation or desolation. " (*Aerea in the Forests*, 117/*Aerea dans les forêts*, 156).

This surge of charm occasionally lent to certain people is, I would say, a strange, dreamy intensification of the paradoxical property that consists in not belonging. It is a kind of wave or swell of being. A heightening of certain people's (or of an island's) being themselves. *Seuls, évidents.* It is indifference, I mean to say; it is indistinction emitting its own spectrum of beautiful colors. When Adam evokes this "disturbing charm," he does so in connection with the colors—"various shades of brown and violet, light and dark gray, ocher and pink"—that the gloomy dark volcanos of Cecilia showed him one morning, just before noon, when the oblique rays of the sun started crushing the outward shapes of things and their surface colors under an excess of luminosity. Then "I saw the gloomy volcanoes slowly turn various shades of brown and violet [. . .], bringing into play all the nuances and intensities of their own particular rainbow." *In darkness too are rainbow colors.* Featurelessness too has beautiful features. One might almost think one had come upon a variant of Giordano Bruno's memory of Mount Cicada and Mount Vesuvius. On the island Cecilia, when the sun sinks in the west, it gives back color to the surfaces of things; it returns to the world its outward attributes. And then the volcanoes, whose attributes are not superficial or even attributable—the volcanoes, "which refuse every influence from outside"—return to their "inert gray."

Comment passer?

Remedios's smile "springs from some unknown region of being," we read (*Aerea in the Forests*, 103/*Aerea dans les* forêts, 132), and it strikes Adam "in a region of the heart equally unsuspected." It seems to pass, then, from somewhere within Remedios that she has no knowledge of, to a similarly unknown spot within Adam. I think it must be a secret.

I suggest this, thinking of other Hocquard pages bearing on secrets. For example, a secret is always someone's, he says—someone in particular's. It is always "mine," he writes, in *Cette histoire est la mienne*. However, this does not mean, he hastens to clarify, that I *have* a secret, keep it, divulge, or conceal it. No: a secret is a secret. One must understand it literally. *My secret* means what is secret *from* me. It is what escapes me (*Cette histoire*, in *ma haie*, 486/"Secret," in *This Story Is Mine*). It is my very own not-mine, the property that consists in not being one, I would say—my life, which comes to me gone. Gone from the word go.

In *Aerea* life passes from Remedios to Adam as if it were a secret message. A confidential communication, just between two. One half suspects, then, that life, or being, is a letter bearing a secret—that being is a secret communication. Which should cause us to think again of the importance of letter writing for Hocquard, and of his emphasis on a letter always being *to* someone, from another one—*entre deux*. But life being a *letter*, that passes between two, also suggests that *literality* is the way *across*: that something "autoliteral," like a secret (a secret is a secret) offers the way through an impassable dilemma (*natus* ou *regressus*). Life being a *letter* (passing between two) implies that a *tautology* traverses the forest, pure aporia, even though a tautology *is* an aporia (nothing follows from it, it follows from nothing; there is no before or after to it, no front or back; it isn't a sentence, Hocquard often stresses, for it doesn't feature anything like a sentence's *one-way-through*; it is, I insisted earlier, sheer disjunction).

Now, you may remember these lines, cited earlier:

A bridge is made of three
the central element is inexpressible

This third is *is not* (*Theory*, 22)

They were cut out from a poem that begins, "A hippopotamus is black / crosses a room." I believe this is the crossing we must think about—the way through, the communication between one corner of a room and another, or one lookout and another, which is to say between one world and another, some one and some other one. For I think we must consider "A hippopotamus is black" as the subject of the verb *to cross*. Moreover I expect we must read "A hippo is black" the way we learned from Hocquard to read "Maylis est jolie": as a tautology. That is, *à la lettre*. This letter, if you will, crosses a room.

Here is the whole poem (notice the shimmering fabric at the end—blue, perhaps, or green—and the "timbre": "stamp," in English, as well as "sound quality," "tone color." "Intonation" is a kind of postmark).

Un hippopotame est noir
traverse une pièce

La pièce du milieu
est plus silencieuse
est plus lumineuse

Un pont est fait de trois
l'élément central n'est pas énonçable

Ce troisieme est *n'est pas*

La lettre qui manque n'a pas d'enveloppe
est la plus silencieuse
la plus lumineuse

L'hippopotame
passe un pont de lettres

La robe de soie est un timbre (*Théorie des tables*, 22)

A hippopotamus is black
crosses a room

The room in the middle is quieter
is brighter

A bridge is made of three
the central element is inexpressible

The third is *is not*

The missing letter has no envelope
is the quietest
the brightest

The hippopotamus
passes a bridge of letters

The silk dress is a stamp (*Théorie*, 22)

When Wittgenstein and Russell first met, Wittgenstein refused to rule out the possibility that there was a rhinoceros in the room where they were conversing. Perhaps the hippopotamus here is related to that rhino. I believe Hocquard's view is that what matters is not whether a rhinoceros is or is not in the room, but rather that a rhino is a rhino, and *crosses* the room. "Traverse la pièce." Any child can see that, Hocquard writes at one point (*ma haie*, 407), suggesting that it is *une évidence*, and causing me to wonder if it is (like the hippopotamus) black.

In any case, a letter crosses a room—or again, a tautology is a bridge (perhaps a bridge of letters). And of the bridge's three elements, the middle one, "indicible," is *is not*. At the center of a tautology, then, is *is not*. I mean, right in the middle of a tautology there lies a darkening area where *is* is not and *is not* is, where *is* and *is not* can't be distinguished, reminiscent of dusk on the rooftops of Fez, when one cannot tell a white thread from a black. Or again, the central element of a bridge is a *neutral* medium, the element of indifference, indistinction. The smile I've tried to describe must be the expression of this neutrality; it must be something like the unique characteristic of the unrecognizable; the special (the secret) attribute of a secret.

All this implies, I believe, that the middle—of a bridge, of a tautology—is an internally contradictory whole: *both* being and not. Yes and no, white and black both at once, indistinguishable. The central element is being, simply being (the whole of it, the entire extent of it *from the word go*, if you will—a complete journey from past to future, birth to death), inasmuch as being's *not* is *it*. And this means that the central element is the whole and also a hole: a synopsis, Hocquard suggests in one poem (the complete play, if you will, within the play), and also a *trou* (*Un test*, XXVI). In the middle they become indistinct. If you recall the expression I have used more than once, "sheer disconnect," or "sheer disjunction," you might think of some sheer, gauzy material, and imagine stark separation to be diaphanous, too, or a little vaporous.[16]

Thinking once more of another phrase I have used before—a phrase of Hocquard's this time: "They have in common what separates them"—I want to suggest that two observation stations (two island lookouts, two solitudes) have in common what neither has. In other words, they share a secret. A life.

They have in common what is proper to no one. It simply does not belong. But it *passes* between two. Life is the secret communication of a secret, just between us.

"Mourir nous a fait naître"

Hocquard recalls the newborn in Quignard's "Inter aerias fagos," terrorized, looking back like Orpheus: "Orpheus turns. Eurydice is lost to him" ("Lament," in *This Story Is Mine/Cette histoire* in *ma haie*, 485). His lament, Hocquard observes, rises in the void opened by what has escaped him, and ever after, elegy has tried to fill up the lack birth leaves us with. It seems the pain of loss must be shared and explained in song and story, being too heavy a sorrow for anyone to bear alone. But Hocquard, "the reverse elegist," understands that words have no hold at all on loss. No hold on life, that is, which escapes. Birth is precisely that instant when, as we've suggested, language suddenly clams up. A clap of silence. "Violent silence inaugural." Instead of "la fable," "l'éclipse." The pain of the loss is "indicible." The astonishing joy "ineffable." Words lack for this lack. Please read this literally. The words that lack are the lacking ones: the missing words are the words for it.[17]

They are the words that are not heard, and they form the secret message that passes between a one and another one.[18]

"L'accent du neutre"

But Hocquard goes on to speak of Orpheus's lamentation, from the perspective of the "reverse elegist," and he says that it tells the secret of an idiot ("Lament," in *This Story Is Mine/Cette histoire*, in *ma haie*, 485). You might imagine the arcana lodged in a mind that unfortunately is a sieve. And the toneless communication of this oblivion. From the reverse elegist's perspective, Orpheus sings the grief that escapes him, the pain—or for that matter the joy that is not his, or anyone's, but rather the special grief, or the singular delight of no one at all.

This idiot Orpheus reminds me of the halfwit who, it seems, would sometimes sit down in the middle of the rue du Dadreb in Tangiers when Hocquard lived there, obstructing traffic and singing in a crude, unlovely voice. Only donkeys could get around him, cars just had to wait till the tuneless song was over. This idiot's inertia, Hocquard writes, was not a pose or a strategy of any kind, and it had no consequences. It appears rather similar in this regard to Pessoa's indifference (I mean, his uniqueness). It does not show up anywhere on any scale of personal strengths and weaknesses. The halfwit's disposition is unqualifiable. Simple. "On the rainbow scale of merits, it has no color." Elsewhere—in the same vein, I believe—Hocquard evokes a cafeteria that

Charles Reznikoff came upon while walking around in New York City: Mrs. Smith's Cafeteria. No inviting name, he observes; nothing especially attractive, just "Here is Mrs. Smith's cafeteria, come in if you want." "My *art poétique*," he writes, "became Mrs. Smith's cafeteria" (*ma haie*, 448).

L'accent du neutre, the accent of the neutral, is a phrase of Pierre Alferi's, in an essay about Maurice Blanchot, Henry James, and secrets.[19] Toward the end of it Alferi writes that though of course Blanchot's voice is not "the voice of the neutral," nevertheless the appeal Blanchot tirelessly makes to *le neutre* tempers his voice. Alferi calls this inflection "l'accent du neutre"—clumsily, he fears, since Blanchot's accent is precisely the timbre that nothing in particular lends to a voice. Maybe it resembles the expression on a face one does not see. It could be the special timbre of the unheard. (A silky quality, perhaps, on occasion?) In any event, I have no doubt that Alferi is thinking of Hocquard, his friend (and, to put it clumsily, his onetime mentor), when he writes, at the very end of his essay—adapting the last sentence of James's *Sacred Fount*—that nothing can supply, now that Blanchot is dead, his *intonation* (*Brefs*, 156).

It is tempting, Alferi observes earlier in his text, for admirers of Blanchot to imitate his tone, which as a consequence disappears behind what Blanchot himself always avoided: "un pathos, une thématique..." Blanchot imitators abound, Alferi remarks. I expect this is the situation Hocquard refers to in an account of his own intellectual itinerary called "La bibliothèque de Trieste" (*ma haie*, 15 ff). In these pages he describes his disillusionment when, around the beginning of the 1980s, notions such as "lack," and "loss," which should be taken *literally*, began turning into rhetorical clichés. They started exuding a lugubrious melancholy, he recalls; moreover, though by definition they had nothing at all to offer in the way of models or methods, they began producing their own brand of conformity. He dramatized his rejection of this development—he emphasized his distaste for the conceptual and affective varnish applied to, let us say, "le désoeuvrement"—by turning off abruptly in what, on the face of it, looks like a very different direction from Blanchot's, and from Lacoue-Labarthe's. He stressed at every opportunity his down-to-earth activities like typesetting, unpretentious pleasures like detective fiction, and his admiration for plain-spoken American poets like Reznikoff. In a rather dour text bearing on *Le Renversement*, the first poetry book by his friend Claude Royet-Journoud, he describes the dismal world that Royet-Journoud must reverse (*renverser*)—a world that sounds very much like the forest in *Aerea*, engendered in fear, and like the world of Blanchot, for it evokes the themes and the desolate moods one might call *blanchotiens* (Kafkaesque, Beckettien...).

There was an accident, Hocquard writes, summing up this universe (the one that needs reversal): an accident heeded too late.[20] Consciousness, thought, language are by definition tardy. They can only ever try to represent, *après coup*, the circumstances of a disaster that is always anterior, further back. One thinks here of Blanchot, of course: of his many pages on an origin anterior to any beginning, more ancient than anything that has ever begun and from which nothing ever issues, *l'essence de l'oeuvre* back and back toward which writing turns. If anything at all survives this retreat, this "désoeuvrement," it is just a book, and the most it can do, in Hocquard's eyes, is show, "par procuration"—via analogy, or in a miming, theatrical manner—the *appearance* of an origin, its own, which it cannot reach. Thus it finds itself deported from itself, and in the manner of *A la Recherche du temps perdu* expends itself in quest of its start, progressing toward the moment it could begin, which turns out to be where it ends—where it begins again, that is, not to begin yet. You might picture it turning in circles without start or finish, trapped in itself, and expelled back into itself with every turn. It forms its own *dehors* with no *dedans* to relate to; it is a bleached, denatured territory like Hérodiade's. Nostalgic or ironic thoughts hover over it, Hocquard writes—thoughts of warmth that could substitute living features for masks (*Un privé*, 64).

Mort-né

Nothing that exists is really alive on this terrain, or in this world, he goes on—not because death ever put an end to life, but because it preceded, and because life has never begun. Whence a sort of inaptitude for living that Hocquard senses, he says, in a writer like Roussel (*Un privé*, 64, 65). Even if he isn't thinking specifically of Beckett's *Not I*, he must be thinking of Beckett in general as well as of Kafka and Blanchot when he writes, "From then on whatever 'emerges from the earth' can no longer be 'I,' but 'he,' impersonal and errant subject, born in fear and a prey to opacity and night" (my translation).

For his own part, Hocquard doesn't care anything about what comes before. He is opposed to turning back, looking back, and just as disinclined to look *deep*, à la Mallarmé (famous for saying that "by digging so deep into verse, I encountered two voids. [...] Luckily, I am utterly dead"). Hocquard has no patience for this "approfondissement." Luckily, he is utterly superficial. He favors "direct observation," looking straight ahead and contemplating what is before his very eyes. Moreover, he is committed to writing in the first person, pretty much exclusively.

> Octobre. Le retour des rouges-gorges. Ce que j'ai sous les yeux.

Reading him carefully, and dwelling on the enigma of birth (the death of us), and all the while recalling that for some time, at least, in the 1970s, he was allied with Lacoue-Labarthe, close to Blanchot's writing and attuned to the work of other writers in Blanchot's orbit like des Forêts, suggests to me not so much that, after all, his thinking is closer to theirs than he wants to let on, but rather that in his vicinity *they* now sound a little different. I think one can perceive a dull color or timbre that their admirers may have drowned out, if one happens to hear Blanchot hummed in Hocquard's unlovely voice. Or if one chances to have Hocquard's accent in one's ear when reading some book or another of Lacoue-Labarthe's. I mean, the accent of indistinction. For I have heard joy and sorrow without being able to tell the difference in Lacoue-Labarthe's *Phrase*, when the *Stabat Mater* resounds, and a mother's tears flow because of children "nés sans naissance." Sorrow and joy. "Joie et douleur." "No affect, no pathos. Grief and joy, that's ample" (107/trans., 75). "Douceur et douleuer ensemble." "Sweetness and suffering alike" (25/trans., 17). This alters my sense of Lacoue-Labarthe's sadness, and places a slight stress on the sentences where he says that it is nothing. "Cela ne me concernait pas." "It was no longer of any concern to me" (44/trans., 30). If anyone asks you about the abject, the superb "jolt" that casts you up like flotsam on a shore, "né sans naissance," there is nothing to say, he observes, except that it's nothing, nothing serious. "Unimportant" is how Blanchot describes it (*L'écriture du désastre*, 27/ *The Writing of the Disaster*, 13); "of no concern." To put it clumsily, Hocquard damps the music that sounds in the distance when Blanchot writes, and that tends sometimes to swell up around Lacoue-Labarthe, so one can at least imagine one hears their unforgettable expressions in an undistinguished undertone, or as intermittent asides, and realize that this is as it should be.

3

Palindromes

"Toujours, traduisant"

Alix and Jacques Roubaud did not exactly share a language. In *Le grand incendie* we learn that on Alix's mother's side she had French, and on her father's side English, and that the French was that of Anglophone Ontario, in Canada, while her father's English was that of a French Canadian born and raised in the United States. In English, Roubaud notes that Alix had an unusual accent—not foreign, exactly, and not identifiable as coming from any particular locale—while in French her accent, it seems, was that of French high schools abroad. For Roubaud's part, his mother was a distinguished "angliciste," and perhaps, he suggests, if he had had the choice, he would have preferred English as his first language (if not Provençal). Cambridge English was the language that he and Alix met in; it was the language of their everyday exchanges, of their marriage and their joy yet, Roubaud writes, it never was entirely theirs. It remained somehow inalterably remote, and strange. "At all times we were translating." "Toujours, nous traduisions" (*Le grand incendie*, 336-37/*The Great Fire*, 259).

One thinks of this when contemplating Roubaud's double oeuvre, the overall plan for which—as well as the firm decision to undertake it—came to him in a dream just after the suicide of his youngest brother: for this twofold work (a reason to live instead of dying) is comprised of a poetry Project to be accompanied by a novel (*Le Grand Incendie de Londres*). And Roubaud imagines the two elements—the Project, the novel; or verse, prose—as two languages each a translation of the other. Each would mirror the other. And the work, then, would never speak either language as a native, only as a language seen from elsewhere, "in the mirror, darkly" (*The Great Fire*, 128/*Le grand incendie*, 171).[1]

The two languages would share a single source, he suggests: an "Adamic" language, which he compares to the silvering of the mirror. And he thinks of this primordial language as a silent one: the silent tongue of the dream from which his initial decision to undertake his lifework arose (*Le grand incendie*, 171/*The Great Fire*, 128). The novel, Roubaud suggests, gazes, from its (odd) title (a translation of the dream's unspoken language), into the inner space of the dream, and this gaze touches on the dream's duplicity: the double language carrying it along. "C'est qu'il est touché là à la duplicité du rêve, à la double langue qui l'entraîne" (*Le grand incendie*, 174).[2]

The two languages deriving from the one unspoken tongue stand, in Roubaud's imagination, in a palindromic relation to each other. For one is associated with darkness, the other with light. Thus light, the erasure of darkness, faces darkness, light's shadow—"light being the palindromic obliteration of the shadow; the shadow, the palindromic trace of the light" (*The Great Fire*, 258/*Le grand incendie*, 335).

Roubaud has an attachment to doubles of many kinds, and to palindromes in particular: he dwells, for example, on the role of a horizontal mirror at the center of George Perec's great novel *Life a User's Manual*, which assures the reversal, over the course of the whole work, from "W" (for Winkler, a primary character) to "M" (for "mort" or death).[3] Or—another example—he describes the mysterious inscription, "*moor eeffoc*," with its suggestion of a heath wrapped in fog, which Dickens encountered on a fogged-up pub window one gray day in London: this wasteland turns out to be the bleak inverse—"a palindrome translated from a mirror language"—of the indoor refuge, the "room" in "coffee room," read from the other side of the pane (*Le grand incendie*, 174/*The Great Fire*, 131). This shelter (the "room" in "coffee room") might be thought to figure the room and the house, which are linked in Roubaud's mind to the "place of the dream" from which his decision—to live—arose.[4] Inevitably accompanied by a sinister double.

Leaving aside for now other such symmetries in Roubaud's pages, I will emphasize a possible world that is palindromic: a world for two—or rather a world for a one that would be two. Not solipsism, Roubaud says, but "*biipsism*." While Alix lived, such was their world. It was a world with two languages, each a translation of the other.

Biipsisme

Roubaud initially undertook his six-branch narrative in what he calls "a state of biipsism."

> L'ordre dans le monde, mais avec deux commencements
>
> Différents, inséparables
>
> (from "Une Logique," *Quelque chose noir*, 49-50)

> The order of the world, but with two beginnings.
>
> Different, inseparable
>
> (*Some Thing Black*, 47-48)

In this world of one (one consciousness, one tongue), that *one* (*un*) would reflect and be reflected by its palindromic double (*nu: bare*). And this would be the beginning of a double language.

> Le nombre *un*, mais comme bougée dans le miroir, dans deux miroirs se faisant face: son palindrome, début d'une double langue, *nu*.
>
> (*Le grand incendie*, 209)

> The number *one* [*un*], but, as though shifted in the mirror, in two facing mirrors: its palindrome, beginning of a double language, naked [*nu*].
>
> (*The Great Fire*, 157)

Le grand incendie was undertaken in that double world, made of her photographic images, and his words—the *biipsism* of showing and saying, "montrer, dire." There was in that world one language understood twice, or doubly—in words, and in images; in saying and in showing. I picture them doubling each other on either side of the one language that doesn't say anything, or show anything, but says what can't be said and isn't.

> Dans ce monde la double langue, palindrome de la pensée et du miroir, la même langue comprise doublement, et nous, toujours, traduisant.

> Dans ce monde, ses images;   mes mots. Le biipsisme
> des images et de la langue.   Montrer, dire.
>
> > (*Le grand incendie*, 210).

In this world the double language, palindrome of thought and mirror, the same language doubly understood and ourselves, at all times, translating.

In this world her images;   my words. The biipsism of the images and language.   To show, to tell.

> (*The Great Fire*, 158; translation slightly modified)

One life is not enough if a person is to live. For it takes a lifetime to be born. A cruel logic which derives from the "auto-énigme"—a logic briefly foreshadowed in the preceding chapter of this book and which we will encounter head on in chapter 4—determines this. One life is not enough—but love's double design might suffice. Its palindromic logic might sustain a world always perceived twice over, always understood in two versions, with each version a translation of the other one.

Danielle Collobert's intuition is, I think, related: a life requires another to address itself to. Whence, in part at any rate, the brief, repeated scenes of parting, on her pages—of separation from another to whom saying would say—as well as the scenes of pursuing, approaching, meeting. But whence also the frequent sensation of being mired in an embrace, sunk inside another body, imprisoned. The other (to whom saying would say "I") tends not only to be gone, far beyond reach, but also to be walled off by its own oppressive nearness. It walls in, holds back a life, swallowing the words. The worst, though, is there being no other at all. Say I live to—to whom?

> [...]   une page blanche—
> couleur aussi des murs à peine éclairés—et des mots—en
> saccades—tout autour—seulement—plus personne d'autre
> ici—absence—rien à dire à
>
> > (*Dire II*, in *Oeuvres I*, 212)

> [...]   a white page—
> also the color of walls barely lit—and words—in
> fits—all around—only—no one anymore
> here—absence—nothing to say to
>
> > (My translation)

je parole s'ouvrir bouche ouverte dire je vis à qui
(*Survie*, in *Oeuvres I*, 416)

I speech opening mouth open to say I live to whom
(*Survival*, in *Crosscut Universe*, 42)

Roubaud emphasizes this impasse in the pages he devoted to Collobert, but not without recording, earlier in his text, a sort of pause in her "chemin d'effacement." For he pictures her following a path of effacement where successive hopes, in words, of one kind or another, that would be possible, wear down to nothing. The pause—brief respite—is a momentary, precarious balance, Roubaud writes, "where it seemed there was a 'you' and an 'I' simultaneously, whence some possible duplicity in the face of the approaching cut-off." And he cites this passage:

> Tu tremblais dans mes mains et je fige ici le tremblement. Assis au bord du fleuve longtemps tout près, large et calme sous le soleil, rousseurs des bords, longtemps dans les reflets, les dessins rapides, le passage des choses dans l'eau. Eblouissement. L'air si doux, nuages légers, stratifié sur la cour déserte. Simple articulation, fin des mots, de l'effort, un son envahi par son propre écho—la résonance d'une vague sur l'autre—l'ondulation à l'infini. Accalmie.
> (Cited from *Dire I*, by Roubaud in "Danielle Collobert," cip Maresille, 36)

> You were trembling in my hands and I fix the trembling here. Sitting for a long time very close at the edge of the river, wide and calm under the sun, reddish at the edges, for a long time in the reflections, the fleeting patterns, the passage of things in the water. Dazzling sight. The air so soft, light clouds in layers above the deserted square.
> Simple articulation, end of words, of effort, a sound invaded by its own echo—the resonance of one wave upon the other—infinite fluctuation. Respite.
> (My translation)

For his part, Roubaud knew, for a few years, a world of one, but who was two—a single consciousness operating on an alternating current, perhaps; an awareness of being alive hovering tacitly between two palindromic versions of it.

> *La pensée de l'extérieur, dans ce monde, le nôtre alors,*
> aurait été celle des choses aparaissant à une conscience

alternant, dont seules auraient existé réellement les perceptions, utopiquement unies, tiennes et miennes, à l'in-
térieur de l'ile des deux:

Le frigidaire, le four, les lumières faiblissantes, les cris
et les bruits, enfants, sans hostilité, rumeurs, entre nous
la table,   pensée,   de la cuisine.
(From "Une Logique," in *Quelque chose noir*, 49-50)

Thoughts of the outside, in this world of ours, would have
been of things appearing to our alternating consciousness,
and only those perceptions of yours and mine which reached
utopian fusion would really have existed on our twosome
island:

Fridge, stove, fading light, shouts, noises, children, not
hostile, clamor, between us, thought, the kitchen
table.
(*Some Thing Black*, 47-48)

Had this island for two lasted (fridge, stove, thought, the kitchen table), then the entire project, Roubaud's use for life, might not have failed. '*Le grand incendie de Londres*' might not have had to materialize as the account of what *Le Grand Incendie de Londres* would have, or might have been, had it been anything. But, as it happened, Alix died, and '*le grand incendie*' just went (via six remarkable volumes, its whole life in him, as Roubaud puts it), from the nothing it was before being named, to the final nothing that consists in its never having been anything but a name (*Le grand incendie*, 187/*The Great Fire*, 141). "Now," Roubaud writes, in 1985 or so, '*le grand incendie de Londres*' is "just the tomb of its own only possible world."

In the early pages of the novel such as it is, Roubaud copies out a poem called "La lampe." Its starting point had been a photo by Alix, and he "now" takes it up again because he is unable to write anything new—at least, no new poem. Moreover, "La lampe" suggests to him the image of his current prose writing, his "minuscule 'projet' actuel," pursued doggedly in the last dark hours of night, by the light of his lamp, until the daylight, gradually entering his window, washes out the lamplight (*Le grand incendie*, 43-46/*The Great Fire*, 29-31). In this "Rhythmic Composition," as he also calls it, the same small rectangle of words, four full typewritten lines ("a paragraph? a strophe? a matrix for a strophe?") repeats twelve times across two facing pages, with tiny changes in each new iteration. Departing thus, slowly, from its initial orientation, the little text gradually revolves and eventually it turns itself around 360 degrees, so that at length two images (two sequences of six variations) end up reflecting each other on either side of the book's central fold—where it is hard not to suspect something sank and disappeared, leaving two mirroring phantoms behind.

Or again, where it is tempting to fantasize the imaginary meeting of two companions, an *I* and a *you*, perhaps. For with each repetition of the little text one word, *slowly*, moves slowly a little more to the left, while a blank spot moves at varying speeds in the opposite direction, toward the right—and they cross, "de manière virtuelle," Roubaud explains, between the sixth and seventh "stanzas"—in the fold of the book, in the "fictive interval that separates the end of the first page from the beginning of the second" (*Le grand incendie*, 43-46/*The Great Fire*, 29-31).[5]

We will come back to this composition (with its virtual, its fictive midpoint), but will note here, in passing, another pattern featuring two languages translated back and forth, each into the other, and—in between, I'd like to think—a third, silenced tongue. The protagonist in *Eros mélancolique*, Mr. Goodman in his graduate student days, speaks both French and English, like Jacques Roubaud and Alix. Neither is his own tongue. He is always translating, he remarks, from one to the other: "toujours traduisant." In his case it is all because he was raised by two different branches of an extended family, the French and the English one— his mother (with whom he'd hidden in the south of France), having disappeared during the war. *Her* language, his mother tongue—neither French nor English— he forgot. He had to suppress it violently as a child. One presumes it was German, for Gutmann is among the family names in Mr. Goodman's complex family tree. Once, when he was grown up, at a party in Paris where he knew nobody, he heard a voice speaking English with a slight, unplaceable accent. "Elle sonnait légèrement étrangère." This voice had about it something like the murmur or rumor of a memory (*Eros mélancolique*, 77). One suspects it was a tinge of German that reminded Goodman faintly of his lost mother and her silenced tongue.

I mean to suggest a link between this mute language, and some "primordial" one, the unspoken one of Roubaud's dream (from which the two palindromic modes of his project derive). And I propose to associate poetry, too, with this stillness: poetry that doesn't say anything, just says—poetry that occurs within a particular person as the private memory of his or her own language (the self-revealing one). I want to connect the *absentee*, as it were ("l'absente de tout poème"), with a puzzling dream, a perplexing self-memory.

The silenced language in Goodman's befogged perception might be taken for a language that no language is; a "purely virtual" one, worse than lost,

Palindromes / 77

which "began," if you will, by disappearing, and left behind like ripples the play of two mirroring translations. Goodman, whose memory was stirred at a cocktail party by a voice with a faint foreign accent, and who undertakes a "quest" (a time quest and a memory quest) whose "secret object," though never specified, must be the owner of that voice, eventually comes to mock himself as a pitiful Orpheus whose Eurydice evaporated before he'd even met her. "Quel bel amour que celui qui est perdu avant même d'avoir commencé," he observes sardonically to himself (*Eros mélancolique*, 198). What a fine love that is lost before having begun.

Traduire, Encore

Hocquard, like Roubaud, is a translator. And since he is also a promotor and publisher of translations, it might seem surprising that he doesn't think any text ever really passes from the language in which it was composed into any other language. But *getting across* a difference or a distance—starting on one side of a strait, say, and arriving on the other shore—is not at all the way Hocquard thinks of crossing or traversing, or communicating. "Une lettre," he writes, "n'arrive pas" (*Théorie des tables*, 38).

Rather, "une lettre"—a secret secret just between two—"une lettre dit maintenant" (*Théorie des tables*, 23). That is, it says "stop." For "Now means what happens / hasn't happened won't happen" (*Theory of Tables*, 41). It means what occurs, preceded and followed by nothing—interrupting time's continuity, *achrone*. Now is a kind of accident with nothing behind or ahead of it, that splits space apart and wrecks its homogeneity. But then again, *now* is also the *whole* of time, or of space (past and future at once, behind and ahead indistinguishably), slicing into the middle of things. It is the whole of a lifetime, let us say, ripping the center out of a life. Adam's description, in *Aerea*, of a fisherman's experience when suddenly he feels a fish bite, applies to this. For when he feels that "touch" at the end of his line ("the ineffable moment of the sign of recognition")—when he feels that "déchirure" which only Remedios' smiling gaze can soothe—a man holds the whole of his life, we read, past and future, in his hand (*Aerea in the Forests*, 112/*Aerea dans les forêts*, 149-50).

We have come again to the whole that is a hole—to the meeting of two (before and after: "quelle rencontre ineffable!") that separates them. Separates us, rather. For it all happens "entre nous." Secretly.

So, pushing a Norma Cole poem, say, from American English across into French is not Hocquard's concern. Such is not the point of a translation in his view. The point is to "gain new ground," he says: "gagner du terrain" (*ma haie*, 401). The point is to open up the in-between I have just (re)described (the *entre-deux*, the *entre-nous*): a blank spot, Hocquard often calls it, "tache blanche," whose unsuitability for development of any kind he likes to underscore. "*No man's land*," he says. "Espace inoccupé, sans sujet" (*ma haie*, 403). A space with nobody in it, without any "subjects," like a tautology.

The "new territory" translation can open up (between two languages and also inside one language)—the new territory explored, I suppose, at Hocquard's Bureau sur l'Atlantique, and at the translators' meetings he organized at Royaumont outside of Paris—is not a "terrain de rencontres, d'échanges, de dialogues, de discussions, d'influences, bref de communication," but a vacant lot. Hocquard calls it a *distance,* and characterizes thus his modus operandi with Michael Palmer—who translated his *Théorie des tables* from French into English and whose *Sun* Hocquard translated in turn, from English into French. He says he and Palmer had little to share. Indeed, it seems they barely corresponded, at most a few amusing postcards, and very infrequently exchanged a book or two. They had practically nothing to say to each other, "especially not points of view on anything at all, not even *on* translation." On the rare occasions when they would cross paths, they would settle a few questions at a table in some hotel or café. "Besides that, each of us plays by himself, off on his own side. An unsynchronized game, out of alignment—played at a distance—a game of distance" (*ma haie*, 411).

The two of them, Palmer and Hocquard, translators each of the other, are rather like mariners and fishermen who share the sea. "Their interests intersect," Hocquard observes. "Without meeting, they go their own way" (*Aerea in the Forests*, 112/*Aerea dans les* forêts, 150). Humans and falcons share the city of Paris in a similar manner: it seems that twenty or so falcon pairs live in Paris, where they have been reproducing since the Middle Ages. They are said to nest in certain bell towers. Their hunting area is thought to stretch dozens of kilometers in all directions. "Based in the capital, they are supposed to go looking for their daily nourishment all the way to Royaumont." I don't believe, Hocquard continues, that I have ever seen a single falcon in the sky above the city, and I suppose most Parisians are also unaware of their presence. He says he finds this story instructive, since it shows that "two territories ignorant of each other can coexist in one space, without interference or connection" (*ma haie*, 409).

He dwells rather relentlessly on *décalage*, distance, indeed on mutual unawareness: "Necessary discrepancy *between* a voice and its echo," he writes. "Between a phrase and the same one again, sounding the same, and not quite

... "Indispensable discrepancy *between* a voice and its echo, *between* one and another language. But also *between* us" (*ma haie*, 409-10).

Just between us there is a sort of intimate oblivion, it seems, or oblivious confidence. The point of translation is to enlarge it. To intensify life.

Langue inouïe

Hocquard has said that he enjoys reading American poetry in French translation, because no French person would ever have written such a thing—nor would any American.[6] No doubt he means that American poetry in French opens up a different French inside the French all French people know: a "new territory." An American poem translated into French introduces between French and French (French and the same thing, but not quite) a blank spot, "tache blanche." But perhaps the main thing in a poem written in English but read in French is the sound of a language not spoken by anyone French or by anyone American or British or by anyone at all: the language, I would hazard to say, that no one speaks. I imagine Hocquard's pleasure at hearing it echoing in the nondescript terrain his various translation projects have opened up.

No one speaks it: not you, he, she, or I—not the first person or the second or the third, but "person" speaks this language. Person, unqualified. Simple. Whose words have the sheen of colorlessness.

Person, undifferentiated, who broke into three. Or folded three ways. Complex, triplex impersonation. Three faces. Three masks, or personae.

It is faceless being, I expect—unmasked—that speaks no one's tongue. The tone is not just impersonal; it is unimpersonated. In any event, translation can give rise to *effacement*—which Hocquard also calls nakedness. *Etre nu*: an event, the simplest. *Etre le cas*.[7]

Faceless, impersonal person. "Un cas san sujets." "It then," Danielle Collobert wrote. "Il donc."

> Il donc—Il—abandon de l'impersonnel—de l'infinitif—enfin résigné—incarner—de la chair douloureuse—s'incarner comme l'ongle du pouce—Il donc
>
> (Epigraph to *Il donc*, in *Oeuvres I*, 293)

> It then—It—abandon of the impersonal—of the infinitive—at last resigned—to embody—with flesh in pain—to embody like the thumbnail—It then
>
> (*It Then*, 13)

"Le deuil du présent"

Many of Roubaud's protocols (the exercises, that is, or rituals he practices) involve counting things: steps when he is walking or going upstairs, strokes when swimming, syllables and lines and stanzas when he composes poems. He knows that there were 1,178 days between the day he first met Alix and the day she died. And when, after her death, the same number of days have passed, he notices it. Between the days before and the days after, he pictures a symmetrical, palindromic relation, where to each dismal day there corresponds, on the other side of the divide, a radiant one. And vice versa. "To each day of love," he writes, "my numerological obsession links a day of mourning."[8] The 1,178th day of grief reflects, then, reversed, the happy day he first met Alix. And in between, time unfolds in two directions at once, stretching gradually backward into the past, and forward into the future, on either side of a median absence or night—an axis, which Roubaud has elsewhere called the present, the present instant, or sometimes "le mur du deuil."

And also "now"? "Le maintenant de la poésie"? ("Poetry is NOW," Roubaud often emphasizes [e.g., *Poésie, etcetera*, 114].)

In any case, a wall; certainly a wall, the wall of mourning. "Mur ou miroir," Roubaud adds; "miroir muré" (*Poésie*, 179). Wall or mirror; walled mirror.

The theory of time that he develops presupposes what he calls "le deuil du présent." Renunciation of the present. "Le présent, j'en suis persuadé, n'a pas de réalité," he writes. "The present, so I am persuaded, has no reality; it is always virtual, real only in the past, when it is no longer" (*Poésie*, 17). There is no such thing, if I may put it this way, till there is not. Not any more.

This is the "solution"—a make-believe one, he says—that Roubaud proposes to the ancient paradox of the instant (how can there even *be* such a thing, given that it differs continually from itself, and that therefore you cannot possibly tell when it ceases, etc.: "du pur Zénon," Roubaud writes). Time, according to his own personal "solution," is just an indefinite drift, or slog, like his own (for he is an inveterate urban pedestrian), up the street and down, then down another street and up again (one always goes up a street or down, he observes; "on monte ou descend," even when the street is level. You can tell because of the numbers on the houses, which rise on one side and descend on the other). And this endless itinerary up and down, down and up is what Roubaud calls time. "This descent (or ascent) which nothing stops, this is what I name in my own mind time" (*Poésie*, 17). Time labors on then, as if accursed, up the slope Roubaud calls the *futur antérieur* and down the one he calls the *passé postérieur*. The present—drawn back into itself, as I imagine: blacked (whence *le deuil* and, as I imagine, the curse)—leaves its past futurity to mirror and be mirrored by the inverse, its future pastness.

Collobert:

> ... être là—juste à l'instant même—quelque part même pour un instant—déjà une approche—pouvoir se maintenir un peu dans le présent—peut-être si la sensation était plus forte—si on pouvait être sûr que c'est bien ça le présent—qu'on ne déborde pas déjà—à la seconde où l'on essaie de se fixer là—dans cette position—dans cet endroit du temps—dans le creux—s'y maintenir (*Dire II* in *Oeuvres I*, 224)

> ... to be there—right at the very instant—some place even for an instant—even an approach—to be able to stick a little bit in the present—perhaps if the sensation were stronger—if one could be sure that that's what it is, the present—that one hasn't gone beyond it already—at the second one tries to stick just there—in that position—in that spot of time—in the hollow—to hold oneself there (My translation)

According to Roubaud's theory, the most you can say of this little hollow, this exact instant, the present, is that at some future moment it will have been an instant in the past. "The present instant is the one which *will have been* a given past instant at a given future instant" (*The Loop*, 221/*La Boucle*, 238).

A past, then, that lies ahead: such is the present instant. A "futur antérieur" prefiguring a "passé postérieur." Roubaud provides this definition in a three-line poem titled *présent*.

> futur antérieur
> ⊗ préfigure
> du passé postérieur[9]

A gone-ness that is still coming, as I take it—a foregone obliteration that approaches. "Nuit, tu viendras ... Night, you will come."

The light, present to itself, which nothing else can or need illuminate and which is thus given over immediately to invisibility, approaches from the future. I mean, the somber radiance of the present-to-itself puzzle, the self-riddle's black illumination. It will come. The self-memory.

Beware of enigmas, Roubaud warns.

4

Beware of Enigmas

Hével havalim

Throughout his work, Roubaud returns to conundrums of the kind he warns against. Logical traps, he calls them. For example, particular phrases that no one, unless he is lying, can say—not, at least, if he means to say anything at all. Such as, "I believe it is raining, but it isn't." Or, "I think nothing other than this: what I think is true."

Or again, "I am sleeping."

We will return to these "pièges logiques" before long; for the moment let me simply observe that paradoxical occurrences of "something which cannot be said" appear to have a particular attraction for Roubaud, similar, I suspect, to the attraction that windows framing night's pitch black exert on him. In any case, one such "unsayable" lies at the origin of his entire lifework, guaranteeing its failure.

l'inachèvement
⊗   absolu
          comme fin unique

he writes, in a trident (*Tridents*, 202) whose title is "gril," his abbreviation for '*le grand incendie de Londres.*'

The work is double, as I have indicated: composed of a poetry Project that was to be accompanied by a novel. *Le Grand Incendie de Londres* would have recounted the poetry Project as if it were a fiction. But the novel failed because what it had to recount was something that cannot be said: "quelque chose qui n'était pas dicible" (*The Great Fire*, 159/*Le grand incendie*, 212). It was supposed to recount the enigma that the poetry Project contained (*The Great Fire*, 148/ *Le grand incendie*, 196).

Now in the course of *Le grand incendie* Roubaud reflects on Bartlebooth, in Perec's *Life a User's Manual*: he comments on the lifelong work that Bartlebooth planned and undertook and *almost* completed; he dwells especially on its failure. Roubaud observes that Bartlebooth's project, with its elaborate set of strict constraints, must be taken to stand for Oulipian projects in general. It shows that projects founded on formal constraints have their failure built into them—the impossibility of their completion. In Perec's novel, the figure of this impossibility is the letter *M*, mirror image (as we've observed) of *W*, and death's initial. *M* is the shape of the black hole left in Bartlebooth's lifelong undertaking. It is the signature that the whole unfinished work comes to bear. Moreover it is, Roubaud affirms, what all constraints try, by leaving a void, to say and at the same time not say—or, in Di Bernardi's translation, to show and hide both (*Le grand incendie*, 331-32/*The Great Fire*, 255-56). As if saying exactly what it is that cannot be said were always what is at stake ultimately in works based on constraints. And showing that there is something nothing can show.

In any event, we might delay here a moment, thinking about Roubaud's commentary on Bartlebooth's Oulipian program because we are just approaching the inevitable failure, according to Roubaud himself, of his own double project. He lays out and discusses the numerous axioms underlying its prose wing and the constraints informing this aspect of his project in chapter 5 of *Le grand incendie de Londres*. He defines the whole project as his alternative to voluntary death, yet also states that it had to break down because it was from the start called on to say something unsayable. My inclination to reflect here briefly on Roubaud's reading of Bartlebooth's failure is also motivated by the fact that in one of Roubaud's own novels, *Eros mélancolique*, the main character, Mr. Goodman, finds himself abandoned at the last moment by *his* Oulipian project. It inexplicably derails, leaving a shambles; his feeling is one of "dereliction."

Bartlebooth's project was conceived so as to last exactly as long as he did. I gather it was his way of *using* his whole life, all up. Having systematically completed all the many stages of the project's programmed composition, he was to reverse or undo them all just as systematically so that the entire project would be completed and also neatly erased when Bartlebooth himself came to his end. But one procedure very near the conclusion of it all proved impossible. The last piece in the final jigsaw puzzle would not fit in the last empty spot, and Bartlebooth died facing this "black hole," as Roubaud puts it.[1] "Déposition pure, inaccomplie," one might think, staring at this black.

"The riddle remains a riddle, even after the corpse's eyes turn into hollow shells" Roubaud writes, in a similar context, in his own *grand incendie* (141/ *The Great Fire*, 187). "L'énigme reste énigme jusque dans les yeux troués du cadavre." One might well recall that sentence, especially "les yeux troués," upon encountering the "trou noir" that he sees at the end of *Life a User's Manual*. "Trou noir," black hole.

It is no use living, you cannot fill it up. *A quoi bon?* What's the use? What's the use of a user's manual.

Speaking in 1989, in *Le grand incendie*, of the double project he conceived in 1961, he says that what he still has left to do, now that he is over fifty, in order to complete even the current, modified version of the poetry Project's prose wing is pointless. I expect this is largely, if not entirely because the "state of biipsism" he was in when he took it up has not existed since 1983. It makes no difference if I continue or not, he writes. "De toute façon, c'est un tombeau." "In any case, it's a tomb" (*Le grand incencie*, 183/*The Great Fire*, 138). "Un tombeau," "un trou noir." Between the first and the last branches of his long prose work he throws paragraphs, chapters—"moments," "insertions"—one by one, he says. "I throw them into a hole that will not be filled—even at the end" (translation slightly modified). "Je les jette dans un trou qui ne se remplira pas, jusqu'à la fin."[2]

> Vanité dit Qohélet
> hével havalim
> Hével dit Qohélet
>   tout est vain

Roubaud translated the book of Ecclesiastes in 2004.[3]

> "I can no longer say my name" —*D. Collobert*

The impossible-to-say thing that determined the failure of '*Le grand incendie*' seems to have been a riddle. I cannot tell, or ask you the riddle, because *that* is the riddle: what is it?

Beware of Enigmas / 85

This is the riddle bearing only on itself—the "self-riddle" that I introduced in the first pages of this book, and have referred to on and off since. "L'auto-énigme."

Like light for Dennis Ps. at Mr. Goodman's evening seminars—like light that nothing else can illuminate—the self-riddle is its own sole solution. Identical to itself, it is the riddle of identity. And like poetry, that doesn't say anything, just says (says what it says by saying), the self-riddle doesn't ask anything. I mean, it doesn't inquire into anything *else*, other than itself. It just asks. Asks what it asks by asking. "What am I?"

The form of this self-riddle is the riddle-form of poetry—poetry that says, but not anything possible. Not anything sayable. Rather, something that cannot be said and isn't. This *form* is the enigma that the poetry Project contained, Roubaud states (*The Great Fire*, 148/*Le grand incendie*, 196), and the untellable thing that the accompanying novel was to "recount." This is to say that the auto-énigme is the puzzle, the trap, the logical conundrum (the built-in disaster) of the entire, two-part project itself.

In Roubaud's books, it appears more than once as the question the young knight Percival failed to ask at the palace of the Fisher King. In order to ask it he would have had to know the answer. That is, he would have had to know what the question was. Or, as Roubaud sometimes puts it, "been in a condition to know."[4] To know himself, I expect. As it is, he must approach this condition haltingly and belatedly throughout the whole of the life granted him in the pages of Chrétien de Troye. And the reader of Chrétien as well, similarly tardy, should progress, in this same long quest, toward this same condition. The condition of one able to understand, who (s)he is.

On occasion Roubaud presents the "auto-énigme" or "self-riddle" via a possibly apocryphal account of Gertrude Stein's last words. Just before entering the operating room from which she did not emerge alive she is supposed to have murmured, "What is the answer?" and, after a silence, "Then, what is the question?" (see *Le grand incendie*, 186–87/*The Great Fire*, 140).

This question (what is the question?) implies that a voice somewhere in her head or in the light fixtures in the hospital corridor had said, in answer to "What is the answer?" "The question." Causing her to inquire, "Then what is the question (if *it* is the answer)"?

I suppose a voice might have answered, "What is the question?" (for *that* is the question), but there was no need, since Stein herself gave that answer when she asked the question (what is it?). I expect, though, that she gave the answer (in the story, at least) without knowing or giving it, without knowing or giving anything. She said "tout rien": all-nothing or, in Rosmarie Waldrop's translation, "absolutely nothing."

"She neither revealed nor kept anything back—neither showed nor hid anything. She said, but nothing. "L'énigme reste énigme jusque dans les yeux troués du cadavre."

"Etrange lien," Roubaud exclaims elsewhere, "entre l'identité et la mort."[5]

You could imagine, thinking about the story of Stein's last words, that the answer to the riddle, of identity, comes at the end of a life, or, more desperately, that it *is* the end. This is not exactly the same picture as in Chrétien de Troye, where ultimately—Percival having achieved the condition of one who is able to know—"the question asks itself all on its own and receives its answer from itself" (*La Fleur inverse* 36). In the Roubaud conception of the tale however, a life proves impossible to complete (a life, a quest, a "project," a book). The end leaves a hole, its signature. "Trou noir," "tombe noire," "yeux troués du cadavre." This would be Roubaud's somber prose-narrative way of thinking.

Along this way, or path, one must imagine, I believe, that the answer comes the way *some thing blacks*. The way some thing—a question, let us say—finally reaches itself. Let us imagine a question reaching itself at the end of the quest, the quest for itself that it has been; let us imagine a question reaching itself at last, its own pitch-black solution, and thereupon dragging the whole world along with it out of the world into the dark. "Whoever solves the riddle loses the light of day," Roubaud writes in *Le grand incendie* (187/*The Great Fire*, 141). A person arrives at his birth, you might think, when at last his life has had time to dawn on him as the impenetrable enigma it always was. One's origin, or identity is, as it were, the kind of snark called Boojum.[6]

"To link thus a birth to a death—if possible—absurdity," Collobert writes (sounding like Beckett, whom she knew).

> comme un espoir de naissance—on dirait—dans cette
> destruction—dans le continuel échec—dans cette fuite en
> avant—jusqu'à la fin—relier ainsi une naissance à une
> mort—si possible—absurdité   (*Dire II*, in *Oeuvres I*, 243)

> a faint hope of birth—you might say—in this
> destruction—in this continual failure—in this flight
> ahead—all the way to the end—to link thus a birth to a
> death—if possible—absurdity   (My translation)

> longtemps chercher—par tâtonnement—approche—
> s'avancer parmi les débris—sans rien reconnaître—avec
> tant d'horreur—tenter de se retrouver là—ne trouver de
> ressemblance avec rien d'habituel—de normal—aucune
> forme—c'est presque ça—sans forme—sans lumière—dire
> c'est moi—et ne rien recouvrir de ces deux mots—deux
> sons—à peine prononcés—à peine saisis—et plus rien—
> pas même une fraction de seconde—le temps d'une
> évidence—toujours au delà—à côté—non—pas même
> à côté ... (*Dire II*, 222-23)

> seeking for a long time—groping—approach—
> advancing among the debris—recognizing nothing—with
> so much horror—trying to find oneself there—finding
> nothing resembling anything familiar—normal—no
> form—that's almost it—without form—without light—say
> it is I—and reach nothing but these three words—three
> sounds—scarcely pronounced—scarcely grasped—and nothing more
> not even a fraction of a second—time for a
> clue—always beyond—off to the side—no—not even
> to the side ... (My translation)

In Collobert's *Meurtre* there is a brief narrative that begins when the narrator, fleetingly, recognizes someone. "I went into the café and saw her right away in the back, facing me. [...] An old woman, a very old woman, and the resemblance." "Une vieille femme, très vieille femme, et la ressemblance."

She is wearing a raincoat and just looking into space; then she makes a note on a sheet of paper, puts it in her bag and a little later leaves. The speaker follows. They take a bus, without speaking. When the old woman stops at another café, the speaker goes in too; they stay there for a long time, then take another bus, and so on. In Roubaud's work, too, there are itinerary-texts like this one—long trudges marked by a series of stopping places, like stations in some drab ritual. Or enigmatic episodes along the twisty route of some quest. Or dream. We will encounter at least one of these later. In his text in memory of Collobert, Roubaud evokes the narrative from *Meurtre*, which I have just cited, and suggests that something is *completed* when at last, at the last stop, the narrator's gaze, and the dead gaze of the very old woman, lying on a bed in her raincoat, meet. Something is completed, but then again, not. "For 'the inner eye' has finally met the 'outer eye.'"[7]

> I look at her. I go back down. The door doesn't close. I am lost in the streets. The drizzle turns milky blue. The day is torn.
> (Murder 44/Meurtre, in Oeuvres I, 54-59)

Roubaud's own text breaks off with these lines from Collobert's *Survie*:

> je partant voix sans réponse articuler parfois les mots
> que silence réponse à autre oreille jamais
> si à muet le monde pas de bruit
> fonce dans le bleu cosmos
>
> assez assez
> exit
> (Survie, in Oeuvres I, 420)

> I leaving voice without response to articulate sometimes words
> that silence response to other ear never
> if to muteness world not a sound
> plunges into blue cosmos
>
> enough enough
> exit
> (Survival, in Crosscut Universe, 41)

Better not to persist doggedly to the last station, the quest's conclusion. There are questions, Roubaud sometimes advises, that should be left "hors question." Too dangerous.

> One should not solve riddles; do not answer the questions asked by the sphinx. The enigma must remain *hors question*—outside questions and questioning—no less than *hors réponse* (beyond answers). Otherwise, catastrophe.
> (La Fleur inverse, 36; my translation)

Shun the radiant black fact of nothing's being there, no one. Horrible black, horrible poetry which says, but not anything, not anything sayable, but me. Who I am. To hear it, I imagine, is to feel my life and death confounded, no distinction whatsoever between my world and none, language perfectly plain and totally mute, poetry's all and its nothing. Vesuvius and Cicada melted into each other, all doubt wiped out.

Vers de dreit nien

At the beginning of the lyric tradition to which Roubaud feels most akin lies William of Aquitaine's famous poem about nothing, "vers de dreit nien." Subsequent troubadours allude to it often in their songs of love and this makes for what Roubaud, in *La Fleur inverse*, calls the fragility of the trobar: its vulnerability to ridicule, its tendency to deride and parody itself for ideas like absolute devotion to someone totally unknown, for paradoxes such as *I love a lady but I don't know what love is.* For really, love like that is just nothing. Raimbaut d'Orange, a favorite of Roubaud's, begins a canso in this way (in Roubaud's translation):

> Ecoute mais je ne sais ce que c'est   seigneurs ce que je commence
> (*La Fleur inverse*, 41)

> Listen, but I do not know what it is   my lords, that I am beginning

Songs of love like that are *dreit nien*. "Gouffre pur d'amour," Roubaud writes in *Some Thing Black*, his most desolate book. Sheer abyss of love. "Je t'aime jusque là," he writes, as if love, like light itself, and "death itself-self," were, in its perfection, a pit of nothing. Or at best pure folly. A fine lover, the one who lost his beloved before ever finding her, and a fine love the one that before getting off the ground is over. Roubaud dwells on ridiculous love like this long enough in *La Fleur inverse* to make one suspect that when, in *Poetry, etcetera*, he says poetry is *amour de la langue*, he means *amour de loin*: like Jaufre Rudel's for a lady he never knew.

In fact, the whole affair—*le chant l'amour la poésie*—looks to be so foreign to the world that one could only ever make it up, a fantasy. (Why, one of the minor characters in *Eros mélancolique* asks himself, is love so strange that I can only dream it?)

In the dialogues that comprise a good deal of *Poetry, etcetera*, Roubaud takes up the troubadours' gesture of alluding, sardonically, to the *nothing* poem of Guillaume d'Aquitaine, and to the *I don't know* motif (I don't know whom I love, what love is, what I am saying). At least, so it seems to me—when, for example, in what could be perceived as a mildly flippant gesture, he says that what poetry says when it says, but not anything is "un je ne sais quoi" (*Poésie*, etcetera, 79/*Poetry, etcetera*, 78). In fact, it is striking, how close to nonsense he brings poetry in this polemic—how close to a sheer nothing—he who is poetry's champion. When his imaginary interlocutor asks him if he couldn't please add some term or other for clarity's sake at the end of the expression *la poésie dit* (poetry says), he obliges by proposing the word *kekchose* (an allusion, I expect, to Queneau's "néo-français"). "La poésie ne dit pas "quelque chose" (something), mais kekchose," Roubaud writes ("sump'n" is Guy Bennett's translation).

> "Let's call what poetry says but what cannot be said **sump'n**."
> "Can it be shown?"
> "Nope."
> "So, it's not said, not shown—is it kept silent? Is poetry a silence?"
> "Only a public silence.
> Poetry keeps nothing silent."
>
> "Many people, who confusedly feel that sump'n is not something that could be said, find poetry saying sump'n an absurd activity, and poems nonsense."
>
> (*Poetry, etcetera*, 77-78/*Poésie, etcetera*, 78)

Elsewhere, in a poem, Roubaud again insists on brushing up against nonsense, nothingness, and alludes once more to a widespread distaste for poetry: it gets a hairbreadth from a demon, the demon of silence. No wonder so many people recoil from it nowadays, disguising their dread as indifference (see *The Plurality of Worlds of Lewis*, 72/*La pluralité des mondes de Lewis*, 72).

More Logical Traps

In *La Boucle* (*The Loop*) Roubaud presents the "logical trap" that captivated him when he was a boy: a summer afternoon, a table set outside for a family meal, the outer wall of a house rising up as a backdrop, a balcony outside the upper-story bedroom windows, and from there, sounds of a little commotion among children. A voice asks, "Are you asleep?" And another, "naive" one answers, "Yes" (*La Boucle*, 402-3/*The Loop*, 378).

> I was so seduced by this logical trap that I've held onto it, preciously, ever since, wrapped up together with the sun-drenched table, the tablecloth, the glasses on it; with the laughter, the silence of the windows, their curtains drawn for the afternoon nap of my youngest brother, Jean-René.

This nap-time scene chez les Roubaud makes me think of Percival, half asleep in the dining hall of the Fisher King, watching strange and radiant objects being carried to the table. Perhaps this is because of the family table, with its cloth and glassware, bathed in sunlight, and just above, the curtains drawn across the windows of a silent sleeping chamber, a little like a veil concealing a mystery—and because of the question, and the answer, a thing that cannot be said, except in dreams. At any rate, dining table, shining glassware, voices and silence compose the wrapping in which Jacques, the eldest Roubaud son, long preserved a trap, "un piège logique," as if it were a treasure. He unwraps the *Are you sleeping?* trap quite often in the course of his work, and examines it. He places a little set of "pièces logiques" in the middle of his poetry book *La Forme d'une ville change plus vite, hélas, que le coeur des humains,* and demonstrates there a few things a wide-awake person cannot think, any more than a slumbering person can affirm, in answer to someone who asks, that he is asleep. (Yet what if that person were talking in his sleep—asking questions in a dream and dreamily answering?)

I suspect it is an impossible poetry-thinking that Roubaud (or someone, sleepless) keeps approaching and renouncing in these puzzles—mocking and desiring, desiring and fleeing. Perhaps the stubborn, illogical desire is for the blacker black hidden in the "other night" (the one "that is coming," and has no end). Maybe Roubaud does not want to be blinded to that awful radiance by lesser rays.

One of the "pièces" or "pièges logiques" nested in the middle of *La Forme d'une ville* features someone who wants to think his thought is true. He prefers not to think anything *else*; he does not wish to train his thought on this or that, on any particular thing at all and then find his thought about *it* to be true. He declines to think anything at all about the inconstant, deceptive, rotten world. He just wants to think he thinks true—to think the pure truth truly: "véritablement le vrai / le vrai pur."

But, as his patient interlocutor tries to explain, if he won't think anything else, which he could then think true (if he won't take seriously the question "But *what* are you thinking is true?"), he won't be thinking anything, that could ever be ascertained to be true or not ("La vérité," in *La Forme d'une ville*, 143-45/*The Form of a City*, 128-30). He won't be thinking anything, any more than poetry says anything, given that there is nothing *else* that can say what, just by saying, it says.

The stubborn thinker of "le vrai pur" is advised to think of something else.

Maybe it is still he, obstinate, who, in another of the "pièces" or "pièges logiques" tries to think, not that he thinks true, but that he thinks false. His efforts recall G. E. Moore's famous paradox: "I think it is raining though I see that it is not." For he insists he believes both that the weather is bad *and* that this is a mistake ("Il pleut," in *La Forme d'une ville*, 121-22/ *The Form of a City*, 109-10). "Tu ne peux pas," his interlocutor informs him. You can't think that; you can't think one thing and the opposite both at once, it is impossible. You can't deny a thought that you simultaneously maintain. You can't maintain that a thought you're maintaining is maintained in error—although poetry, as Roubaud observes elsewhere, does not obey this law of noncontradiction. And although another poem in *The Form of a City* evokes the frightening experience of doing almost exactly that, on an occasion when it is practically impossible *not* to think what one simultaneously thinks impossible.

Une rue

du fond de la rue
viennent
sont venus
droit
ces nuages
si droit
que cétait impossible
impossible que la rue
ne les dirige pas
impossible

que jusque dans la nuit
viennent
soient venus
sur une trajectoire
si exactement semblable à celle de la rue
véritablement seuls
les nuages
(une trajectoire
si droite
qu'elle faisit

peur)   (*La forme d'une ville*, 142/127)

A Street

from the bed of the street
come

came
straight
these clouds
so straight
it was impossible
not possible the street
had not steered them
impossible

that even at night
come
came
these clouds
on a course
so exactly like that of the street
all by themselves
(so straight
a course it was

scary)   (*The Form of a City*, 127 [translation slightly modified])

Clouds

The impossibly rigorous procession of these clouds, straight down the street, "jusque dans la nuit" (all the way into the night, I would say, thinking of other occurrences of this phrase in Roubaud's pages), reminds me of other clouds in his books: of the ones, for example, that he has often described appearing at dusk from behind the Eglise des Blancs-Manteaux in Paris, and sailing straight into the bay of roofs visible through two windows of his apartment on la Rue Vieille-du-Temple. He used to watch them every evening in the months after the death of Alix, watch them advancing as always, inexorably from the west as daylight receded; he would watch them through the two windows between which she had placed her photo of them.

Cette photographie, ta dernière, je l'ai laissée sur le mur,
où tu l'avais mise, entre les deux fenêtres

Et le soir, recevant la lumière, je m'assieds, sur cette
chaise, toujours la même, la regarder, où tu l'as posée,
entre les deux fenêtres,

> Et ce que l'on voit, là, recevant la lumière, qui décline,
> dans le golfe de toits, à gauche de l'église, ce qu'on
> voit, les soirs, assis sur cette chaise, est, précisément,
>
> Ce que montre l'image laissée sur le mur...⁸ (*Quelque chose noir*, 91)
>
> This photograph, your last, I've left on the wall where you
> put it, between the two windows,
>
> And in the evening, catching the light, I sit down on this
> chair, the same, still, and look at it, where you put it, between
> the two windows,
>
> And what one sees here, catching the light as it fades, in the
> bay of roofs to the left of the church, what one sees,
> evenings, sitting on this chair, is precisely
>
> What the picture shows, on the wall... (*Some Thing Black*, 89)

Eventually he recognized, in the clouds entering the bay of roofs, a monster from his childhood: the scary and excitingly mysterious Monstre de Strasbourg from the tales he'd made up for his siblings after dark as a boy in Carcassonne. By 1983, time had finally converted this mere mystery into the black enigma it really always had been (*La Boucle*, 373-74/ *The Loop*, 351-52). It had always been coming for him ("nuit, tu viendras...").

Mr. Goodman too—when he is a professor of mathematical crystallography at the University of Edinburgh—contemplates the evening clouds from his apartment where grief has temporarily paralyzed him. He too eventually recognizes in their regular procession into the aperture formed by the roofs of the church and the houses lining the square, the ghost of a monstrous event from the past: the disaster, I suspect, that all photographs, as we later learn, suggest to him: an imminent, brutal disappearance.

> Les nuages, à leur habitude, sortaient dans le silence de derrière l'église presbytérienne, dans le golfe de toits entre l'église et les maisons du square. Les nuages arrivaient lentement, venant de l'ouest comme toujours, porteurs du soir précoce et de la lumière finissante, désolée, sur les maisons, sur l'église, sur les arbres du square; déviaient dans les fragments de miroir collés sur le mur. [...]
> Dans le mouvement des nuages, alors, dans l'image même du bord des toits de l'église où ils lui apparaissaient d'abord, dans la forme de la pierre,

il sentit la présence d'un monstre, qu'il savait avoir connu, longtemps, longtemps avant: le spectre d'un événement monstrueux revenu le hanter, depuis toutes ces années qu'il pensait à jamais oblitérées dans la mémoire.[9]

The clouds, as was their wont, would emerge in silence from behind the Presbyterian church, into the bay bounded by the roofs of the church and the houses on the square.

The clouds would arrive slowly, always coming from the west, bearers of the early evening and of the receding, desolate light, on the houses, on the church, on the trees of the square; they would stray into the mirror fragments glued to the wall.   [...]

In the movement of the clouds, then, in the form of the stone, he felt the presence of a monster, which he knew he had known before, long, long ago: the specter of a monstrous event, come back to haunt him from all those years he had thought obliterated forever from memory.

(My translation)

"Jusque dans la nuit"

Even into the night a Roubaud meditation persists, full of foreboding, but "almost happy" ("Jusque dans la nuit," in *La pluralité des mondes*, 63/*The Plurality of Worlds*, 63). It is a vision of things shedding their particular attributes, the bits and accidental pieces of world, I expect, that attenuate their essence, which would be sheer form. Gradually they put aside the robes their forms had worn by day, leaving these features of their particularity, "parfum de leur *haeccéité*," on the last visible stairsteps down into the shadows. They appear "themselves-selves," or almost—their practically featureless bulk wrapped in golden transparency, "la transparence dorée" of their nakedness. They recall descriptions Roubaud quotes elsewhere, from the troubadours, of a lady's nudity appearing luminous in a darkened chamber. Having left off the vestments that had adorned their forms, showing faces that seem the face of "la première, & philosophique matière, écaillée de toute qualité" ("the first, & philosophic, matter, scraped clean of any qualities"), the radiant objects contemplated at dusk reveal all save their "most intimate opacity that they defended to the last"(*La pluralité*, 63/*The Plurality*, 63). "Au fond des jambes ouvertes, cette tache sombre," as Roubaud writes in a different poem (*Quelque chose noir*, 111/*Some Thing Black*, 109), the exact spot where light stops, "exacte là / Où tu deviens noire" (*Quelque chose noir*, 96/*Some Thing Black*, 94). "Between your open legs, dark patch," "exactly / Where you turn black." This intimate opacity on which a prohibition bears is light's withdrawal into its own invisible beauty, the black beauty of light itself. Itself-self. It is desire's secret object (you, you yourself), absolutely inaccessible. "Gouffre pur d'amour." "Je t'aime jusque là" (*Quelque chose noir*, 15/13).

"I deemed myself almost happy to enjoy this rarest of visions," we read, in "Jusque dans la nuit" ("Even into the Night"): almost happy, as I understand it, to behold the forms of almost nothing appear: almost the pure forms of form.

> (...) I deemed myself almost happy to enjoy this rarest of visions which at the same time stirred such forebodings of disaster as I could barely endure. But so as not to succumb to something like despair, I kept turning my eyes away from such contemplation, as if it were forbidden. (*La pluralité*, 63/63)

"I know I couldn't have thought my thought was wrong," Roubaud's trapped logician eventually acknowledges, in another of the *pièces logiques* ("L'occasion," in *La Forme d'une ville*, 140-41/ *The Form of a City*, 125-26). I know that on that particular occasion, I couldn't have thought either rightly or wrongly that my thought was wrong, unless I'd also thought that on that occasion *some other thing* I thought was wrong. And moreover, he grants, I couldn't have dreaded on that particular occasion, rightly or wrongly, something it was not reasonable to dread if I hadn't on that occasion had *an altogether different unreasonable fear*. But I would so have wished to have but the one thought, he says: the one fear.

> peur
> peur
> peur

My shameless paraphrase continues: I would so have wished not to think anything *else*, not to endure any other fear. I would so have wished that no particular occasion would preserve me from the perfectly separate, the totally unlike—from the one thought and the one fear. Indeed I want no particular occasion to preserve me from the occasion that would come ... that would come depriving me of the one thought, the one fear forever.[10]

One thinks of the blank face of truth removed from the vicissitudes of particular occasions—I mean, one thinks of *the* particular occasion (its closed countenance) on which all occasions, including especially that very one, black out.[11]

>   Quelque chose noir qui se referme. et se boucle. une
>   déposition *pure, inaccomplie*.   (*Quelque chose noir*, 76; my emphasis)
>
>   Some thing black which closes in. locks shut. *pure, un-
>   accomplished* deposition.   (My emphasis)

Beware of enigmas: never try to grasp them, Roubaud advises.

Never act, that is, as if the object of your longing, the goal of your quest were something to capture. Respect "l'interdit de la vitre" (*Eros mélancolique*, 266). Believe in the shape that hovers in a mirror or shimmers on a translucent pane, a barrier comparable to Tristan's sword laid between Isolde and himself. Spare your eyes the complete dissolution of things, bared of every outward attribute—even if that black, that nakedness is all you would so have wanted. Believe in the image that trembles on the surface of a pool, that swims into focus at the top of a well or emerges dripping from its tray in the darkroom. Suspend your disbelief, leave things a little in abeyance, let them hesitate, flicker, and in this temporary delay, watch the fitful movement of shadows on the bumpy surface of a wall on a colorless evening—a fountain agitated by a gathering of shy nymphs.

> La lumière pourtant continuait, affaiblie mais réelle, à s'aventurer dans les interstices d'un mur qui, mes yeux s'habituant, puisque l'ombre (étant à la fois grise et pâle) échappait aussi bien à l'éclat qu'à l'obscurité, non à la couleur noire mais à l'indistinction, semblait entourer une fontaine agitée de tremblantes nymphes nues; peut-être une illusion, née de mon imagination, ma pensée toujours peu capable de supporter la dissolution maintenant presque entière des objets.
>
>   ("Jusque dans la nuit," in *La pluralité*, 65)

> The light, however, real if weakened, continued to probe into the cracks of a wall which, as my eyes adjusted not so much to the color black (the half-light, being both grey and pale, was neither bright nor dark), as to the lack of distinctness, seemed to surround a fountain splashing with naked, trembling nymphs. Perhaps an illusion born of my imagination, my mind still not very capable of bearing the now almost complete dissolution of things.
>
>   (*The Plurality*, 65)

Knights of the Round Table

Roubaud's observation—which I have cited before—that a "strange link" seems to exist between identity and death, appears in his book on Arthurian romances, *Graal fiction*. "Etrange lien (...) entre l'identité et la mort." His own prose writing bears a special and explicit relation to the Grail narratives as he understands them.[12] This is especially true of his autobiographical narrative (i.e., the six twisty branches of *'Le grand incendie de Londres'*). For riddles lie behind the medieval Grail Book, and indeed *launch* it. Riddles such as Who am I? These give rise to certain formal characteristics and determine a particular narrative logic, in the Arthurian legends just as in *'Le grand incendie de Londres.'*

Gawain, in the Grail stories, is the name of the knight whose name is most his own, Roubaud observes: of all King Arthur's knights, Gawain is the one who most completely knows and owns his name; he carries it better than anyone (*Graal fiction*, 87). And thus his name can also serve to name all the knights, for it names the chivalric life itself, in which a knight is supposed to learn of his lineage, perform feats of valor, experience love, win tournaments and in this way discover and take possession of his name.

Lancelot's name, in contrast to Gawain's, is a puzzle. Much of the Lancelot branch of the wildly forking Grail Book bears on the gradual discovery of this name. Its first disclosure occurs when the young knight lifts the stone covering the tomb where he will eventually be buried and reads upon it, "Ici gerra Lancelot du lac, le fils au roi Ban de Benoic." "Here will lie Lancelot of the lake, son of king Ban de Benoic." "Etrange lien ainsi noué entre l'identité et la mort!" (*Graal fiction*, 220).

Lancelot will hide this identity as long as possible, calling himself (and being called by others) well over a dozen different nicknames and pseudonyms. The formal importance for Roubaud of this bewildering web of the true name's disguises, distortions, partial revelations, and splits cannot be overemphasized. The spreading patterns of similar situations and repeating motifs obscurely supported by an underlay of name fragments and remnants—the delays on the way toward the recovery of the whole name (the detours within detours, the abandoned paths)—inform his own brand of narrative. *'Le grand incendie,'* too, one gradually sees, holds, and hides, knotted up in its odd title, several scarcely recognizable fragments of a prior life. Vivid but truncated and scrambled memories of a life before the beginning of the book. The hope for the book was that by the time it ended it would have retrieved these shards and gathered them into a composition such that the title, given from the outset, would prove to be its key. Or again, if all had gone well, the book would finally have been assembled from the splinters of a shattered *before*. At last it would have completed the prior life whose proper name its title would then turn out to have been all along.[13] It would have formulated the question—What am I? Who?—to which its mysterious title will have been the answer.

Lancelot never does completely master his identity. Shadows of madness and death keep falling across his path, and this darkness cannot be separated from what Roubaud calls "the fatality of the name—at the same time malediction, tabou, secret, dangerous possession and constantly mislaid" (*Graal fiction*, 221). In his view the entire Grail Book is like Lancelot: dispossessed of itself, bereft of the book it is. For, he says, it isn't just a book about a mysterious grail and a long, perplexing quest for it; the Grail, he holds, is itself a book (183). A plate—a cup, if you will, a precious stone—but also a book. And he cites an old Irish manuscript that reveals, he says, that the Grail borne by a beautiful young girl in the Fisher King's palace "appeared in every way similar to a *textus*"—that is, a richly ornamented Gospel.

That the Grail should be a book implies that the Grail Book is for itself a Grail: the book is a quest, then, whose "object" is itself. This is the narrative logic of Roubaud's own prose, as I've just been suggesting; he recognizes it in other narratives besides the Arthurian romances—in Henry James, for example, and in George Perec (*Life a User's Manual*, especially). His favored type of prose narrative consists in the slowly developing recollection, "réminiscence ou anamnèse," of the "form" that instigates it.

This "form" appeared—in my earlier comments about *Life a User's Manual*—as a black hole: the enigma that remains inscrutable "even after the corpse's eyes have turned to hollow shells." This "form," I tried to show, launches the narrative (initiates a life), and is its built-in collapse. It is the unsayable thing that *Le Grand Incendie de Londres* like *La Vie mode d'emploi*, was to recount. Roubaud proposes, however, another perspective on narratives of the Perec, or James or Roubaud type: on narratives, that is, that share certain formal characteristics with the tales of King Arthur's knights. They are all twisty, branchy; they entangle many different stories and different versions of the same stories within the wandering, halting, detouring course of a very long, never completed tale; they leave some developments half-finished; they add sequel after sequel to others. In this way they might be thought to outdo the insoluble problem that in Roubaud's view faces all prose narrative: the ending. *La Vie mode d'emploi*, with its wealth of separate stories, some interrelated, some not, is exemplary in this regard: Roubaud considers that (despite the "black hole") ultimately Perec's great novel evades the catastrophe that completion entails. That is why, in the statement I tacitly referred to above—the statement that prose narrative of the type he himself composes and admires in the work of others is a slow recollection of the form that instigates it—Roubaud elaborates at some length on the *slow* tempo of this recollection, describing *La Vie mode d'emploi* as "an intertwining spiral of multiple completions and incompletions (lives, life), of the completion and incompletion of memory, of a reminiscence, an anamnesis of the form that instigated it, Grail or Snark" (*Poetry, etcetera*, 257/*Poésie, etcetera*, 247). Describing his own Grail novel ('*Le grand incendie de Londres*'), he stresses the multiple, differing versions it contains of the one "réminiscence" or "anamnèse"—some of them complete, some not, some spiraling around each other, some introduced within another, many intertwined, often entangled, snarled.

> The prose of memory was a prose of intertwining, modeled on the Grail novels and the modes of the constraints; a shadowy version of rhythmic complexities:
> —successions, with no regrets or backtracking, of discrete events, the pages;
> —embeddings, intercalations of new stories, a thousand and one nights of memory;
> —encroachments, simultaneous overlappings toward an end. The end of one story would be the start of another. Loops; spirals;
> —obliterations and their doubles, substitutions; abandoned tales; tales coming "in the place" of a sentence, of a proposition, of a word, of a letter, of the mirror of a letter; deleted tales;
> —and so many others
> 					(*The Great Fire*, 155-56/*Le grand incendie*, 207)

In all this what I wish to emphasize is the "form": at once the narrative's origin and its object, or end. And the narrative itself, instigated by the form: it unfolds as an "auto-quest," so to speak, or self-question (What am I?). This quest is moreover the *memory* of what is sought. The story is the *recollection* of what it does not know (what it is). This recollection is a multiple, inconsistent "anamnèse," featuring abandoned reminiscences woven in with overlapping, complete ones often at variance with each other. An "autobiography." A hazy, seemingly incoherent self-memory. A dream of before its birth.

I mean to attribute to narrative as conceived by Roubaud an odd awareness of something—of itself!—whose having been lies ahead. An oneiric sort of self-consciousness, then. Narrative for Roubaud is a dream of something—a life—that is not, but was going to be, and eventually will have been, already. It is as if prose narrative for Roubaud were an effect of his desolate theory of time, which grants, as we've seen, to the present instant the sole possibility of having, later, already occurred. Prose for Roubaud seems to imply an accursed time, the time of mourning—"le deuil du présent"—and a wasteland setting. Or an accursed world where time can only be wasted. I think we must try to imagine a story that from episode to episode would proceed in the dark about itself—dimly recalling, maybe sometimes remembering wrong, losing the way, confusedly dreaming its winding route toward itself. I think we must try to picture a book whose pages would be written in a language it does not know yet how to read.[14] Every page would have the mysterious character of Merlin's "paroles obscures," those strange prophesies never decipherable until too late, which say to the questing knights of the Round Table, "This is what will have been revealed." *This*, each page of the book I am trying to picture would say, *is what will have been written*.

As I observed earlier, there is a remarkable number of obscure, lost books floating around in Roubaud's many books—ghost books, it sometimes seems, or faint images of books we seem to glimpse through a looking glass; books that seem lost in a dream of themselves. There is *Eros mélancolique*, for example, which, we are given to understand (by Roubaud and Anne Garréta, Roubaud's coauthor), is an unattributable, unfinished work containing several long blanks, which seems to have drifted around the internet for an undetermined period before a link to it fetched up unexpectedly on the screen of Roubaud's Mac in the early hours of a morning in 2008. Roubaud happened to be googling three mathematicians, and "at the intersection of Clifford's algebras, Cayley's graphs and Coxeter's lattice paths," the link appeared. Then there is the lost book, *Le Voyage d'hiver*, which figures in a book by Perec (also called *Le Voyage d'hiver*), and the hunt for which is continued in a sequel by Roubaud, *Le Voyage d'hier*).[15]

Afterlife

The "form" that launches narrative is the riddle-form of identity, "self-riddle." "Question muette," "question sans question," form of an enigma that cannot be said, or shown (or hidden or held back), and is not. This form is poetry's. "Poetry is riddle," we read in *Le grand incendie* (199/*The Great Fire*, 150). Thus poetry launches autobiographical prose—I mean, the blacking of poetry casts narrative like a shadow across a wasteland, in an accursed time.

> Poetry is riddle.
> Poetry is riddle and the novel is a fall from poetry.
> (*Le grand incendie*, 199/*The Great Fire*, 150)

Sometimes—as we have seen—Roubaud appears to lament that he can glimpse form itself only via some particular mode or manner that it happens to assume on some particular occasion, when it is the form *of* some *other* thing, this or that. Only because a lingering remnant of this or that thing's random features still cling to it can form itself be apprehended at all. "Whether it be truly infinite, or simply beyond my reach," Roubaud writes, of poetry, or "form" in "The Idea of Form," "I cannot behold it but asquint, upon a vestige, a delayed effect, a garment, a reversal, a mirror, a shadow" (*The Plurality*, 69/*La pluralité*, 69). Wherever form is perceptible, there the pure form of identity—the self-form, if you will—goes impure.

On the other hand, its purity blacks. "Falls," Roubaud says. The fall of poetry launches the prose narrative, the quest ("poetry is riddle and the novel is the fall of poetry").

Another way of putting this would be to say that my own fall (the blacking of my being who I am) initiates a life. Launches an afterlife, that is—a shadow life, a difficult-to-dream dream of before. It is a hard journey along paths that branch and twist bewilderingly through dense woods. From time to time an obscure prophesy is apt to appear: this will have been life.

Roubaud sometimes suggests that his kind of narrative is a shadow cast at the feet of the self-enigma. "The riddle, in its fall, would cast a shadow of mystery over the novel" (*The Great Fire*, 166/*Le grand incendie*, 220). The story holds a mystery, but no enigma. A mystery story winds through prose; the self-riddle is poetry's.

Roubaud says he knew, in the dream that lies at the origin of his life's double project, that he would elucidate a mystery. He knew upon awakening, you will recall, that there would be a novel (accompanying the poetry part of the work, recounting it as if it were a fiction and telling the unsayable thing within it); and he knew the novel's title; but *in* the dream he was eagerly getting ready for a *vita nuova* in the course of which he would solve a mystery. "J'étais extrêmement pressé, dans la rue grise. Je me préparais à une vie nouvelle, à une liberté joyeuse. Et je devais élucider le mystère, après de longues recherches" (*le grand incendie*, 172/*The Great Fire*, 129: "I was in a rush, in the gray street. I was preparing myself for a new life, for joyful liberty. And I had to fathom the dream's mystery, after long investigations").

Unlike the unapproachable self-riddle, a mystery can spin out at great length as the object of quests and missions—presenting a challenge for researchers, archivists, detectives, knights errant. The "fallen" version of the riddle (the "mystery") can pass along from one story to the next, and the next and the next, from waystation to waystation on the long road replete with detours to the ultimate station—I mean, to the answer, *what this is, who I am.* The knotted family trees of Arthurian legends come to mind; the proliferating adventures of the Grail knights; the confusing web of names disguised and distorted, partially revealed, or split; the knights' "errances," when they stray or get lost altogether. These produce an oneiric effect, Roubaud observes, "comme si on ouvrait devant nous la boutique obscure du sommeil." As if sleep's dim storeroom had been opened to us (*Graal fiction*, 207).

Rues

Sometimes the shadow lying at the foot of the auto-enigma takes the simpler shape of a street, a Paris street among those Roubaud is well known for trudging, and for memorializing, with such a lot of wit and charm, and affection for his old master, Queneau.[16] I think in particular of a scattered family of street poems connected to no specific street (not Rue Volta or Rue Duguay-Trouin, not Rue Tronson-du-Coudray or Rue Jonas ...). These are just called "une rue" or "la rue." Sometimes they seem to appear in dreams. In one poem of this type, that breaks off the way dreams sometimes do, waking you up suddenly instead of getting anywhere or finishing, the dim sense of a street from the past comes over a pedestrian going down another street in the afternoon sun ("La rue," in *La forme d'une ville*, 93-94/"The Street," *The Form of a City*, 80-81). A streetless street with houseless houses enters his head like a presentiment of the past—more precisely, like a premonition of a past that despite being past has yet to come: its houses, которые haven't been built yet, have roofs that haven't yet been roofs.

> Rue sans rue, aux maisons sans maisons, aux toits sans toits—rue du passé.

> Street without street, full of houses without houses, roofs without roofs.
> The street of the past.

I couldn't remember this street, the speaker recounts; I couldn't locate myself on it; I didn't know how to reach it; it would come, however. " Elle viendrait." Already it was declaring its coming presence. "Une rue d'autrefois annonçait, future, sa présence étrange. Elle viendrait. Elle serait du passé venant à moi."

> A street from time past announced its strange future presence. It would come. It would be the past coming toward me.

Like the clouds, I daresay, coming so straight from the street's far end along a course so exactly like the street's that it was scary; a parcel of time was approaching, and would come, like the clouds Mr. Goodman watched as they came inexorably each evening, into the estuary between the stone roofs of the church outside his window. Goodman sensed in their approach a monstrous past.

A coming past. A dream-past approaches from the future. A past that hasn't had its time yet, comes announcing the strange presence it is going to have had already. I couldn't remember "the street from time past," the speaker in the poem recounts, I didn't know how to reach it, but it would come, "elle viendrait." ("nuit, tu viendrais ... night, you would come

les lumières
pousseraient
sur les pentes vidés de jour ...

nuit tu viendrais

ce serait
nuit je verrais

dans le noir le
noir le

noir plus épais ...

Nuit

tu

es venue

les

lumières
ont poussé
sur

les herbes, les pentes
vidés
de

lumière ...

nuit tu
viendrais ...)

"Elle viendrait"—*la rue*, I mean, in this street poem. The street from a past was coming and would come all the way, "elle viendrait"—and when I'd be there I'd know. "Quand j'y serais, je saurais." I think this means I'd recognize my own path, my life, my life *before*, when at last it came to met me out of the future. I'd know it was me. But as it turns out, "au moment même où je le sus, je cessai de le savoir."[17] "The very moment I knew I ceased knowing." ("L'énigme reste énigme jusque dans les yeux troués du cadavre." "Pure unaccomplished deposition.") The time the street from the past takes to come out of the future is the time it takes the future to run out. Time drains away *right on* the swell of its approach—*il s'épuise* à même *son avènement*, if I may put it this way; *s'en va au ras de sa venue*. My life uses up my life-time coming.

usé—avant d'arriver à être
essai-essai

worn out—before managing to be
try-try   (Collobert, *Dire II*, 253)

Try, try, *mais à quoi bon*? What's the use? "In any case, it is a tomb."

Nuit sans date rue Saint-Jacques
La rue tombe noire, noire, la noire rue noire tombe là.
La rue tombe noire, noire, la tombe noire, rue noire, là.
La rue tombe noire, noire, tombe la noire rue noire, là.
La rue, tombe noire, noire, rue noire, la tombe noire, là.
La rue tombe noire, rue noire noir, là, tombe noire, là.
La rue tombe noire, la noire noire rue, noire tombe là.
La rue tombe noire la noire noire rue noire tombe, là.
La rue tombe, noire, noire, là; tombe noire, rue noire, là.
La rue, tombe, là. Noire, noire tombe, noire rue, noire là.
La rue noire tombe; noire la noire, noire rue-tombe; là.
La rue tombe. La noire rue noire. Noire tombe noire. Là.
                                (*La Forme d'une ville*, 248–49)

The street grave, black, black, the black street black grave there.
The street grave, black, black, the black grave, black street, there.
The street grave, black, black; grave, the black street black, there.
The street, black black grave, black street, the black grave, there.

[…]
The street grave, black; black, the black black street-grave; there.
The street grave. The black street black. Black grave black. There.

> (*The Form of a City*, 240. This translation inevitably leaves out the double meaning of "tombe" in French: not only *grave*, but also the third-person singular of the verb to fall, *tomber*. So, the "street grave, black, black" also says "the street falls, black. The black street black falls there." Try to hear both at once.)

5

Is This a Dream?

Roubaud recommends, as we've seen, that one leave enigmas alone, especially *l'auto-énigme*, the self-enigma; he advises that one place one's trust instead in people who talk in their sleep. "Il ne faut jamais déchiffrer les énigmes. Il faut croire les dormeurs." They are the ones who can ask, and do sometimes, talking to themselves softly as they slumber, "Tu dors?" Is this a dream? and they can answer, dreamily, "Oui." Believe in them, Roubaud counsels. I think his advice implies that who you are is like love: so strange a thing you could only have dreamed it up. So, suspend your disbelief and believe the fantasy impressions of life's survivors, those shades who lead a second life preceded by no first, figures resurrected from a past that still lies far ahead, heroes and villains in the story of a story still unknown. Listen for the muffled echo of a language that doesn't exist, of a time that no time is, of an "I" who never has lived. In poems poetry persists dreamily as the memory of that life, no one's. Which must be what Roubaud means, in part anyway, when he says poetry is the autobiography of nobody and everybody (*Poetry, etcetera,* 109/*Poésie, etcetera,* 107).

Another Quest

Believe the dreamers, put your faith in illusions. For it is conceivable that something worldless and impossible might after all allow itself to be approached, in a kind of overlay of appearances. It might appear to appear in a hesitant, wavering dream of a dream, as the image of an apparition—a picture, say, of a reflection in a mirror, like the photos taken by Goodman in *Eros mélancolique*, in the course of his "quest" or, as he also puts it, his "Project." His unspoken aim seems to be to capture a "secret object" in an intricate web of photos taken of windows seen through other windows seen through the view finders of his two cameras. The unknown object of his whole undertaking must have something to do with the voice he once heard speaking English with a faint, unplaceable accent. And it might be lured to enter the composite image of images that he slowly assembles.

That peculiar voice seemed to remind him of something. Possibly of his lost mother, possibly of the wintry clouds, fleeing, anxious, which he used to watch as a child, his forehead pressed against a fogged-up window pane. He watched them hurrying on, reflected on another pane, a watery gray one, a pool of rainwater.

> Ce n'étaient plus les nuages heureux de septembre, mais des nuées rapides, fuyardes, pressées, inquiètes, que le vent poussait l'une après l'autre dans le ciel, des nuages de pluie grise d'hivers, gris. Reflétés dans la vitre de l'eau grise derrière la vitre au verre embué de la fenêtre, ils coulaient en silence dans cette eau triste, comme un torrent.
>
> (*Ciel et terre et ciel et terre, et ciel*, 28)

> They were no longer the happy clouds of September, but rapid, runaway clouds, hurried, anxious, which the wind pushed one after the other across the sky, gray rain clouds of winter, also gray. Reflected in the pane of gray water behind the window's clouded pane of glass, they flowed along silently in that sad water, like a torrent.
>
> (My translation)

Patiently James Goodman—a grad student now, on a research grant in Paris during the 1960s (well before he becomes a professor in Scotland)—patiently this junior researcher photographs the play of light, of shadows upon windows, the effects of urban grime on glass surfaces in autumn drizzles, the reflections of clouds on dusty glass, the black panes at night. He takes pictures of pictures, photos of photography. You might think of comparing him to a noble lover strictly respecting "l'interdit de la vitre."

The Project to which he devotes his fellowship year in Paris has two parts: a study of photography's early history, and the photographic composition I have begun to describe. The latter somewhat resembles the frantic photographic practice of another young man in the same novel, desperately in love with a woman he never ceases to lose sight of even when she is right in front of him. She keeps moving, changing, her features are restless, her gestures impulsive. He can't remember her face if he closes his eyes, he can't really see her when he opens them. She is too variable. He tries to take her picture, to capture a vanishing half smile, a furtive gesture, but she is invisible in the photos. For it isn't really what escapes him he is after, it is the escape. Not something that exists, exactly, in nature, like an object which a person could aim his camera at. Or even like someone he once knew but lost track of, cannot find again, cannot quite remember. What he longs to see, and cannot, is imperceptible: it is the woman's "fuite imperceptible" (*Eros mélancolique*, 27). He wants to possess her perpetual fading. By which he means her live presence: the fleeting expressions of her face, her surreptitious movements of desire. "Nothing covers the distance that separates me from her farawayness," he says. It is not that he wishes he could catch up with her so she would stop being distant; rather, he longs to approach her distantness. But nothing stops her flight, "ne couvre la distance que me sépare de son lointain" (*Eros mélancolique*, 27).

Eventually he gives up on the precise instant, ceases trying to catch the specific expression of her face at one fleeting moment and has recourse instead to repetition. He snaps countless pictures of her, without aiming at anything, without thinking, without even looking, leaving everything up to the blind eye of his digital camera. (Actually, he recites a poem to himself, and at the end of each line, he presses the button.) It was a "mitraille d'instants quelconques," a rapid-fire series of undistinguished moments, and at the end, he sees the object of his love, "l'objet de mon amour." He watches on his computer screen: she appears and disappears from frame to frame,

> s'approche et glisse au noir à nouveau, et revient encore avant de
>
> disparaître dans le lointain ... (*Eros mélancolique*, 28)
>
> approaches and slips into the dark again, and comes back once more
>
> before disappearing into the distance ... (My translation)

Passages

Roubaud sometimes seems to seek a certain fuzziness in pictures, and dwells on his distaste for the kind of photograph that isolates a single instant, catches and holds it still, presenting an object, a face, or a scene perfectly contained at that instant within its own sharp contours, identical to itself. What about the passage of moments, he asks—the glide from one to the next? What about the changes the photo's subject undergoes as the light shifts, or a shadow moves across it and it looks like itself in one way and then in another and another? Nothing could be more inescapably distinct than the sharp, self-same image of Alix Roubaud's death—what Roubaud saw when she died (her hand hanging over the edge of the bed, the blood unmoving at the tips of the fingers). This is a photographic image, he writes; he cannot bear it, but it returns to him relentlessly, reproducing itself with horrible exactitude every time: "la mort même même, identique à elle-même même" (*Quelque chose noir*, 11, 16/*Some Thing Black*, 9, 14). He wants Alix's life, her mutability, her imperceptible receding movement, her farawayness, not this stasis. I noted briefly, earlier on, a characteristic, dark yen of Roubaud's to approach "the absences of clouds," bringing his own thoughts, as he gazes at a cloudy sky, as near as he can to extinction. And I have associated the movement of certain clouds with the inexorable approach of a disaster, the imminence of a brutal disappearance. But Roubaud has other cloud moods, and often contemplates them for hours at a time sailing over the Minervois landscape and on out of sight, overlapping and interfering with each other, wafting through and by each other, bunching up, thinning out, grazing the forms (cumulus, cirrus ...)[1] with which they never coincide exactly but whose movement they are. For, as he eventually writes, "la forme n'est que le mouvement dont elle est la forme" (*La pluralité des mondes*, 72/*The Plurality*, 72). "Form is but the movement whose form it is." And he ponders how to compose a condensation of such changes, a "deposit of likenesses, weave of likeness, threads crossed and recrossed" (*Quelque chose noir*, 15/*Some Thing Black*, 15). Not a fixed contour, and not a definitive void, but a twining and fraying.

> *passages*
>
>   dans l'espace fait
> des passages
>   qui croisent, décroisent   (*Tridents*, 35)

He must have been trying for a condensation or weave of changes in the infringements and overlappings of quasi-identical elements in the succession of short, repetitive poems called *Dors* (*Sleep*). These poems are like clouds, passing and changing, overlapping and intermingling as they go. Roubaud comments on their composition. It was a long, slow process, he says. By the time they were published they had already existed for six or seven years and had been read, aloud and silently, copied and recopied in different manuscripts many times. Each time, something changed. Their "particularity" is "that they are not fixed."[2] Sometimes one version will be "almost identical to another"—"virtually identical, different by barely a word"—yet none is immobilized. "I immobilized no poem." They changed. Each time he spoke them, his voice, saying what was written already, went on a little further on its own, sometimes just to repeat, sometimes to shift an edge, extend it by a word, a line. And thus the contours of the poems move, on each occasion. Each poem, as well as each sequence and subsequence, as well as the entire (65-page) set of poems presents a panoply of minor changes, slow mutations wherein a form keeps stirring, shaping a continuous displacement, continuously altering this shape. "Form is but the movement of which it is the form."

> sleep
> you will slee
> p
> you
> now know this
> s
> leep
>
> sleep
> you can do
>
> it adjust
> your open
>
> legs
> and sleep
>
> sleep
> night scratches
> you
> contain it
> and
> sleep
> sleep
>
> (*Sleep*, 35, 49, 56)[3]

Once Alix Roubaud took a photograph of a long row of cypress trees at night near her in-laws' house in the Minervois. There was no moon. She exposed the film to the faint light of the stars for fifteen minutes. And she rested the camera on her chest during this slow process, so it moved a little with her breathing. The combination of these factors—the dim light, the long exposure, the small, rhythmic movement of the camera—produced a slim, hazy fringe at the edges of the black cypress shapes in the photograph: a grayish margin, a "halo of gray," Roubaud says, which suggests to him that the faint light from the stars, operating slowly on the photographic salts, "hesitated to stamp an image" on the film's thin surface (see *Le grand incendie*, 396-400/*The Great Fire*, 308-11). The image, you could say in French, is not distinct, but "bougée" (blurred). "The boundary of the tree's body dissolves" in the photo, Roubaud observes; the minutes that pass alter it. It is as if a loss were revealed that ordinarily remains concealed from us. The photo doesn't show some *thing* we cannot see otherwise, but a retreat, a fading, a hazing over that we usually don't perceive because, like a camera employed in the conventional way, our vision just registers one instant, then another, not the passage from one to the other.

Roubaud once came to observe of himself, during the long period of mourning after Alix died, that what he feared was not really the pitch black of night (perhaps he even preferred it, as oblivion), or the light of one more bleak day, but rather the passage from one to the other. The fraying of definitions, I expect—the fading of distinctiveness.

> Ce n'est donc pas le sommeil que tu préfères ni la non-lumière que tu crains, ni l'éveil, mais le passage; c'est du moindre passage que tu souffres, de la moindre dévolution ... (*La pluralité*, 62)

> So you do not really prefer sleep or non-light, nor do you really fear the light or waking up, but rather the transition. The smallest transition hurts you, the smallest transfer ... (*The Plurality*, 62)

So he undertakes a kind of exercise (to overcome the pain, presumably): think about passages—about one color bleeding into another, about pale honey spreading over a pale plate ... Which is darker, this white sheet of paper or the white winter sky? Try to see, to say, the shades between violet and blue, red and green.

> Dis que du rouge au vert tout le jaune se meurt; dis cela.
> Plonge du vert, enfonce dans l'ombre une poignée d'aiguilles

de pin; brûle un boulet ovale de charbon, à travers une vitre
de mica, fais couler un verre de miel pâle dans une assiette pâle.
Pense cela. Pense les passages. Peux-tu vraiment penser ce rouge-au-
vert, ce vert-au-jaune? Pas ainsi. Comment?

(*La pluralité*, 88)

    Say that between red and green all the yellow fades out, say it.
Plunge some green, thrust a handful of pine needles into the dark.
Burn an oval ball of coal over a mica pane. Pour a jar of pale
honey on a pale plate. Think it. Think these transitions. Can you
really think this red-to-green, this green-to-yellow? Not this way.
How?

(*The Plurality*, 88)

There is something, he remarks, near the beginning of *Le grand incendie*, that he would like to "take" or "capture" in prose, the way a photographer *prend quelque chose en photo* (*Le grand incendie*, 19/*The Great Fire*, 10). It is a *passage*—not so much from red to green, green to yellow, as from earlier to later. A quiet lapse of time; a slow, peaceful change in the light. Something not so different, perhaps, from a flow of pale yellow honey over a cream-colored plate. He takes a photo by Alix as an "example." He calls it "la photo de Fez." Actually, it is a double image; it exists in two versions, one rather dark, one lighter.

    It is a rectangular image, all in grays and white—a rectangular image of several other rectangles: one a photo of Fez hung on the wall of a hotel room in Fez, another the dark frame around this photo; then a mirror, hung on the same wall as the photo. In the mirror a rectangular piece of the facing wall can be seen reflected. And on this square-shaped wall-fragment glimpsed in the mirror there appears, in the lower left, a section of the cone of light from a lamp. The lamp itself does not appear; just "a visible curve," Roubaud writes: just the trace of a single generator of the cone of light from the lamp. It stands out "like a darker gray hill in the picture, beginning at the lower end of the almost square mirror, rather near its left corner, and rising along an approximately thirty-degree slope" (*The Great Fire*, 8/*Le grand incendie*, 17).

    This photo, taken at night by the light of the lamp, is doubled by the same picture taken at dawn when daylight has entered the room. Together the twin images tacitly reconstitute the interim hours between the dark of night, when the lamp burns above the bed, and the morning, when daylight has finished slowly introducing a more hesitant geometry than the one determined by the electric lamp in the darkness. Gradually dawn has spread throughout the room, covering the wall and washing out the light from the lamp still burning over the bed. What pleases Roubaud, as he explains, is the implicit incursion of daylight into the lamplight—the gradual disappearance of lamplight into day—and the whole long night (the "span" of quiet hours) implied in this unspoken, imaginary process. He would like to "capture" an imaginary course of time like this. A tacit spell of time, you might say.

He made a beautiful try in the "rhythmic composition" called *La lampe*, which I have already at least partially described, dwelling—the first time I introduced it—on its palindromic form. (I stressed the way it revolves, via twelve slightly differing repetitions; and I emphasized its simultaneous backward and forward movement across two facing pages—with "*slowly*" moving, from one iteration to the next, slowly from right to left, and a blank spot moving at various speeds the other way; I pointed out the "virtual" meeting, of "*slowly*" and the blank, in the "fictive interval" at the fold between pages.) Here, now, is the "stanza," in the first of its twelve versions: one recognizes the room (*la stanza*) in the *photo de Fez*—the grays and the white and the rectangles ...

> the lamp   evaporates   on the bottom   mirror   rectangle
> it fills up with light   moreover   with gray and white   of a light
> the mirror rectangle   with a light   with gray and white   and the
> wall   fills up with the lamp   with a light   *slowly*   and furthermore
> (*The Great Fire*, 29/*Le grand incendie*, 44)[4]

Roubaud indicates that this poem's mode of existence should really be oral. The various manuscript versions (typewritten or printed) that exist of it are essentially scores. So a voice is intended. It should pronounce the word-segments aloud, falling still in order to separate them, now pausing longer, now less, at an undetermined tempo, with possible pitch variations, in a space punctuated by the heads of assembled listeners. Thus in Roubaud's mind the conditions in which *La Lampe* gradually turns around on itself resemble those of the poems in *Dors*, whose forms keep stirring, shifting, and creating among themselves a weave of alterations, shifts, displacements.

One thing only is determined from the start of the slowly changing four-line "room" that is *La Lampe*: the silence wherever the shifting blank spot reappears in the score must last just perceptibly longer each time than do the varying pauses between other spoken segments. So, listening, one would be just barely able to sense the gradual advance of a stillness, from end to end of the stanza—and imagine the slow entrance of daylight in a room somewhere, in a hotel room in Fez, stealing softly over the lamplight and erasing it.

When I spoke about *La Lampe* earlier, it was largely to suggest a disappearance just at the axis of its symmetry—just at the "fictive interval," where a purely "virtual" encounter might be thought to occur. A plunge into a "nuit médiane," a median night. Till now, in other words, I have mainly wanted to suggest a *trou noir* just at the "present instant," when what was still going to be, and what will already have been—a life!—would *be*. My emphasis here, though, is different: here I have wanted to stress the quiet glide of change in the "rhythmic composition," and the softly shifting form of this glide. But other thoughts, too, come to mind in the presence of *La Lampe*. The rectangular shape of the photo, for example—and of the poem in each of its slightly altered repetitions—is suggestive. Especially since the "photo de Fez" seems to be a rectangular picture of other rectangles: the photo within the photo, its frame, the mirror, the portion of wall reflected in the mirror … All this recalls for me the same geometrical figure (rectangle) appearing elsewhere in Roubaud's writing: quite often, in addition to being the shape of a photo (and a mirror), it is the shape of a window. Remember the photography composition of the young James Goodman, in *Eros mélancolique*—his photos of windows seen though other windows seen through the view finders of his two cameras. In *La fenêtre veuve*, in a description of Giordano Bruno's home town, Nola, we read of nine towers, clad in white, each having at its top a single opening, "une petite fenêtre." Each little window is framed in black, "bordée de noir," like a piece of stationery bearing the announcement of a death, and like the photo on the wall in the "photo de Fez," where one of the rectangles is "the dark frame" around the photo in the photo.

Then, too, in the *Prologue* to *Exchanges on Light*, which presents a sort of outline of the *Exchanges* ("La Forme du poème"), we come upon "a lit window, only one; its rectangle." It is indicated three times ("only one," "only one," "the only one"). In its rectangle, "a shape begins." A form starts to show. It begins coming into sight at the end, or practically the end of a gradual darkening and silencing process indicated between indications of the window: "Night, and silence; and silence; silence." Then, rain stops, "no rain"; and wind, "no wind." Stars go out "one after the other; no stars." The lone illuminated window shows—just before the end of this deliberate passage toward "nothing"—the beginning of a shape. It appears to me similar to the "visible curve standing out like a darker gray hill in the "photo de Fez" ("beginning at the lower end of the almost square mirror, rather near its left corner, and rising along an approximately thirty-degree slope").

A shape just begins to show, then, in one glowing window, in the "program" for *Exchanges on Light*—and then the window's light goes out: "Window dark

/ blown out." In *Eros mélancolique*, too, an unaccountable white streak starts appearing on James Goodman's negatives. He cannot figure out what unexpected shadow it can possibly be the record of. At a loss, he calls it a material trace with no material cause. A thing which does not exist in nature. This is all just before his entire photography project derails, forsaking him.

Roubaud's own suggestion that in "La Lampe" he would like to capture something in prose the way a photographer *prend quelquechose en photo* brings up the thought of a hunt, and presages the close association in *Eros mélancolique* not only between James Goodman's photography project and a quest (with its "secret object"), but also between photography itself and the hunt, notably *The Hunt for the Snark* by Lewis Carroll, who was a photographer, and who warned about the especially dangerous kind of Snark called Boojum (whose captor, if ever it is caught, disappears, along with it). Whatever photography tries to capture is Boojum, Goodman suspects.

As this book begins to veer, haltingly, away from the black sun in Roubaud, and, via a kind of blur, in the direction of a white one—and as we turn from some thing impossible toward potentialities—Jacques Jouet enters with an *entracte*. He is expert at many different roles, and likes to change often, but here he will play the activist, whose outspoken ambition is to banish the word *impossible* from the French language. Can Do! says his banner. Yet at the same time he is barely there, which is why the title of the following divertimento is All and Nothing.

6

Interlude
All and Nothing

Jacques Jouet is an Oulipian, like Roubaud, and hence a champion of potential: La Littérature Potentielle.[1] He was born just after the war, in 1947, which makes him about ten years younger than Roubaud. He joined the company of Oulipians in 1983, and the Oulipo has been the principal environment of his extraordinarily productive writing activities ever since. In the Oulipo we speak "le potentien," he says; we read and write it, too, "in order that new things should happen. And they do!" (*Ruminations de l'atelier oulipien, de l'improvisation et du potentiel*[2]). He rejoices in the great multiplicity and variety of these new things: countless variations on old forms, novel formal inventions and variations on them, sequels and prequels to stories both famous and obscure. He contrasts this happy prolixity with the censorious "moderne," which is always ruling out one thing or another: down with tradition and with commonplaces, with regular versification and fixed forms; out with syntax, in with parataxe; forget plot and characters, the imperfect subjunctive and the preterite (*Ruminations*, 20). A plague, Jouet cries, on all protectionism of this sort. He mocks the jitters that pedagogy and writing workshops inspire in writers who entertain a haughty, aristocratic vision of art. He laughs at their nervous "anti-popular, anti-public-life and, basically, anti-republican" stance (22). Words are social animals, he says, and form in poetry is a social value (*Cantates de proximité*[3]). We will come back to this.

A lot of potential lies in formal constraints; form itself—preferably quite strict—is a principle of invention and novelty. Jouet, and the Oulipo, are formalists. Jouet doesn't mind pointing out, to anyone who thinks formalism is stiff and old hat, that antiformalism had its most glorious hour under Stalin, and resulted in many dead poets. Moreover, lest Oulipians' affection for traditional forms, and their lively (antimodernist) interest in literature's past look like some kind of neoclassicism (or neobaroqueism), he stresses with some impatience that the past is no golden age. Rather it is a field of perpetual productivity: "un terrain de perpétuelle fécondation" (*Ruminations*, 19).

A practitioner, like his Oulipian colleagues, of many diverse forms, Jouet invented, earlier in this century, a new one called *A supposer*....

"A supposer qu'on me demande..." These words ("suppose someone asks of me...") are the first in any *A supposer* poem. Or, as Jouet more commonly says, in any *A supposer* phrase. "Phrase" means sentence: a long and complicated one filling a page. "Suppose someone demands of me...," and then comes some impossible challenge. Suppose someone asks me to write, say, about the sense of justice I perceived among union activists in Lens as they prepared to take their seats on a board of labor relations. Suppose I have to get it all into one single sentence. Or, suppose someone really insists I must evoke in *writing* (only one sentence), a *visual* image. Each time Jouet rises to the occasion, proving that nothing is impossible for poetry.[4]

Were someone to ask him to put a visual experience into writing, he'd take the Max Beckmann lithograph called "the Street," he says—immediately launching into the "impossible" sentence, which he describes in advance. I'd take 'The Street,' " he says—the smashed faces, the lump of a woman, the drunken clown, the rat—and go to work on them. "Je les mettrais sur le métier, ces gueules cassées, cette grosse dondon..." In the weak light of a street lamp in rainy Berlin, he'd put them back on the drawing board, and keep going back over them, relentlessly improving the scene; "je la mettrais et la remettrais sur le métier" (*Cantates*, 14) Words respond fast to this hypothetical workover. As the "phrase" expands and thickens, the reader feels them rising to the occasion, hastening to back each other up, or then again to qualify or contradict each other. Impatiently, one clause barges into the middle of another, which resumes further along, changed. Words and clumps of words unceremoniously assemble in this way, pushing and shoving. Left to themselves, they are cold, Jouet observes, but in a long, convoluted "phrase" they warm up, keen to approximate, even provisionally, their complex, turbulent whole. This is what prompts him to say they are "social" and to assign a "social value" to form in poetry.

There is plenty of panache in the "Nothing-is-impossible-for-poetry" stance, but Jouet does not only want to demonstrate his dexterity. He also wants to show just what *a lot* is possible: how *many* poems can be churned out if the conditions are right. Literature produced in bulk appeals to him. Potboilers, for example, sometimes make him happy, and this is due, he says, not so much to their content (narrow escapes, vengeance, star-crossed love, enemy brothers, and so on), as to their workmanlike competence.[5] He admires the sheer know-how of record-holders like Souvestre and Allain, coauthors of the *Fantômas* series, which appeared monthly, filling thirty-two volumes, from 1911 to 1913. He enjoys juxtaposing the famous torment of writing (Mallarmé's "hantise,"[6] or Beckett's "failures") with that practical, routine savoir faire. He has long made quite a point of treating poetry like a nine-to-five job.

> Je veux que l'activité poétique descende aux conditions
> de travaux quotidiens, pisse-copie et journal de tous les jours de
> poésie.
>
> (*Poèmes de métro*[7])

> I want poetic practice to descend to the condition
> of everyday jobs, an ordinary, daily news kind of poetry.
>
> (My workaday translation)

This commitment to poetry as column inches calls for a poem every twenty-four hours. Several of the fixed forms Jouet has invented share this basic one-per-day rule. The *poème adressé du jour*, for example: one of these is composed each day for a period of time determined in advance, and mailed that very day to a particular person. The *poème de métro* is also a daily form, to be composed and written in the subway, where the regular alternation between shadow and light seen as the train passes from bright station to dark tunnel and back (white/black/white/black) suggests a small but fruitful set of formal constraints. "Contraintes de situation," Jouet calls them, and here they are. You compose a *poème de métro* in the course of one ride. It has as many lines as there are subway stations on the route, for you compose the first line in your head between the time you get on and the first stop. You write this line down while the train is stopped. The second line is thought up when the train moves again, and written down during the next stop. Jacques Roubaud described the procedure in a sonnet he himself composed on the fast train from Paris to Toulouse on January 8, 2001. The subway in motion stirs words up, he says, in somebody's head; a line jiggles around and then, when the train stops, cages itself up. Freeze frame.[8]

No *writing* while the train is underway; no *composing* while the train is stopped. You write down the last line of your poem on the platform of your final station. If you have to change trains, you must begin a new stanza in the new train. No revising. The concentrated effort required by the rules provides all the polish a *poème de métro* wants.

What appeals to Jouet is not the "poetry of the *métro*," but the poetry the metro produces—with his collaboration, to be sure, but just barely: he plays a minimal role in an otherwise mechanical process ("ma présence écrivante," he says, "tout juste organique dans le machinique" (*Poèmes de métro*, 186-87). Ideally he would like his poems to happen without him: "sans que moi" (*Poèmes de métro*, 180). A dependable mechanism is a good bet in this regard—a form whose gears mesh so well that just by running, it's a poem.

He produced one metro poem every day for a year, then ceased, though not without publishing the whole year's worth in a book (*Poèmes de métro*). And for four years running he kept a poetry diary. He started it in 1992 and entered a poem each day, with the date, till 1996. In 1998 he published this journal, called *Navet, linge, oeil-de-vieux*, in three hefty volumes.[9] The one-a-day rule produces a lot of poetry.

Some of it is dull; much of it is hard to understand, but none is ever unfinished or unacceptable. Even the least promising line cannot fail altogether: "Il ne peut pas ne pas donner au moins son minimum" (*Poèmes de métro*, 29). It can't deliver less than its minimum. Quality matters, but not that much. Or rather, there is a kind of quality that poems get by being numerous, and turned out regularly. Jouet says he expects something from them that he couldn't hope for from poems written under other circumstances: it is the quality of something that just about always comes out fairly well. But to which no particular value sticks.

You might wonder, thinking of Hocquard, if he isn't pursuing the special character of the unexceptional.

In any event, Jouet hauls poetry along on the subway the better to spring it from the sacred precinct to which it tends to get consigned, and to demonstrate that it is not impractical or "oppositional," marginal or alienated. Not "modern," in other words. His poems are written and circulate locally: via the Parisian mass transit system, for example, or through the mail or, in the case of a poetry collection called *107 âmes*, by way of a census.¹⁰ He wrote *Cantates de proximité*: Local, or Neighborhood Cantatas. He composed them while visiting several different groups of people working together on some job or project, mainly in northern France, but in a few other places as well, notably Africa. One group was rehearsing a play, others were organizing a strike, training for a basketball tournament or trying to recover from mental illness. Each visit resulted in a portrait of the group and its efforts; each portrait is a local cantata, combining several different forms ("phrases," of the *A supposer . . .* type, "récits," "poemes de rencontre," "listes"), much as a Bach cantata combines chorales, recitatives, arias. Indeed, *Cantates de proximité* reflect Jouet's "reverence" for Bach,¹¹ who was a steady worker with a lot of knowhow. He wrote a great deal of formally rigorous music for regular local use. Prior to being published in a book, the *Cantates* were handed around by the schoolteachers, social workers, actors, and technicians among whom they were composed.

Nothing being impossible for poetry means nothing is excluded. Jouet compares poetry to a political form, the Republic, which he considers Utopia mainly because it lies between no borders whatever. It cannot turn anyone out. Likewise poetry cannot rule out anything and nothing is off limits to it. No form is too old or too new, no subject too vulgar or too abstruse. It is "encyclopedic" as well as "local." Recondite as well as everyday, conceptual and concrete both—even dreamy while down-to-earth. Its perfection, if there were such a thing, would lie in the sheer wealth and diversity of its forms and aspects, types of reception, styles of production. Just so the Republic's task is to fashion itself out of everybody. That is why in principle it cannot tolerate the death penalty. Moreover its strength resides in being concrete and ordinary ("la chose bien présente, le terrain du tout-concret"), not epic or puffed up with ideals, or even universal. Rather, local. Which by no means implies its virtues can be identified with some particular territory (France, say, or "les USA"). The republican subject, Jouet says, keeps one foot in one country and one foot in another. Her motto is "le cul entre deux chaises" (ass between two chairs), and her totem is the passport.¹²

"La littérature potentielle," an "art sans frontières," happens in passing between one thing and another, like a subway ride or a gust of wind or a passerby. The works Jouet admires are never masterpieces, he says: never the culmination of anything, still less a stunning break with the past. Rather they are old and new both. Jouet considers the distinction between tradition and innovation (canonical and experimental works) irrelevant. For every work composed in "potentiel" is a transition—between whatever form it has just emerged from and the next ones, ahead, that are about to follow it (*Ruminations*, 21). "Le potentiel," Jouet writes, "n'est [...] autre chose qu'une pensée du transitoire" (22). Potential equals transitory. We Oulipians do not expect to persuade skeptics of our outlook, he says; they can prefer their impotence, if they like; in any case, "We will never become potentates because our slogan is *Il faut être absolument potentiel!*" (22).

"Il faut être absolument moderne," was Rimbaud's, but that is for potentates, it seems. Jouet's "potentiality" is a different, diffident "pouvoir."

"Classy!" he exclaims—unexpectedly—in *Ruminations*, concluding his definition of potentiality. "Elle s'affirme en s'effaçant: la classe!" (21).

Potentiality affirms by effacing itself. What style! Scarcely there but gone already. Michelle Grangaud suggests that what a poet like Jouet is good for is rendering unto blankness its due.[13] I am reminded of Hocquard's admiration for Paul Badura-Skoda. Apparently he played the piano so well that Hocquard got a sense of the music's disappearance (*Cette histoire est la mienne, ma haie*, 470/"Badura Skoda" in *This Story Is Mine*). The nineteenth-century poet Tristan Corbière—"I don't care if he was great or mediocre," Jouet says—neglected to lament that in his time the great days of poetry were over. Rather, Jouet observes with admiration, he stated once perfectly in just twice six syllables that the rejuvenation of poetry always depends on the poet's manner of negating all he affirms, withdrawing all he advances. Corbière's twelve syllables are

> Ce fut un vrai poète: il n'avait pas de chant
> (quoted by Jouet in *A supposer...*, 15)

> He was a true poet: he had no song

That's style, I expect. The glamour, I mean, that comes of shrugging it off. To be sure, Jouet disapproves of style—a writer's individual style, that is: his signature. Jouet dismisses that along with other haughty, aristocratic notions, preferring Queneau's ninety-nine styles in *Exercises de style*, and saying that for his own part he aims to have so many that he'll have none at all. One senses in him the rare and indifferent disposition of someone who neither attaches any special importance to his activities nor ever considers renouncing them. "Souffle ta part dans le vent," he recommends. "Blow your share into the wind which doesn't ask itself if it should quit blowing." He'd just as soon it not be he writing, as I said: "J'aimerais autant pas que ce soit moi" (*Poèmes de métro*, 180). Happily, a writer can dissolve, by writing more, not less. And the greater the variety the better. "Il y a moyen de se dissoudre dans le monde par la quantité, la diversité de ses écrits, c'est le mien." There's a way to dissolve into the world via the quantity, the diversity of one's writing, and that way is mine (*Poèmes de métro*, 180).

No doubt Jouet's wish for poetry in bulk relates to his thoroughness: he would prefer to neglect not one of the potential structures or compositions contained within a given set of constraints. He has experimented with many different forms and genres, and he may well share Georges Perec's ambition to traverse the entirety of contemporary literature and produce in his work a grand catalog of the literary potentialities of his day—writing at least one of every type of literature that a person of his time could possibly write. As if literature itself were a huge combinatory system, and it were a matter of elaborating all its possible permutations. Maybe each of these transpositions would have a quality of its own comparable to the particular sound emitted by each individual sonnet in a sonnetorium.

A sonnetorium is a construction like an enormous aviary, home not to birds but to sonnets. Ideally it would house the totality of all possible sonnets—the realization of each and every potential sonnet that the sonnet form holds within it. An American named Merrill Moore (1903-1957) built one at his house in Squantum, Tennessee, to accommodate the 10,000 sonnets he wrote, in addition to the 1,000 he actually published in a single volume.[14] Jacques Roubaud learned about Moore in the 1990s, when he was conducting some research on "sonnet recordmen." Moore was his best find.

Roubaud had spent the 1960s studying sonnets, getting "sonneticity" into his head, and composing his own first poetry book, which was a book of sonnets. In the course of his work he observed among the characteristic traits of the sonnet family a tendency to multiply, proliferating in sudden spurts. For example, right after Petrarch's *Canzoniere* there was a sudden surge of sonnets in Italy—"une soudaine surchauffe de l'économie sonnettistique." Astronomical numbers of sonnets were composed, by the most unexpected people (bishops, popes, and merchants; Machiavelli and Bronzino). A veritable epidemic, in France also, around 1547, in England a little earlier, 1530. Roubaud himself narrowly escaped catching sonnet fever in the 1960s: he might have ended up like Tomaso Baldinotti (1451-1511), who wrote 3,500 sonnets in the last few years of his life after retiring to the country. "Li miei sonetti fanno come el fungo," he wrote, in a sonnet (*Poésie*, 180). My sonnets sprout like mushrooms.

I am opening here, within this Interlude, a smaller one on Roubaud, Roubaud the Oulipian, to whom so far I have given scant attention. During his apprenticeship as a sonneteer, he realized that sonnets are like spheres: each is closed, its end buckling up with its beginning, its surface curling around the sense hidden at its heart and yet, like the topological sphere, each holds within it a veritable swarm of cloudy and weird structures not at first apparent (*Poésie*, 147).[15] So he proceeded to compose sonnets according to a principle of variation and distortion, expanding the range of plausible modifications ever further, ever more aware of the sonnet form's "axiomatic elasticity." He unsettled the meter, blurring the count of syllables, twisting the alexandrin every which way in the vicinity of the caesura; he experimented with fifteen different rhyme schemes; he shortened and elongated sonnets. He wrote "pruned," "truncated," and "excised" sonnets; also double and triple sonnets, and prose sonnets. Someone might think that in this sonnet game pretty much anything goes, but Roubaud was and is diametrically opposed to such an idea. He means to advance continuity and discontinuity at once, tradition, and innovation simultaneously. "Order and adventure," as Apollinaire's slogan has it. His joy is to contemplate the vast, strange, and wonderful potential of a single form, itself diminutive and centuries old. He was particularly glad to follow up on John Cage's mention to him of the American from Tennessee. For contrary to the mild worry Cage had planted in his head, Moore hadn't really resorted to shooting off huge machine-gun blasts of sonnets in the hope that a couple might hit the bullseye (the Beautiful). He was aiming rather for the sum of features proper to the sonnet world, or better, a sort of virtual sonnet chorale: a performance of sonneticity, a rendition of everything the sonnet's got, as it were, by 100,000 assembled performers, all giving at *least* their minimum. Each poem rings in its very own way *because* it is just an element of this whole. It wouldn't have found its own voice otherwise.

Jouet might be thought to be aiming for a comparable chorus when he composes sets of poems, such as the volume of metro poems, or the book of *poèmes adressés*: each tome would at least approximate the totality of poems that can be enabled by whatever particular combination of formal constraints is in operation. Or at least all the poems they can enable when he, Jouet, is wielding the pen. If another hand took over, there could well issue a fresh proliferation. However, it could also appear that Jouet's impulse is to use and use up—indeed, *exhaust* all the possibilities harbored within a particular set of constraints. Warren Motte suggests as much, without so heavy a note of pathos as I am tempted to sound here; he associates Jouet with "the literature of exhaustion" and says his wish is to "expend himself utterly within literature."[16] Jouet's impulse to neglect no possibility might be paired with a will to wear them out. And himself.

His sanguine affirmation of inconsistency can occasionally flare up melodramatically and produce a jarring juxtaposition. For example, the mild contradiction in his notion that a person can matter less by writing more. At the end of one subway poem he asks if there is necessarily anyone at all—any subject, "sapiens, ludens"—behind poetry's lines, and answers

> Il peut y avoir impudiquement quelqu'un et, une autre fois, terriblement personne.
>
> (*Poemes de métro*, 18)

> There can be shamelessly someone, and then, some other time, horribly no one.

Rank subjectivity, and then without warning the silence of the grave. Poetry lives a jagged life, exaggerating what it abruptly cancels, marring what it perfects (*A supposer . . .* , 15). Jouet can imagine it as a fight to the finish. Two antagonists—like "le hasard" in Mallarmé, and "le coup de dés" (fortune's blind mechanisms and the Master gambler's ultimate coup)—wear each other down to nothing. Or, some rigorous and shapely program in one corner and in the other a practiced mind determined to wring out an unforeseen possibility. Jouet claims to invest his confidence solely in such combative rivalry.

> Je n'ai confiance qu'en ce combat:
> forme forte et pensée forte du stylo, qui sont capables
> de se stimuler, dans le cadre de leur annihilation commune
>
> (*Poèmes de métro*, 181)

> I have confidence only in this combat:
> strong form and the pen's strong thought, which are able
> to stimulate each other, in the framework of their common annihilation
>
> (My translation)

Only such a duel fought to the finish has a chance of producing poetry that dissolves among the everyday comings and goings of the world: loops out of a particular "situation" and loops back in again. Emerges from some locale (school, gym, hospital), and circles right back in, to settle like dust on the world whence it came. For, each getting the other all worked up, humming machine and extravagant voice (shapely formal program and impetuous thought) wear each other down to nothing. It doesn't always go so well. Such a mess just to die. "Oh! mourir sans s'en faire et sans tacher partout!" (*Poèmes de métro*, 224).

While it lasts though, the confabulation of subway poems that Jouet assembles gives each one a quality of its own due to its being just one voice in a clamor, one participant in a family reunion, a company, or a set.

Roubaud's first poetry book was a set of sonnets. A set in the mathematical sense. Its title was the sign for belonging in set theory, ϵ.[17]

Now *jeu* in French means *game*, of course, or *play* (as in *jeux de langage*, or *jeux oulipiens*); it can also mean *set*: a complete series, a full assortment or collection. A pack of cards, for example; a set of chess pieces, a bunch of keys … And it can mean *interaction*, as in *le jeu des pistons*: the play of the pistons. In Roubaud there is such a thing as a "jeu de jeux." A sonnet comprised of sonnets, for example. This "second degree sonnet" provided the initial organizing principle for the sonnet book whose title Roubaud borrowed from set theory. He had always known, ever since the dream in 1961 that decided him on his life's project, that the first element of it would be a sonnet book, by which he understood not just a selection of sonnets but a Book: a rigorously constructed, encompassing design, a poetic form in itself. Each sonnet, perfect all alone enclosed within its narrow borders, would also entertain specific relations with all the other sonnets; each would open thus onto the larger, overarching structure, the book, which would in turn reveal certain formal and other properties its individual elements would turn out to share. Sonnets each of whose lines would be a sonnet was the first idea he had for structuring this set, or *jeu—de jeux*.

Similarly, he envisages a "jeu des jeux oulipiens": a "Grand Jeu." I picture a giant set composed of countless oulipian inventions—past, present, and even future; I imagine a vast formal composition revealing the myriad interrelations among the forms that compose it, thus conferring on these forms their kinship, their belonging together. Roubaud compares this great set (or great poem) to "Le Grand Chant des Troubadours," which is to say, to the great song that all the songs of the Troubadour poets compose together. This "Grand Chant" is the *world* of the trobar, and a "form of life," as Roubaud puts it, referencing a "pseudo-Wittgenstein" (*Poésie, etcetera*, 215). By "form of life" he seems to mean a living association composed of many companion lives on which it—the collectivity—bestows a shared vitality. A "form of life" is something like a great company for living. The Oulipo, with its *jeux* and *jeux de jeux* (with its numerous members both living and dead, its regular meetings, its customs, its contests and collaborations) could—validated in this regard by a fictitious sage (the pseudo-L.W.)—approximate, or foreshadow, or perhaps partially recover, a possible life.

At the time he was composing his first sonnet book, Roubaud did not know *Cent mille milliards de Poèmes*—Raymond Queneau's famous sonnet-machine, the book whose pages, cut in flippable strips, hold all the possible combinations and permutations of ten sonnets' one-hundred and forty lines—or one hundred thousand billion poems: *Cent mille milliards de Poèmes*.[18] But *le Livre*—the Book dreamed of, planned, sketched, abandoned by Mallarmé—was already on his horizon. Mallarmé's Book could never really have existed—could it?— but fascinating notes, fragments, hints, and clues remain. Phantom books of which just a shred is left, sometimes in the memory of a mentally ill person, or a solitary mourner, turn up on and off in Roubaud's writing, as I have mentioned already, in a slightly different context. You might think of them as varieties of some Grail Book. Perhaps they hold the elements of a whole possible world. Dubious, though, sometimes doomed, they may simply bear witness to its loss. Or to its illusory character from the start.[19] Thus the fear of perdition accompanies, "éloge inverse," the idea of a poetry world (*Jeu des jeux; Grand Chant* . . .), the way a sense of utter vanity accompanies the dream of belonging. Defeat shadows the quest that all Roubaud's "jeux," no doubt, partake in to some extent.[20] The hope of restoring a wasted land, or a scattered family, a half-forgotten "form of life" cannot escape despair or derision. When Roubaud introduced the game of go as an additional organizing principle for his sonnet book, he decided on the number 361—which is the number of pieces in the "jeu"—for the number of poems in his book. And since in go 180 pieces are white and 181 black, each sonnet in Roubaud's book, likewise, is either white or black. This is indicated by a little white or black circle beside each one. And in addition to its place in the sonnets of sonnets, each has another place—its place in the sequence of the first 157 moves in the match of go played by Masami Shinohara and Misuo Takei, analyzed in the April 1965 issue of the *Go Review*. The white pieces belong to the stronger player in the match, who appears to be winning. Roubaud says that the black, the losing side, is his (*Poésie*, 500).

"Nothing," Roubaud allows, could be a name for Kekchose—for what poetry says, you will recall, when it doesn't say anything—as long as "everything" is too (*Poetry, etcetera*, 79/79). Jouet observes that poetry rings twelve strokes, and we know it is zero o'clock. "Douze coups": "zéro heure" (*Poèmes de metro*, 18). There is nothing it cannot say, and nothing is all it wants. Or at least it preserves implacably a double impulse to say everything and to say nothing whatsoever. The fact that the last line of one day's metro poem got written on the platform at the station La Muette, is duly recalled in the next day's poem.

> Le hasard apparent de LA MUETTE d'hier
> Est à rappeler positivement pour continuer à parler de la poésie
> Qui pourrait être au moins aussi justement que l'armée dénommée
> > la Grande Muette
> > > (*Poèmes de métro*, 12)

> The apparent stroke of luck yesterday—LA MUETTE—
> Should be remembered in all seriousness the better to keep talking of poetry
> Which could, at least as aptly as the army, be named
> > the Great Mute

An enormous dog appears on the platform of another station, wearing a muzzle, but wearing it like a necklace, which reminds Jouet of poetry, voluble poetry whose silence, far from being imposed on it from without, defines it as much as quills do the porcupine.

> Un énorme chien, sur le quai, dont je ne connais pas la race, porte certes
> > une muselière
> mais il la porte en sautoir, et je pense à la poésie parlant
> dont la muselière ne serait pas ajout externe de censure, mais un organe
> aussi topique pour la définition de l'espèce que la coupe de cornes inégales
> > chez le rhinocéros d'Afrique
> ou que les dizaines de javelots miniatures plantés sur le dos du porc-épic.
> > (*Poèmes de métro*, 16)

> An enormous dog, on the platform, whose breed I don't know, is wearing
> > to be sure, a muzzle,
> but he wears it like a string of beads, and I think of voluble poetry
> whose muzzle would not be a censure imposed on it from without, but an
> > organ
> as pertinent to the definition of its species as, for the African rhinoceros
> > the cut of its unequal horns
> or the dozens of mini-javelins planted on the back of the porcupine.
> > (My translation)

Alternately or at the same time the language in poems hangs open like the door to a vacant room, and sings. "Béer et chanter": that's poetry for Jouet. The hiatus at the heart of the very words *poésie* and *poète* (*ohé!* and *ohè*) gives the mouth itself a chance, he notes, to fall open, dumb and empty, while nonetheless spitting out its all: "La bouche bée son vide en crachant du plein"

(*Poèmes de métro*, 14). But do not forget, on account of these extremes, poetry's averageness (an everyday job, and so on). And its in-between-ness (pure transition . . .).

"Entre nous" is the title of five of the twenty-five separate groups of poems in the metro poem volume (other groups are called "Voice," "Measure," "Murmur," "Atelier," for example) . They contain the only personal material in the book, so "entre nous" certainly means "in confidence." "Que ceci reste entre nous": Let's keep this to ourselves. My dreams these nights, Jouet confides, are all blood, breasts, and childbirth. But "entre nous," meaning among us—among us all—also seems to be the name of poetry's preferred locale.

May this remain among us, then: this poetry that seeks its way neither on some oppositional outer fringe nor in the realm of self-improvement—which has a civic sense and is not above causes and commitments but never claims to be especially good for anyone. May it find among us the path it seeks in regular, measured activity like the heart's, the menses', the metro's; may it find its way "dans la moyenneté" (*Poèmes de métro*, 103): in the mediumness, that is, which the subway performs from station to station, being as it is in the middle of everything, and mixing in with everything as it does, and being so similar, Jouet observes, to the collapsible-expandable bellows of an accordion. May the prolix, promiscuous "poetry of proximity" find its medium way on the rails between nothing and everything and on to nothing again, from white to white again via black. Jouet would like to write such a lot, as we've observed, that it wouldn't really matter it was he, writing anything. Would that it were the human species—yawning empty and belting out its plenty.

7

Fin' Amors

"La lumière, là/la lumière"

It seems that snow once fell in the night and covered the garden behind the house in Provence where Roubaud lived as a child. Snow was very unusual there. He tells in *La Boucle* (*The Loop*) how one morning he woke to see it shining at dawn, not in the sun's light, but with its very own radiance. He pictures it still as "luminous density through and through; it is entirely present, in a full and gentle whiteness without any night" (*The Loop*, 39/*La Boucle*, 40). This pure white snow-light illuminated the garden, all the shapes and forms in it, and illuminated the sun itself—a white sun, which received, rather than gave light. This is not the Black Sun, Roubaud explains—that hides and withholds light inside itself out of disdain, "ou par énigme," or that casts a profusion of black light. This rare snow-dawn with its empty white sun is precisely not the black night of the soul when the pitch dark of light's absolute perfection proves inescapable; when God turns out to be exactly nothing, and the demon familiar to Roubaud, the *what's-the-use* demon, cannot be beaten. ("A quoi bon?" "Il n'y a rien." In these words his youngest brother, Jean-René, explained why he could not live.)

The pale sun glimmering in early morning snow light is not this black sun. Nor is it the golden sunshine Provence is known for. It is a white sun, a snow sun; its white has the properties, Roubaud writes, of a fall, a privation. Its loveliness conveys a sense of the irrecoverable. I think the white sun is different from the black the way sorrow is different from dereliction. That is, the way the loss forever, of someone who was once everything for you differs from the disappearance, before you can even have approached her, of someone you have long desired.[1]

Perhaps it is only a coincidence that both Roubaud and Giorgio Agamben, to whom we will have reason to refer at some length later, should assign a particular significance to the word *privation*. Not the same significance but, to my ear, related. If, in Roubaud, privation names one mode of unhappiness, distinct from another, in Agamben it serves to distinguish between two kinds of potential. There is not, in his understanding, just one kind—an ability yet unrealized (to hear or see, for example)—but two, and the second is the ability not to. So, the potential for seeing is one thing, but there is also the potential to not see, a capacity for blindness, which Agamben calls a "possibility of privation." It is because humans have this potential, for privation, he says, that they can see shadows.[2]

Roubaud is a reader of Agamben, and borrows from him, but the reader of the present book will judge, as it continues, whether it is only in my imagination that Agamben's "privation" resounds quietly in Roubaud.

In any case, when Roubaud first read the poems of Guido Cavalcanti, two lines in particular pierced him, he says, with exquisite delight. He adds that he uses the term *exquisite* the way it appears in the English expression "exquisite pain." Here are the two lines of Cavalcanti.

> aria serena quand' apar l'albore
> e bianca neve scender senza venti
>
> calm air when the dawn appears
> and white snow descending without wind

He felt emerging in these lines the "explanation" of the dawn snowfall he remembered from long ago: that is, he sensed in the couplet a luminous cold that tempers the bitter cold of night, calms the wind, blankets the ground and the creatures on it protectively. It looks after them and takes care of memory (*La Boucle*, 44/*The Loop*, 43).

Roubaud associates the sudden serenity of the air at dawn described by Cavalcanti with the sudden appearance of a new truth at the dawn of Western lyricism in vernacular tongues (*La Boucle*, 44/*The Loop*, 43). At the origin of medieval love poetry, then, the black sun (*vers de dreit nien*), and also a white one.[3]

"Who is she who comes, gazed upon by all, causing the air to tremble with light?" ask two other *exquisite* Calvalcanti lines.

Chi è questa che vèn, ch'ogn'om la mira
e fa tremar di claritate l'âre?

The answer is obvious in the poem: the lady, *la donna*. For Roubaud, though, as he explains, it is the snow that comes, making the air tremble with light, and making him tremble. "The vibrating clarity that it carried with it was contained in its name," he writes: "Memory" (*The Loop*, 44/*La Boucle*, 46).

For my part, I associate the morning snow's vibrant white radiance with the "secret object" of James Goodman's "quest" in *Eros mélancolique*. I think it bears a relation with the *appearance* that he tries to welcome (or conjure, or capture) in the web of photographic images he slowly assembles. The quiet, snowy air whose name (pulsing with light) is Memory is linked, I suspect, to whatever, or whoever Goodman was dimly reminded of by the voice with the unplaceable accent. He didn't know who it was or what; he could not simply have aimed a camera at it, but it might conceivably drift into view somewhere in his lattice of images and images of images.

Here is the reason I make this association—between the white sun of memory and the secret object of Goodman's quest. The image that he places in his photo composition, in a series of shots taken at 11:00 p.m. on a succession of different dates, is either a plain white square, or a shot of a "micocoulier de Provence." This is a tree he had loved as a child hiding out in the South of France with his mother. He'd been surprised to come upon it again in Paris: a gray-barked tree with leaves "d'un vert lumineux," paler green on the underside, and slightly fuzzy. "Il aima cet arbre." He'd thought to himself as a boy that "afterward," in the garden of the house where he would live with his parents when the war was over, there would be such a tree. At the 11:00 p.m. spots on the clock, so to speak, of his photo Project, he placed, then, either a picture of this tree or a white square. And he foresaw this "alternating couple of melancholic squares" slowly tracing through his entire, gradually developing composition a pattern resembling the path of rhyme words through the stanzas of a sestina.

> The alternating couple of *melancholic squares*, the virtual white sun and the micocoulier, would begin to trace by contrast, among the others, something like a spiral, by virtue of the permutation that drew the hours along and, simultaneously, the bits of space photographed at these hours.
>
> (*Eros mélancolique* 201; my translation)

Goodman had considered a black square for the 11:00 p.m. spots, because eleven at night is for him, we learn, "l'heure noire." It was at eleven o'clock one July night in 1944 that he woke up to hear his aunt talking worriedly downstairs with other grownups. She said, "It's eleven o'clock, Esther will not come back."

She did not come back. She never came back.

(*Eros mélancolique*, 135)

But he decided against the black square, in favor either of a white one, or a picture of the micocoulier, for once in Provence he'd awakened to see snow making the sun white, and he considered his own melancholy to be white, not black—not the "nuit noire de l'âme," but white. "The white of his particular melancholy got its properties from a disappearance, not from the loss of a desired object lost before ever being reached" (137).

A deprivation gave his white sadness its whiteness, just as, on one unusual morning, snow trembling in the air gave the sun its pale radiance. Goodman's melancholy has the luminous pallor of memory, which preserves his sense of loss.

It blankets this feeling just as snowfall does the cold ground and the creatures on it. Thereby it safeguards the apprehension of a world *before*. It looks after the life of the worldless. It is the silvery semblance of that life, its fantastic appearance—like the inner shadow of the impossible in a poem.

In a subsequent volume of his autobiographical prose, *Poésie: (récit)*, Roubaud observes that all his beginner poems from the 1960s—all the ones he didn't tear up—referred back, with every word and image, to words and images from before his brother's death in October '61. All those early poems were placed at a huge, heavy distance, he says, from the time of their composition. They belonged on the far side of a wall, "le mur du deuil," wall of mourning. He placed them long before the spot in time where the present is not. And the light that fell on them, coming from that faraway *before*, cast its practically absolute irreality on the streets of Paris, where Roubaud walked, up and down, reciting poems by heart, composing others, counting the syllables, the lines, choosing the words. "It lit the streets of the city with an almost absolute irreality" (*Poésie*, 179; my translation).

I think of the rue Saint-Jacques at night: "La rue tombe noire, noire, la tombe, rue noire, là." And then of Paris thoroughfares bathed in the light of another world, unreal, the world before. "Elle était là," Roubaud says, of this light, in *Poésie*: "toujours là," anterior to everything that words said, that numbers counted.

> La lumière, là
>
> la lumière
>
> là, là
> dans la rue
>
> la lumière
>
> la lumière bue,
> la lumière, là
>
> la lumière,
>
> là (*Poésie*, 13)[4]

"Rien que la lumière"

When he sublet an apartment partway into his fellowship year in Paris, and investigated all it had to offer a photographer, the young Mr. Goodman had never felt—even though he'd known a much more spacious photography studio as a teenager—so intensely at one with light.

> Light ...; nothing but light; light when it falls, light acting on the film where the image of light can be discerned, the light from the window; reflected in water, concentrated in the window; refracted by the mirror; condensed by the film; seen in a room where, again, the sun's light, refracted by the window, compressed by a door, refracted by the mirror, and so on ... repetition of light like repetitions in music.
>
>   (*Eros mélancolique*, 89; my translation)

PHOTOGRAPHY

Photographers and troubadours share a place in Roubaud's thinking because the trobar and photography are similar "inventions."[5] In at least two different texts about photography, Roubaud emphasizes its early history (the young James Goodman's research topic). And his treatment of this subject recalls the troubadours' invention of love: their discovery, that is, of something that does not exist in nature. Something so odd one can only dream it.[6]

"Rêver la chimie de la lumière" is the title of one section of *Eros mélancolique* (202). The lovesick Goodman dreams the chemistry of light. He prefers dreaming it to explaining it, in the essay (the "Mémoire" [dissertation])—that was to form the first part of his Project. He likes the idea of dreaming light's chemistry "historically, via a meditation upon the images, the techniques and intentions of photography's first initiators." Of course, this oneiric methodology is not really called for in a Mémoire, but the second, secret part of the Project (the photographic assemblage, "l'image d'images") required it.

The three heroes of the Preface to the Mémoire—Daguerre, Talbot, and Sir John Herschel—were in large part, we read, "a dream of his own" (203). Which means Goodman dreamed *for* Daguerre et al. the idea of photography which he, in the 1960s, considered they had already developed fully—though this was impossible in the 1830s. "Nothing had been accomplished yet at that time, the achievement could only be a future one" (303). Talbot and the others were invaded by Goodman's thought, "envahis de sa pensée, anachroniquement," inasmuch as they couldn't have fully imagined what he, much later, thought they had already brought into being. Photography. For his conviction was that the name—*photography*, the writing of light—"invented" by John Herschel, was not just a label but gave birth to something that did not exist in the natural world.

> —La photographie est ce qu'elle est
>   dès qu'elle a un nom
>   et parce qu'elle a ce nom, photographie—   (204)
>
> —Photography is what it is
>   as soon as it has a name
>   and because it has this name, photography—

Photography was the proper name of a future thing. It named a thing that was exactly what was going to be.

In a brief essay of his own on the beginnings of photography ("Première Digression sur les débuts de la photographie"), Roubaud suggests that his own interest in photography is similarly aroused by its name, which gave it a kind of advance being: that of a thing that is going to materialize. "The invention of the name," Roubaud writes, "coincides with the existence which begins, and the name shows this existence, designates and orients it in a very particular way" ("L'Invention du nom coïncide avec l'existence qui commence et la montre, la désigne et l'oriente d'une manière très particulière" ["Première Digression," 210]). *Photography*—the name—is in this regard similar to the title—*Le Grand Incendie de Londres*—of the novel that Roubaud had been going to write. This novel would have been, had it not inevitably failed, the story of

its own gradual coming to be what it was from the start, due to its title. As I suggested earlier, had the novel succeeded, it would have been the story of its own eventual discovery (like an Arthurian knight's) of who, or what it was. It would ultimately have answered to its name—which appeared in Roubaud's mind soon after the death of his brother and just before he embarked on his own double project. He knew the name upon awakening from a dream, you will remember. He knew nothing else about the novel, or how he would ever write it, but he knew there would be one, and the name of it. His dream informed him. And from then on, that name named what was going to happen
... except that it never did, as we have observed.

But, pretty much in the same way that the name of a novel came to Roubaud, the idea of "photography" as the proper name of something future was "the first, constitutive truth" of Goodman's Mémoire (first half of his Project). And this "truth" had come to him earlier in his life, we learn, in *Eros mélancolique*, upon his awakening from a dream.

It seems to be photography's "not-of-this-world" character that captures Roubaud's attention. Its kinship with dream and fantasy, and memory. He underscores the ghostly feeling it elicited especially in its early history when it was thought to create "objets-images n'existant pas dans le monde naturel" ("Première Digression," 210). When daguerreotypes were circulating, to gaze at one was to see the image of another world, impalpable, beyond the looking glass. Shadows, fleeting and intangible, can be captured, Roubaud recalls William Talbot's having said, and held by photography, our "natural magic." Dream figures swim into view, comparable to the immaterial form of a beloved lady that enters the eye of the lover according to the troubadour tradition and is reflected on the eye's watery surface, a phantasm.[7] Sometimes, when Roubaud mentions a long-desired lady appearing naked and all luminous in a dark room, *chambre noire*, it is hard to tell if this happens in a bedroom at night or a darkroom (a stanza—of a poem—is a "chambre," too).

Although initially it sought to imitate the world of sensations, and tried to reproduce colors rather than forms, photography had the good luck to fail. "Photography is really born only from this failure, this poverty," in the young James Goodman's view (*Eros mélancolique*, 207). Its function is not to mimic nature; it is not, regardless of what it first thought, a kind of painting, or even a kind of drawing. Rather, it writes; it is a formal writing like mathematics (*Eros mélancolique*, 208), and poetry. "After the disappearance of pigments, and very soon thereafter, the loss of colors, the world appeared colorless, written by the silver salts in black and white" (*Eros mélancolique*, 207).[8]

The colorless world of forms that we come upon in the poem called "Jusque dans la nuit"—the "neutralité apathique" of the evening scene—suggests the colorless world of early photography. We have glanced at this poem already. It begins with a description of things' "dessaisissement" at twilight. The removal of their properties. The gray shape of a fig tree, a wall, stairsteps, and a shovel leaning against a shed—all detached from their particular characteristics (color, texture, . . .). "Who, or what," we read, "can have so denatured the world?"

As daylight recedes, objects gradually drop their attributes, you will recall: they shed their specific features and present a face that seems that of "la première, & philosophique matière, écaillée de toute qualité." They almost show, I suggested earlier, form itself, not the form of this or of that, but the naked form of form (and they grant an almost-happiness mixed, you will remember, with "forebodings of disaster I could barely endure"—similar, I expect, to the dread all photos inspire in Goodman, despite his near-obsession with photography: for all photographs announce, he feels, a brutal disappearance, "immotivée, incongruë, imméritée" [*Eros mélanclique*, 105]).

It is things' "dessaisissement," in any event—their having shed every mere accessory at the beginning of "Jusque dans la nuit"—it is their being scraped bare of their attributes that raises the question, from whence comes this unnatural world? This colorless world of love, of phantoms, this world of forms?

NUDITY

Emmanuel Hocquard considers photography to be a mode of thinking that is particularly well-suited to the contemplation of a thing's bare being. Or a person's. A person's simply being the one he or she is. "Alone, evident." Whence the title of his 2009 book, *Méditations photographiques sur l'idée simple de nudité*.

Nudity is the simplest idea, he states. A common French idiom calls it the simplest getup, *le plus simple appareil* (the one you are born in). Anne Portugal uses this expression as the title for a poetry book that revolves around Susannah's discovery bathing in her garden. Norma Cole's English translation of this book is called *Nude*.[9] Hocquard refers to Susannah and the elders, and at the same time to Anne Portugal (*Le plus simple appareil*) in his *Méditations photographiques*.

No ornament at all is an ornament—*une parure*—the simplest. Simplicity itself is an *imperceptible* embellishment. The present book keeps returning to this ornament—the singularity of the utterly undistinguished. The beauty of

Maylis, say, which is not an attribute of hers. It is just her being she ("seule, évidente"), and if this is after all a property, it is the one that consists in not being one—or in lacking or escaping. If it is a property it is the fake one, it does not belong: "fausse propriété," fake estate. Or "naked lie." Think of Pessoa's unique distinction: none. Indifference. One might imagine the invisible adornment, simplicity, as a torrent that washes and rinses away all distinguishing features, and/or think of nudity rising up gradually in a bath that erases the face. When Hocquard writes that the old voyeurs rinse their eyes in Susannah's nakedness ("se rincer l'oeil" means "get an eyeful," but also, literally, "rinse out your eye"), he is certainly thinking of the following two lines from Portugal's *Le plus simple appareil*—

> deux vieux qui se rincent
> les yeux me plaisent   (*Le plus simple* ... , 63)
>
> two elders getting
> an eyeful please me   (*Nude*, 53)

While they rinse their eyes, Susannah, as Hocquard has it, bathes in their gaze. "Her nakedness and their gaze swap by surprise," he observes (*Méditations photographiqiues*, 32). "Sa nudité et leur regard s'échangent par surprise." That is, nakedness bathes in the gaze it drenches; the exposure or surprise occurs in both directions at once. "[L]a nudité est surprise," Hocquard states. It takes whoever surprises it by surprise and exposes whoever exposes it. "Quelle rencontre ineffable!"

Instantaneous reciprocity, without start or finish. "Achrone."

"Le tournant de l'ouvrage"

Anne Portugal is about eight years younger than Hocquard; her first poetry books came out in the 1980s and by now she has published a dozen. She is a teacher, in Paris, of writing and contemporary literature, and a translator as well, like Hocquard and Roubaud. Like Hocquard, she has a taste for grammar—rigorous but unconventional grammar—and especially for syntax, which she likes extremely complex. At best, "impossible." She favors "acrobaties syntaxiques," syntactical acrobatic tricks.[10] Architects' blueprints and surveyors' equipment are stimulating models for the construction of her poems, for these often involve delicate spatial relations, multiple perspectives, shifting lines of sight and abrupt changes in scale.

There is no doubt that her poems' intricate syntactical composition contributes to their perplexing character, but opacity is not the goal, or gravity—the enemy of poetry, she says. Nothing is hidden. Or thick. Compared to Hocquard, whom it would be easy to find icy cold, Portugal is exuberant and very funny. Her most recent book, *et comment nous voilà moins épais* ("here we are again and look, less thick") appeared in 2017; the preceding one (2010) is also delighted to be lightweight and is called *la formule flirt*. In *définitif bob* (2002), "l'espace littéraire" is the virtual expanse of a video game.[11] You might think that Portugal often looks for a way to slip her poems into some game or gambit: the public relations game, perhaps, or advertisements for beauty products, or the treasures of French literature and art. Her poetry books have come out at relatively long intervals, and she has on occasion explained that this is because of her laziness; but another explanation is that for each new book she must find a new gambit, another formula or device: "It takes me years," she recently commented, "to experiment with different models and try different systems, in order to create new kinds of verse."[12]

Her poems in *et comment nous voilà* are so slim, she has said, that they can slip into pages already written, as into beds already slept in. "They say you have to sleep around to succeed, and in this book there is a lot of that—stretching out and falling asleep."[13] I am calling on Anne Portugal to brush into my book a bright stripe symmetrical to Danielle Collobert's dark one.

Like Roubaud (he is an influence), she sets a high value on verse: "Je suis tourmentée par le vers, qui disparaît aujourd'hui," she recently said.[14]

It is the turn at the end of each line that preoccupies her especially—the ploughman's regular turnaround. The word *vers* ("verse," and also "line of poetry") winks from time to time from inside words for turning, turning back, reversing, turning upside down. "Renverse" is an example. It congers up a change in the wind or a turn in the current, or again an accident: "tomber à la renverse" is falling flat on one's back. "Que fait le texte quand il tourne?" she asked, in an interview with John Stout.[15] Poems never answer this question, she observed; they just fail and send it back again. Whence the "revers" in some of her poems, which you might take, momentarily, for a flippant gesture, a brush-off (the back of her hand). It could be a "setback," though, when it appears, for example, in the last line of the next-to-last poem of *et comment nous voilà moins épais*. It might be a setback there, but also a "return," a backhand shot in tennis. Or, perhaps it is just "vers" all over again: "re-vers." "Recommence," the line, and the poem, ends. Begin again.

> [...] dès
> lors il allait se montrer d'un revers recommence
>
> (*et comment nous voilà*, 115)

The first words of this poem are "amis des plaisirs communs" ("friends of mutual pleasures").[16] They link it, in my mind, to the poem on the facing page. For this preceding poem appears to be about a public park, "propriété de la commune aire de jeu" ("owned by the local authorities a playground"). The two poems both have to do with shared pleasures and common space. They look alike as well: each is a rectangle, seven even lines from top to bottom, justified at both margins (all the poems in this third and last part of *et comment nous voilà* have this strict rectilinear shape, and many other poems by Portugal—the ones in the first part of *et comment*, for example, or the ones that compose *La formule flirt*—present a somewhat less hard-edged version of the same small block of print). The first of the pair of poems in *et comment* that I am speaking of here may well be referring to itself—to the square it forms on the page—when it begins, "le square est un jardin public de petite dimension / propriété de la commune aire de jeu" ("the square is a park of smaller dimensions / owned by the local authorities a playground"). Sometimes, indeed, Portugal's poems seem to offer themselves as a setting: a small public garden, say, or a park. Or a little stage. They propose an improvised environment, a festive décor for amusements enjoyed in common. Sometimes even an experimental or make-believe locale for living together. A sort of midsummer night's dream.

I refer to the play by Shakespeare mainly on account of the talking lion. The first section of *et comment nous voilà* is an exchange, stretching over thirty-two four-line poems, between a lion and a hermit, planning their life together in the desert. Their colloquy is called "la colocation": the two of them will be, somehow or other, housemates. Theseus's question in *A Midsummer Night's Dream*—"I wonder if the lion be to speak"—serves as the epigraph to their schemes. Theseus is wondering about the rude mechanicals' play (to beguile the "lazy hours" between after-supper and bedtime). But I have in mind as well another allusion of Portugal's to midsummer. It appears in "The Garden." There she refers to a central place: a "disposition placed at a mid-way point, mid-August," she wrote. She said that poetry seeks this milieu's formula. I wonder if she had the Feast of the Assumption in mind. She does not say. She does stress "nothing final, nothing sublime." I picture a semimiraculous balancing act, and think of the seesaw and the swing set that figure among the pieces of play equipment in *Le plus simple appareil*. Or again of some of the other outdoor activities introduced in that book—"pratiques de plein air" suitable for the very, very light: "se diluer dans l'air," "s'évaporer dans l'air" (dissolve, evaporate into the air). But Portugal, when she mentioned the midway point, mid-August, which poetry wants to map, just called it "a motionless state," its halfway point measured by some gardener's string ("The Garden," 41). The talking lion in *et comment nous voilà* brings to mind a more fanciful summer midpoint. Still, how to picture—make ready, design, draw into place—a "vie à deux"? Or "à plusieurs"? How to prepare a milieu for shared amusements, lay out a garden, install a "propriété commune"? What are the necessary adjustments, realignments? Is there a formula for it? These are questions that poetry confronts in books by Anne Portugal.

The penultimate line of the poem that begins "le square est un jardin public" turns on the word "entourage." Which suggests, I believe, right at the "tournant" of the text (just where it turns), an unobtrusive encircling—the sketch of a circle—the contour of a locale or milieu. An "environment," in Ian Monk's translation. A good environment for shared pleasures, possibly. For a company, even ("entourage"). But the sketch contains disorder along with peace: the line and its upset.

> [...] autant d'un entourage
> tout ensemble contenant ligne dérangement avec

Here is the poem in its entirety.

> le square est un jardin public de petite dimension
> propriété de la commune aire de jeu qui peut se
> développer sur du béton conduit dans le schéma
> donc des catastrophes il est d'abord puis autre part
> devenu si général publication d'appartement à la
> manière dont on le regarde autant d'un entourage
> tout ensemble contenant ligne dérangement avec
>
> (*et comment nous voilà moins épais*, 114)

> the square is a park of smaller dimensions owned
> by the local authorities a playground that can be
> developed on concrete thus resulting in the scheme

of things catastrophes it has to start with then subse
quently become so general a publication for lodgement
from the way we look at it as much as an environment
all together containing a line of disturbance with

(Translation by Ian Monk)

I imagine this small square of verse to be a pocket park, a diminutive piece of urban planning. Often I picture Anne Portugal as a gardener. She has said that floral arrangements are not for her, she prefers to stick with the gardener. And there is the gardener's string that draws the summer midpoint, that "motionless state," into place. Moreover two poems in her early poetry book, *De quoi faire un mur* begin, "le jardinier sait"—"the gardener knows."

> le jardinier sait
> l'opération
> le tournant de l'ouvrage
>   [...]   (*De quoi faire un mur*, 65)

> the gardener knows
> the operation
> the turning of the work[17]
>   [...]   (My translation)

And then again:

> Le jardinier sait
> diviser mon temps
> pour avancer
> chaque pas est folie dans ce pas
> que je n'ai pas à placer
> là et qui sait la fin du tour.   (*De quoi faire un mur*, 31)

> the gardener knows
> how to divide my time
> to move ahead
> each step folly in that step
> which I do not have to place
> there and which knows the end of the road
>   (Trans. Serge Gavronsky, in *Six Contemporary Women Poets*, 39)

The mix of measure and folly in what the gardener knows here is arresting—the mix of meter and lurch or stumble. Not to mention the step, or pace that is simultaneously a loss of footing ("ce pas / que je n'ai pas"; "... que je n'ai pas à placer / là"). Much as I admire "the end of the road" in Gavronsky's translation, I regret a little his not having kept "tour," because of the stress I wish to place on turning, "le tournant de l'ouvrage," and also because the poem itself makes a little tour, describes a small circle, if you consider the first line to say "the gardener knows," and the last to ask "who knows?"—thus suggesting, perhaps, a steep drop-off just around the bend. At any rate, I often think of Anne Portugal as a gardener, tending neat, straight-edged beds, tying things up sternly to stakes and trellises, cutting them back. Laughter, she says, is her pruning shears ("The Garden," 39). In "le square est un jardin public," however, I picture her at work developing a small playing field, on concrete which she pours into a strophic form: a "schéma," as I take it, featuring the turn of the "vers," the turn and return, strophe and "catastrophe"—with "schéma" also calling to mind a "schéma d'aménagement," an urban development plan. Perhaps this square is "d'un abord catastrophique," as you might say of some particular place that it is "d'un abord difficile," or "facile," or "risqué": hard or easy to get to, or risky to approach.

LE BORD

Portugal's lines often turn on a "crochet" (a sudden swerve), or a "détour." Her poems, I mean, are often edged with words like "bend" or "edge." They flaunt their "bord," their border, their hem ("ourlet"). Occasionally they do it with a flounce, "un volant," which might also be a shuttlecock, batted back over the net. They joke about enjambment, frequently creating a little tussle at the line break between continuity and interruption, smooth and rough, a link and a gap. "Servir de lien / à l'écart" is an example. These two lines are the last in a five-line poem (from *De quoi faire un mur*, 25). It's a nonstop train that "serves as a link to the split"—it's an express leaving from a holiday resort, barreling along, not without "dreaming in the distance" ("[il] rêve au loin"), and thus briefly echoing Apollinaire's sweet melancholy, but only barely. On! No local stops, this train services only the split, "l'écart."[18] In a different poem (still from *De quoi faire un mur*), an elastic band in the middle of one line turns into a thread by the time it arrives at the turning point—a thread, "un fil," which, retaining the elasticity of the rubber band may well stretch over the line break but, instead of a "fil conducteur" (a continuous, guiding thread), it proves to be a thread to break, "fil / à rompre," between two furrows (or drainage ditches). "l'isotopie de l'élastique devenu fil / à rompre entre deux digues."[19]

For all the speed in Portugal's verse (see the lamborghini in *et comment nous voilà*, with its "ad / justable" steering wheel, "roulant bien," rolling well toward the "bas de la page," leaving everything else behind ["in the rearview mirror there is nothing"])[20]—for all this high velocity, she is really the enemy, in a way, of continuity. Like Hocquard who wants "l'éclipse au lieu de la fable"—brusque interruption in place of sentences that follow one upon the other, telling stories—she claims to be incapable of narrative. "Ce qui m'intéresse moi, c'est la coupe," she told John Stout. "What interests me is the cut. And everything that happens in the area of the cut." The edge or border of her poems, their "bord," can be a brink. "There is terror in verse," she remarked in a recent interview. "A void, an abyss."[21]

Navigating the risky edge is among the mapping and exploring operations in Portugal's poems. Plotting its course is largely what requires the adjusting, aligning and realigning procedures. At least, this is my intuition. Here is a text in which the *placement* "en profondeur," of the poem's irregular edge would seem the whole point of writing. It is the last poem in *De quoi faire un mur*. "Face étroite" is its name for the poem's edge, I believe. Narrow surface, tight margin for maneuver. This suggests the perspective of a rock climber who scales a wall of stone or brick by the dangerous, narrow face. The climber is the stone mason, though, too—or maybe the bricklayer. "L'appareilleur." And to her—if her plans, her preliminary diagrams and framing (just barely compared, in passing, to basting stitches in a sewing project) are worthy—to her, then, the narrow cleft, the tight path shows itself.

> disons que de manière
> à attester sa face étroite
> de sorte qu'elle soit en profondeur
> que le bâti fasse accroire
> la fente le petit chemin
> d'un mur la pose en chant
> révélée à l'appareilleur
>
> let us say that in order
> to attest to its narrow face
> in a way such that it be in depth
> that the plan be plausible
> the crevice the little road
> of a wall places it in song
> revealed to the installer   (My rough translation)

Composing a poem for Anne Portugal may well be (frequently, not always) to locate, to draw, or retrace a border's path. Sometimes to install it and possibly to develop its vicinity (as one might develop a mall, an alley for strolling, down the middle of a busy thoroughfare, such as Broadway in Manhattan). Here is another brief poem from *De quoi faire un mur* that may suggest as much. It seems to picture water, lapping at a quay, as a clear ruler, and appears to wish to underscore how this transparent straight-edge traces from end to end of the page an orchard path.

> Au contact des matières du quai du port à l'eau
> soulignons
> avec la règle transparente d'un bout à l'autre de la feuille
> qu'elle trace
> une allée de vergers et d'autres   (*De quoi faire un mur*, 9)

> At the point of contact between the material of the port's quay and the water
> let us underscore
> with the transparent ruler from one end to the other of the page
> that it traces
> an allée of orchards and others   (My rough translation)

The edge of a poem—its course, what happens in its vicinity—is a question for poetry comparable to the question for a gardener of plotting out a stand of trees, or for a city planner of installing a marina. It could remind one of a race car driver's problems, steering his course, or of the risks a girl takes hurtling down the sidewalk on a bike. Nonetheless it is related, in my view at any rate, to the blueprint for shared amusements, "plaisirs communs" (e.g., walking among fruit trees along an embankment). How to design a life of pleasure, a life together? Attention: the setting which I imagine is sometimes sketched at the edge of a poem, au "tournant de l'ouvrage," can prove a minefield, like the "zone" named in one poem. I suppose it is not for nothing that the Bermuda Triangle shows up in *Le plus simple appareil* (although a better reading of the lines I have in mind could be that the painter standing at an enticing fork in the road is wearing Bermuda shorts). "Tranche," the thin edge of a book, or a blade, is another name for the "bord" to which I am attaching such a lot of importance. Not to be distinguished, then, from the "coupe." Anne Portugal remarked in "The Garden," that her way of loving and laughing involves an ax (40).

SUSANNAH

The Portugal work to which Hocquard refers in his photographic meditations on nudity—*Le plus simple appareil*—is, as I indicated earlier, a send-up of the Susannah story. Portugal "degreases" it, as she told Serge Gavronsky, by way of a secret without mystery ("The Garden," 41). The elders, *les vieillards*, get released from their role as lecherous spies (ogling the lovely Susannah bathing in her private garden). Or perhaps they become inspired to play this role in unexpected and hilarious ways. They turn up as a periscope on a submerged submarine, as photo enlargers, scaling things up; as ophthalmologists examining Susannah's cornea.

> ses genoux touchent les genoux du vieillard
> qui lui prend la mesure de son oeil droit
> 11. 43. 15. en o. p. h. t. a. l. m. o. l. o. g. i. e.   (*Le plus simple appareil*, 48)

> her knees touch the knees of the elder
> who sizes her up with his right eye
> 11. 43. 15. in o. p. h. t. h. a. l. m. o. l. o. g. y.   (*Nude*, 40)

I am convinced that Hocquard is, if not one of these elders, one of the elders that Portugal mentioned in her text for Gavronsky: one of the poets, that is, a little older than she, whose austerity—whose dryness—she says she particularly reveres. My hunch is that Hocquard's coolness and intellectual rigor constitute a high standard in her judgment, even though, as she said, given her particular temperament (not at all chilly; baroque, rather, or even kitsch), laughter must do the work of rigor for her—laughter combined with strict attention to form ("The Garden," 41).

I think that the elders' association with seeing and with all kinds of optical enhancers in *Le plus simple appareil* also links them to the "vigilance" that Portugal considers indispensable in poetry. That is, I expect that in addition to everything else, they *stand guard*, or *keep watch* in the garden tended by Anne Portugal, where poetry confronts a few of what she considers its principal "difficulties" or "problems." In addition to the questions I have myself proposed (how to design a public garden, a "propriété commune"), beauty is an issue. Secret beauty. And exposure. Vigilance is essential here, she has stated, in her text for Gavronsky. "We will keep watch in the garden," she wrote ("The Garden," 40). Hocquard also values vigilance, and dislikes the songs and stories, the habits that are apt to diminish it. I picture him as Portugal's elder companion in watchfulness and imagine that in some way she counts on his being there.

Her thinking and his cross in the neighborhood of simplicity.

In the vicinity of nakedness, that is—near the distinguishing feature of the nondescript. The naked eye, we read, in *Le plus simple appareil*, easily surprises this indifference.

car l'oeil nu
surprendra
c'est facile

l'alignement de tes pensées indifférentes   (*Le plus simple appareil*, 131)

for the naked eye
will surprise
it's simple

the alignment of your indifferent thoughts   (*Nude*, 110)

The naked eye takes indistinction by surprise, then. "L'oeil nu" exposes this "secret sans mystère." And since visual aids of all kinds proliferate in Portugal's book (periscopes, reflectors, rearview mirrors), it is hard to assume that *l'oeil nu* means a gaze without a lens—a microscope or glasses. I think it is an eye unmasked: unimpersonated, that is. Stripped by the nudity that *it* exposes. It is an undifferentiated, impersonal or in-different point of view. The *simplest* perspective. No one in particular's outlook.

Its sight is ravishing—its sight in both senses simultaneously, of course: *what* it sees, and its *own* exposure. Nudity's discovery, I mean to say, denuding the gaze, dazzles the eyes of no one.

BLACK AND WHITE

Hocquard proposes a photographic thinking in *Méditations photographiques*. It is a "pensée surprise." Or thought as exposure. Elsewhere he likes to notice the play of light—flickering reflections among iridescent surfaces (opal earrings, polished fingernails, glassware). Often he dwells on photographic atmospherics: the alternating dark and light, sunlight and shade, on a veranda, say, where white railings cast black shadows on a white floor, or in this description of a smokestack's shadow lying along the deck of a boat.

> When the ship heeled to one side, it swept through space like a dark projector and the light shifted onto other white surfaces, onto other windowed walls, overexposed and bleached like old daguerreotypes, while the spraying

of the water under the bow accompanied, in a parallel, sonorous way, the regular swaying of the bulwark handrail in front of the horizon line.

(*Aerea in the Forests*, 50/*Aerea dans les forêts*, 68-69)

Throughout his work he refers to silver halide photography itself, its mechanisms and procedures: blinking shutter before an aperture, for example. He calls the instantaneous *now* of literality "le temps de la photographie" (*Méditations photographiques*, 14). This is the time of nakedness.

> Puisqu'elle est instantanée, la nudité est sans commencement et sans fin. Elle est achrone.
>
> La photographie ne fixe pas l'instant d'un corps. Mais elle n'en finit pas de donner à voir l'instantanéité de la nudité. (*Méditations*, 16)
>
> Since it is instantaneous, nudity is without beginning and without end. It is achronological.
>
> Photography does not fix the instant of a body. But it never has done with showing the instantaneity of nudity. (My translation)

"Expose the negative, wash the print," he advises in *Theory of Tables* (2). I expect the repeating, reversing procedures involved in photography before the arrival of the digital camera (the negative and positive images, dark for light, then light for dark) would be bound to interest Hocquard, who remembers the alternating flashes of white and black (fish's belly, fish's back). "Brillances et mattités." "Black is light, too," in photography, he writes (*Méditations*, 51). Black is light, as *is not* is. Roubaud is evidently also drawn, in his own way, to the "negative-positive" aspect of photography. He cites Faraday observing that in Talbot's first images "all the lights are black and all the shadows luminous," and Talbot's solution: a second procedure that reverses the blacks and whites again, so that "the lights and the shadows are again in their original position and value" ("Première Digression," 209). Roubaud appreciates the expression *negative-positive* introduced by Talbot, because it brings out the "cusienne" operation that produces photographic images: photography for Roubaud is, it appears, a logical operation of the kind laid out by Nicholas of Cusa in "de

Li non Aliud": "double negation both spatial (reversal of the images) and luminous (exchange between light and dark)" ("Première Digression," 209).

In Hocquard's *Méditations*, photography is a synecdoche for art and thought in general, insofar as these are, at their best, erasing, effacing practices. They subtract, as he sometimes suggests, or impoverish. They want to make perceptible the imperceptible adornment comprised by none at all. You might say, the rainbow colors of neutrality. "[P]hotography (like painting and sculpture, no doubt) allows one to make perceptible [the] non-visible" (*Méditations*, 36).

The nonvisible resides somewhere, Hocquard writes, in all perceptions. Likewise a bit of residual unthought lies left over in every thought. It returns. "Retour de la figure aimée," he writes (*Conditions de lumière*, 80). Not that this un-thought, nonseen, this cherished shape has ever come before. "Revenante inhabituelle," Hocquard says. "Her strange visitation" is Jean-Jacques Poucel's translation. Let us picture the unknown, cherished shape as an image in a darkroom, swimming in liquid, a print surfacing in the bath of developing fluid, a memory. But of nothing. A return, but without precedent.

> la nudité est souvenir. Pas souvenir *de*,
> mais souvenir sans objet. Présence qui
> revient, sous-jacente, dans la chambre noire.
>
> *Sous-venir* serait un verbe de nudité.   (*Méditations*, 31)

> Nudity is remembrance. Not remembrance *of*
> but remembrance without object. Presence which
> comes again, underlying, in the dark room.
>
> To come from under [*sous-venir*] would be a verb of nudity.
>   (My translation)

LOVE VIA SHADOWS

As I observed earlier, photography, early photography, and the lyric verse of the medieval "trouvères" are linked in Roubaud's mind in that both are inventions—*trouvailles*, that is, or discoveries—of something that exists not in nature but in dreams. This turns out to be a perspective on the trobar—if not on photography—that Roubaud shares with Giorgio Agamben.

Agamben is among many figures—like David Lewis, Wittgenstein, Nelson Goodman, Nicholas of Cusa, Basil of Caesarea, F. W. Lawvere, Jean-Claude Milner, the Reverend Father Etienne Binet, and so on—from whom Roubaud borrows. He adopts or freely adapts their learned concepts. I have already mentioned Agamben's "potentialities"; his "whatever beings" from *The Coming Community* will make an appearance here later. But simply as a remarkable reader of medieval literature and philosophy, Agamben makes himself a colleague of Roubaud's. And I strongly suspect that his emphasis, particularly in *Stanzas*, on the medieval "discovery" of the unreality of love must be fundamental to Roubaud's sense of kinship with him. "The novelty of the medieval conception of eros consists in this discovery," Agamben writes. "[This medieval conception] pushes the consequences of the link between desire and fantasy to an extreme which antiquity had merely foreshadowed" (*Stanzas*, 82; translation slightly modified).

I might well have referred to the chapter in *Stanzas* called "Eros at the Mirror" when I discussed the "dessaisissement des objets" as night approaches, in Roubaud's "Jusque dans la nuit." And again, when I emphasized the way things gradually shed their particular attributes in the twilight, before the contemplative gaze of the speaker, till they appear all but nude—sheer forms, bare of material accidents. For Agamben, citing Avicenna, comments at length on this "disrobing." While neither the senses nor the imagination "strip the sensible form completely," the "estimative power" does, he writes. And from this disrobing process the estimative power or "inner sense" apprehends the phantasm's "insensible intentions," such as goodness or malice, suitability or incongruity.

> It is only when the process of the internal sense is completed that the rational soul can be informed by the completely denuded phantasm: in the act of intellection, the form is nude and 'if it were not nude, nevertheless it would become so, because the contemplative virtue strips it such that no material affection remains in it.' (*Stanzas*, 79)

In fact, it was from Agamben (again from *Stanzas*) that I gleaned my sole knowledge of the process, which I mentioned earlier in connection with bare forms in Roubaud, whereby medieval psychology understood the immaterial form of the beloved to enter the eye of the lover and to dwell there, an image reflected on the eye's watery surface.

When Narcissus appears in "Eros at the Mirror" it is not as a figure of extravagant self-love (as modern psychology would have it), but rather as an exemplary paradigm of *fin'amors*, love of an image. *And*, at the same time—in a polarity that, according to Agamben, characterizes the psychological wisdom of the Middle Ages—as a perfect example of love gone mad. Of *fol amour* that "shatters the phantasmatic circle in the attempt to appropriate the image as if it were a real creature" (*Stanzas*, 83). Remember "l'interdit de la vitre" in Roubaud.[22]

IMAGE D'IMAGES

Eros mélancolique, the novel that features young Mr. Goodman's photography research, is a love story and a ghost story. It is set in Paris, in the 1960s. A reader comes to wonder, though, whether the streets and squares, apartment buildings, shops and cafés where the action unfolds have not been recently constructed over top of another city, the Paris of the early 1940s, now emptied, covered with dust, abandoned like the uninhabited room Goodman happens to discover just behind the inside wall of his sublet. A whole family hid there once, the concierge recalls. They all disappeared. There are footprints in the dust when Goodman looks in. Who can have returned, and made these prints?

I only mean to indicate that Goodman's fellowship year seems to unfold on the near side of a thin partition between Paris in the '60s and occupied Paris (with its risky hiding places and meeting places, its secret doors and passageways, its coded messages, its rumors, betrayals, acts of vengeance). Goodman spends his year of research just at the edge of the world of his dead. Stray recollections emerge from it. Old grudges, faded legends. Mysterious footprints and muffled voices also multiply in the normal course of Goodman's everyday life (errands at the bakery or the post office, encounters with the concierge, visits to the dry cleaner). But I do not mean entirely to forget, in this context, the "nonvisible" that Hocquard says resides in all perceptions, and the unthought left over in every thought, and their "return," though they have never been present. "Revenante(s) inhabituelles," "strange visitations."

The love story in *Eros mélancolique*, which is also a ghost story (unfolding slowly as the feast of All Souls approaches), tells how Goodman constructs an elaborate assemblage of images—I am referring, of course, to the second part of his Project (the first being the Mémoire). I have already stressed that this undertaking is an image composed of many other images—pictures of glass panes showing through other panes, with reflected reflections—and I have mentioned Goodman's calling it a quest: a time quest, or a hunt like Lewis Carroll's for the snark. If I now describe the project a little more fully (still without providing much more than an approximation), it is in order to suggest a parallel: between the web of strict constraints that govern its composition, and the strict devotional ritual that a religious quest might demand, or that a courtly lady might dictate. At the same time I mean to reiterate the idea of a formal art that would constitute a sort of spell for summoning a being not of this world, or of any. For capturing it. This device, so to speak, would comprise a kind of phantasmatic circle. It could be a poem or sequence of poems able to hold within it not, perhaps, "l'absente"—not "l'absente de tout poème"—but something like its shadow. An intricate composition of images might just snag in its inner lining the shadow of a worldless being. And this shade might be something like the "forme" that began to show, in the lower-left corner of a solitary window in *Echanges de la lumière* before night swallowed it. Or it might relate to the other shape that started to appear against the square of wall reflected in a mirror in "la photo de Fez," before daylight erased it.

But I should mention also that when Roubaud refers to Goodman's "principles of composition"—his complex "system of constraints"—as a "cahier de charges" (*Eros mélancolique*, 293), he immediately brings Georges Perec to mind, and the famous "cahier de charges" that Perec published along with *La vie mode d'emploi*. Although this is not where the emphasis lies in my own reading of *Eros mélancolique*, let me observe that the disappearance at the center of Goodman's project, and the insistently repeating words *disappear, disappeared, disappearance* in Roubaud's novel, link it still more tightly to Perec—to Perec's *La disparition*, and to the story of his family during World War II. One might think of *Eros mélancolique* as a sort of ritual attempt by Roubaud to recover his friend Perec's lineage, or to offer a kind of afterlife to *La vie mode d'emploi*, the way his short narrative *Voyage d'hier* provides a sequel to Perec's brief *Voyage d'hiver*—a sequel in which great wrongs recounted in and inflicted on the initial text are righted and great losses compensated.

In any case, the rules governing the composition of Goodman's photo montage involve two coordinating grids that he regularly consults. Between them they assign to every shot in the eventual composite image of images two numbers, one indicating the date and hour of day it is to be taken, and the other the portion of the wall with its windows opposite Goodman's apartment that it will include within its frame. Goodman does not plan to pan right across the facing wall in a series of shots taken every day at the same time (through the windows of his own apartment). He has conceived a more complex pattern that will only come into sight slowly, as the project itself proceeds. The construction of the whole thing is designed to take up a specific period of time—the time remaining to Goodman in his sublet—and it also has its own time: its own calendar, its own weeks and days, which do not correspond exactly to those that measure the time outside in Paris. That is to say, it has its own numbered, counted time, like a poem.

Its meter is not so different after all from the apparently arbitrary rhythm of the other, much more agitated photographer in *Eros mélancolique* who, in a last ditch effort to capture the farawayness of his beloved, presses the button of his digital camera again every time he comes to the end of a line in the poem that he recites to himself while looking off into space.

This photographer thinks it must be pure repetition, "la pure répétition rythmique des instants" (28), in league with the sightless indifference of his camera, that surprised the flight of the woman he loved, and drew her remoteness near. I doubt it captured anyone or anything actually existing anywhere, but rather the secret object of the photographer's desire. Or at least its approach—the paradoxical approach, I mean, of the woman's unreachableness. *Amour de loin.*

"La pure répétition," an interesting expression, brings to mind the odd idea of a repetition that would not repeat anything else ("pas souvenir *de*," as Hocquard puts it, "mais souvenir sans objet").

> [...]Présence qui
> revient, sous-jacente, dans la chambre noire.

But if you think of "pure repetition" as repeating nothing save *itself*—repetitions of repetitions—you might think of it in connection with Goodman's images of windows seen through windows, seen through his two cameras' viewfinders. You might recall his enchantment with light reflected, refracted, condensed, from room to room, pane to pane, "répétitions de la lumière comme celles de la musique." Or again you could think once more of the "photo de Fez"—the photographic image of the mirror image of a rectangular patch of wall. Moreover, you might recall another of the principal ideas Goodman planned to bring out in his Mémoire: the one bearing on printing and prints. "Photography, the writing of light, is in fact the pendant, the analogue of printing. To photograph is to print with light" (208). And this might cause Goodman's photos to enter, in one's mind, into a relation with other prints in the world around him—especially the unattributable footprints and fingerprints that contribute to the novel's mystery. Prints, but whose? Traces, but of what?

As if in order to keep this "theme"—pure repetition—hovering in the middle distance, *Eros mélancolique* proposes here and there a few mild jokes about copies and imitations such as one about the Mona Lisa by E. Mérou. This picture of a picture hangs in a café on the corner of la rue de la Rochefoucauld and la rue Notre-Dame-de-Lorette where it presides over a tense tryst between

Goodman and an enigmatic young woman (apparently *it* is not enigmatic at all [see *Eros mélancolique*, 235]). Or again—as if the novel just wanted to sustain the thought, as its plot unfolds, of something like a "phantasmatic circle"— garland of images, coil of traces, echo fugue—there is the voice Goodman overhears on a train, which sounds exactly like the voice of a character in a movie, the poacher in *La règle du jeu*. Goodman concludes that someone is ingeniously imitating the actor, Carette, who played the poacher in the film. But then the train comes to a stop and the imitator of Carette gets off, so Goodman can see him, and it *is* Carette (sounding like someone sounding like him sounding like another). More dramatically, there is the photo that Goodman eventually takes, late in the novel, of the mysterious, the silent young woman who visits him in his apartment. While she sleeps alone in his bedroom, he photographs, with his back to her, the reflection of her nakedness as it appears in a mirror hanging in his sitting room.

His entire existence at this point in his Paris year has become determined by the strict daily and nightly requirements of his project quest, on the one hand, and by the harsh, arbitrary rules that the mysterious woman who has come into his life lays down as conditions for their rare meetings, on the other. All this suggests the intensity of his determination to win an ever-so-unlikely prize by dint of extreme patience and prudence. I think it also suggests an intensive campaign to solve a mystery. For Goodman's elaborate rules, and the two grids on which he lays them out for regular consultation remind me of "la table des contraintes" behind '*le grand incendie de londres*': Roubaud's own "cahier de charges," that is. He lays out the rigorous system of constraints informing his novel in the middle of its first branch, and defines it as "the grid for the mystery's elucidation" (*The Great Fire*, 166/*Le grand incendie*, 220).

Dread, though, must be present always for Goodman, like the "forebodings of disaster I could barely endure" that intrude on Roubaud's almost-happiness as he contemplates the unnatural world at twilight, shedding its vestments, its accidental attributes, and appearing all but naked, unqualified, an assembly of sheer forms, save for the "opacité sombre" they withhold. Love's abyss. Its secret, its forbidden object, lodged as disaster in the elaborate play of reflections—in the musical repetition of light. There light stops—"là où tu deviens noire." There it withdraws into itself, into its black. Just so, the person of the mysterious young woman in Goodman's life communicates to him—when she allows him to look at her at all—the brutal disappearance that he senses in all photographs. "He suddenly had the impression that she was going to disappear. There was something unreal in her immobility" (*Eros mélancolique*, 243).

Of all the terrifying photos Goodman has encountered the worst is the most precious. It is a photo of *before*. Before his birth. It shows his mother as a young girl, and is the only image he possesses of her. She, or someone, wrote on the photo the name of the island on which it was taken, Sark, and added, jokingly, "or Snark?" Her son is reminded, long after her disappearance, of the Snark called Boojum. Then a white streak appears on some of his negatives as he develops them. A form starting to show? "La trace d'une forme?" (214). He can't account for it. He can't figure out what fleeting shadow this stain can possibly be the record of. Nor can the reader make out what relation it may bear to the strange young woman inflaming his desire and subjecting him to her extravagant rules. Or to the woman (her double? she herself?) whom Goodman comes dimly to observe at night moving about in a room in one of the empty flats opposite his own. Finally, he just calls the white streak a material trace with no material cause. A blotch, in any case. It wrecks his project and leaves him inconsolable. "I give up," he states, in English. This is where *Eros mélancolique* ends—with passages titled "Nuits," and again "Nuits," and "Nuit," and "La Déréliction." This is how the novel ends, if you can attribute an ending at all to a book whose two authors, Roubaud and Anne Garréta, present as the remains of an unknown person's abandoned project, incomplete, adrift in cyberspace.

From this perspective one can picture it among the other lost and mutilated books in Roubaud's oeuvre—objects, sometimes, of quests or investigations. In *Parc sauvage* one such book is recovered.

Parc sauvage[23] is among the three or four versions that exist, in Roubaud's writing, of the Provençal childhood that James Goodman forgot. The lost book, retrieved at last in *Parc sauvage*, is the diary of a child, Dora, who seems to have hidden for part of the war in a vineyard called Sainte Lucie at the foot of the Pyrenees with Goodman, James Goodman (known then as Jacques, or Bonhomme Jacques). Her mother's name, Raymonde, is the name that the mysterious young woman in *Eros mélancolique* writes down for Goodman. The diary disappeared when Dora did, in 1944. Nearly fifty years later it comes to light, discovered among some old papers dating back to the war, by the new proprietors of Sainte Lucie. Goodman, whom they manage to contact at St. Andrews College in Scotland, reads the pages slowly, one after the other—including the "geometric messages" Dora inscribed at the end of each day's entry ("paroles obscures," like Merlin's, is my impression). One of these appears at the end of a description of an afternoon that Dora spent dreaming (instead of keeping score at Jacques's tennis match). She dreamed of the mysterious journey to Spain that she was waiting to take—of Guadalquivir and the Alhambra, and of her mother waiting for her there. Jacques had given her a shake when his match was finished, asking, "Tu dors?"

At the end of her journal entry describing that afternoon, Dora added, on a line all its own, "sainte lucie sainte lance lueurs silence heures saintes" (*Parc sauvage*, 55)—which reminds one of Percival, his strange vision of lance and chalice, his silence, and "la question muette." It reminds one as well of the table set outside in the sunshine when Jacques Roubaud was a child, of the gleaming plates and glassware, and of Jean-René's nap inside, upstairs in the house whence Roubaud remembers hearing this question (this "piège logique"): "Tu dors?" And the naive voice that answered "Oui."

In 1992, Mr. Goodman ("Goodman, James"), reading Dora's recovered book page by page all the way to the end, remembers. On the last page he adds a geometric message of his own, in "the language which had become his": "tears at rest."

So, one way of understanding *Eros mélancolique* might be to think of it among the various lost books in Roubaud's oeuvre, or as one variant among others of a single lost book, or as one among other remnants of *before*—one of many, more or less similar recollections that trails off eventually into nothing, like some of the detours stumbled along by the errant knights of the Round Table. But we might also link *Eros mélancolique* a little more specifically with the "place of the dream." The place of the boy Jean-René's dream, perhaps, upstairs *in the house* just behind the family lunch table set outside in the sun. And with the place of Jacques Roubaud's dream too: "dans cette maison." For "in that house" is the name of "le lieu du rêve," we learn, in the fifth chapter of *Le grand incendie*—that long, technical development bearing on the dream at the origin of his lifetime project; on the dream, the decision it commanded, and the project itself.

"Dans cette maison" names "the place of the dream" that Roubaud dreamed soon after Jean-René's suicide; he awoke from it knowing, you will recall, that he had a project, that it would include a novel, and the novel's title. In that odd title the dream says something about its place, Roubaud asserts: through its title the novel looks into the dream's interior and translates from the silence of the dream's language (*Le grand incendie*, 174/ *The Great Fire*, 130).

Later, in Roubaud's ninety-third "assertion" bearing on the dream, the decision and the project, we learn that the name of the dream's place is "l'appartement de Coxeter."

> 'Dans cette maison,' le silence; et son nom: *l'appartement de Coxeter.*
>
> (*Le grand incendie*, 208)

> 'In this house,' silence; and its name, *Coxeter apartment.*
>
> (*The Great Fire*, 157)

Coxeter is the name of the young man from whom Goodman, in *Eros mélancolique*, sublets his Paris apartment. He seems to be a promising art historian; his library suggests he shares certain enthusiasms of Goodman's: photography, for example, and the paintings of Constable. In any event, "l'appartement de Coxeter" is the name of the place, so favorable to the play of light, where Goodman undertakes his doomed photo project and its accompanying Mémoire. We might associate the tattered remnants called *Eros mélancolique* by Roubaud and Garréta very closely, then, with the unsayable thing: with the mute question, "question sans question." With the interior of a dream and the silence that dwells there, the silent language of the dream, saying what cannot be and is not said.

Coxeter is also the name of a mathematician, one of the greatest geometers of the twentieth century, Harold Scott MacDonald Coxeter, 1907-2003. In his field of non-Euclidian geometry, a "building" is a combinatorial and geometric structure composed of subcomplexes called "apartments." Every "apartment" in a "building" is a "Coxeter complex." So a hint of complex mathematical composition inhabits the apartment where Goodman assembles his image of images. Perhaps math left some faint prints there, similar to other mysterious traces of past residents in the building.

Indeed, it seems that mathematics might have had a part in the novel that Roubaud was to have written (accompanying his poetry Project, recounting it). For we learn, again in the fifth chapter le *Le grand incendie*, that because the "enigma" fell (because the "self-riddle," the "form" that incited the poetry Project collapsed), the role that would have been poetry's in Roubaud's novel passed to prose (and the "enigma," as we've gathered, gave way to a "mystery"). Poetry marks the novel, but by lacking, Roubaud states ("elle marque et manque"). Had it retained its role, which was the role of memory, it would have inscribed itself in and as rhythm, via mathematics. But prose took away from poetry the mathematical character of poetic constraints, and inclined poetry toward another mode, the mode of absence (*Le grand incendie*, 206-7/ *The Great Fire*, 155-56).

> Le silence de la mathématique jusqu'au fond de la langue, poésie.
>
> (*Le grand incendie*, 207)

> The silence of mathematics deep into the very heart of language, poetry.
> (*The Great Fire*, 156)

It is as if the departure from Paris of the young man named Coxeter in *Eros mélancolique*, for a six-month period of art-historical research in California, and the consequent availability of his Paris apartment, which he offers to sublet to Goodman, were a discreet signal that mathematics has been removed from the scene, as it were, leaving a quest, a memory quest, to the prose of a novel. Or again, perhaps we should surmise that in the face of prose, math withdrew, into the depths of language, like light itself when it quits the world, receding into its own black beauty. Or maybe math drew back into the interior of Goodman's dream, into the silent language of the dream, poetry. Then perhaps Goodman's story might be thought to bear the print of a disappearance the way '*le grand incendie de Londres*' carries the mark of poetry's absence.

One other related idea about *Eros mélancolique* presents itself. I have suggested that this novel could be regarded as one among several lost books in Roubaud's universe, or as one among many, more or less similar remnants of a single, imperfectly remembered tale (one among a number of troubled, muddled dreams of *before*); but it might also be a *key*. "And I saw at last that the key was photographic, the writing of light" (*The Great Fire*, 148/*Le grand incendie*, 197). *Eros mélancolique*, with its photography emphasis, might even be *the* key: the key to the enigma at the heart of the poetry Project, whose intractableness destined the novel, and indeed Roubaud's entire twofold life work to failure. *Eros mélancolique* could be the solution to the mute question, the self-riddle, beyond even asking, much less answering. Or no: it might be the key not to the enigma itself, but rather to the "mystery," which is the shadow or the "image of the enigma," and inhabits the novel, '*le grand incendie de Londres*.' For the novel *shows*, Roubaud explains—in images—what the poetry Project says, in silence. And the enigma's image has a place, he writes: it is a room ("une chambre"). This *room* is the inverse of a *moor*, a heath, a wasteland. The novel—*Le Grand Incendie de Londres*, had it ever been written—would have described and named this room: "L'appartement de Coxeter" (197/148). *Eros mélancolique* could be the key, then, to writing *Le Grand Incendie de Londres*.

If so, it would be a key resembling the prophesies of Merlin, which never mean anything until it is too late to matter. "I saw at last that the key was photographic," Roubaud writes; "I saw it in the end, too late" (148/197). It is as if in *Eros mélancolique* he had retrieved, when they can no longer amount to anything, several (tattered) elements of the plan that would have led to the completion of his derailed novel. They are hardly foreign to the wide, rich, doomed world of the many books he did write. They belong to that world, they are implied in the intricate, faulty configuration of the whole, which seems thus to hold within it its potential redemption. They seem to be woven into its fabric, but in such a way that it is impossible to recognize them in time, and impossible for them to solve or save anything at all.

8

Diaphanous

Photography by Night

I have mentioned the photograph of dark cypress trees taken by Alix Roubaud on a moonless night in the Minervois. I noted the very long exposure of the film to the faint light of the stars, the slight movement of the camera on her chest and the narrow fringe of haze that appeared at the edges of the trees. It was a sort of vacillation around their contours where, as Roubaud puts it, the dim starlight hesitated to stamp an image. "The boundary of [each] tree's body dissolves; the minutes, passing, alter it." Roubaud suggests that the blurred margin reveals the merging and diverging of each tree's differences and similarities with itself as it stands there through a span of time: the weave of separate cypresses overlapping, penetrating, infringing on each other where each single cypress stands alone. An effect ordinarily invisible to us (we never see the passage of time, only one instant, then another and so on).

But there is an additional aspect to Roubaud's description of the cypress photo: "a stranger and perhaps still more revealing side-effect," he says, of the dim light, the long exposure, the gentle rise and fall of the camera. It is that "each cypress seems to be duplicated" (*The Great Fire*, 314/*Le grand incendie*, 403). Each tree in the photo is accompanied by a gray double, standing very close to it. This cannot be described as a mirror image, Roubaud says: "between them there is no mirror, no reflecting surface." The gray shape at the side of each black cypress is "a diaphanous double," "un double, diaphane."

Roubaud begins his description of the trees, and the night the photo was taken, and the photo itself, by stressing the cypress-blackness. And also the inwardness of the trees standing so uncompromisingly erect in their straight rows on his parents' country property. Black candles, he says; flames of smoke, burning into themselves.

> Even by day each cypress was a column of burning black air, a black body even in daytime, and even in daylight each radiates self-inwardly, like the flame, itself self-absorbed, toward an internal ravagement of air.
>
> (*The Great Fire*, 310/*Le grand incendie*, 398).

They were visible by day on account of their very darkness, "excessive obscurité," for they were all blacker than the black of the mountains in the distance. Yet they seemed to defy the gaze. "[I]t didn't appear possible to show them" (*The Great Fire*, 310/*Le grand incendie*, 398). And by night, each was still more obscure. "In the darkness each cypress is even darker, a double darkness against the dark sealing the black night within its shape [sa forme]: each becomes the epitome of blackness" (*The Great Fire*, 313/*Le grand incendie*, 402).

> The "cypress thing," "black thing."
>
> (*The Great Fire*, 313/*Le grand incendie*, 402-3)

In the photograph, however, the black forms of the trees blur. Their strict, straight contours erode. Each "form-body" loses the substance—that is to say, the darkness—that it encloses. "Du cyprès"—some cypress, that is: a bit of cypressness—seeps out into the surrounding night air, making a gray fringe around the edges of each tree. Roubaud calls it the "diaphanous emanation" of each cypress's "being-black" (of each one's "être-noir," "forme noire").

The blackness then, of each tree bears alongside it, very close, its translucent double. This gossamer twin is invisible by day. But everything—every object and being—has one. It cannot be discovered by a torch or flashlight, the intervention of some bright shaft of light. Rather, weak light, like that of distant stars, persisting for a long time right up against the face of a thing, brings this fringe of haze into view. Relieved of their sharp contours, released from their identity, each dark tree in Alix Roubaud's photo shows an aura around its edges. A halo, Roubaud suggests. Or an angel. "The angel of form, the formal angel" (*The Great Fire*, 314/*Le grand incendie*, 403). The scarcely measurable gap between form and itself, just to the side of itself. A blur. "The angel of blackness" (*The Great Fire*, 315/*Le grand incendie*, 405).

Not Quite in Focus

This blur could be understood, I believe, as a slim border of uncertainty, required by Roubaud, perhaps, in order not to sink. A margin of doubt, disturbing the sharp contours of things, their infallible identity. Holding in abeyance "*l'infaillible* absence qui absorbe toute chose."

When he adopts and adapts concepts developed by other thinkers and writers, his purpose, as I see it, is often to get some help installing an "infime écart" comparable to the one between form and itself. The point is to introduce a little breathing space, some fine distinction or other that could loosen the hold on us of more familiar juxtapositions and forestall apparently inevitable conclusions. Such a margin could create, for example, a little leeway for something not to be absolutely itself—not to be identical, not to be pure—but not on that account to be any other than just what it is. Or again, such a slim border of haze might be able to preserve a distinction between what is said when nothing is, and nothing. I mean to suggest that Roubaud takes an interest in modes of thought that could, for instance, conceive of something's not not being said. Not being said, exactly, but not quite not, either. Or that could accommodate something's not being itself, exactly, but not other, either. Nicholas of Cusa's "Way of Double Negation" is a help in this regard, especially his notion of "not-not" or "not-other." "Le Pas-Autre," "li non Aliud." Roubaud associates this learned prevarication with an invisible black angel: the angel of a thing's definition. Of its identity. An indefinite blur, a fringe of haze, invisible but "infinitely near," adhering to the visage of the definite, the defined. "[C]ollé au visage du défini" (*La Boucle*, 229/*The Loop*, 212).

All of which suggests that modes of thought not obedient to the law of non-contradiction are inviting to Roubaud. He says he has been told that Chinese is a language that distinguishes easily between the negation of something and its contrary. The theory of Lawvere-Heyting is, I gather, intriguing to him for a similar reason (*La pluralité des mondes*, 73/73). I turn again here, though, to Giorgio Agamben, after a brief digression on Hocquard.

Not Other

I suppose that Hocquard is referring to *li non Aliud*, via Roubaud, when he writes, in *Conditions de lumière* (174),

> Possibilité de ne pas être
> comme tu n'es pas C'est-à dire
> non autre
>
> The possibility of not being
> as you are not That is
> none other   (*Conditions of Light*, 174)

Probably he has Agamben in mind as well, for the possibility to not be ("possibilité de ne pas être . . .") sounds like the capacity for impotence brought out in Aristotle by Agamben. "Beings that exist in the mode of potentiality," Agamben writes, "are capable of their own impotentiality. [. . .] They can be because they are in relation to their own non-Being" (*Potentialities*, 182).

It is common to assume that a potential is an unactualized possibility: potentiality is a possible, if not yet realized, actuality. But Agamben (as I observed earlier) proposes that potentiality is also a possible nonrealization: the ability not to be actualized. Moreover, each of these potentials is necessarily in relation to the other ("beings that exist in the mode of potentiality are capable of their own impotentiality; they can be because they are in relation to their own non-Being"). I expect that Hocquard, writing "possibility to not be / the way you are not," is trying out this Agamben manner of articulating—and elaborating a bit on—his own thought about the *not*-being that *is* at the heart of a tautology: the term that is *is not*.

Moreover, he seems to have his own word for the *relation* Agamaben speaks of, the relation between the potential *to* . . . and the potential *to not*. It appears Hocquard has his own name for the relation to incapacity that capable beings depend on (the relation to their own non-Being on which they rely). For he notes, in *Méditations photographiques* (39), that a third term, "un moyen terme," is required between "puissance" and "latence": between power, I gather, and its nonrealization. Between the ability to do something, and the ability to not. An in-between term is necessary in order that the two reveal each other, without ever agreeing and without either one's becoming an attribute of the other. As I take it, an intermediary term is needed between a capacity and the lack or the deprivation thereof, in order for each to be exposed as the other. In order for *is* and *is not* to surprise each other, I think. For *is not* all of a sudden to be, I mean, and for *is* abruptly not to.

Hocquard's "moyen terme" is *nudité*.

Nudity is his word for the neutral terrain between power and impotence; it names the margin of separation that being, and not, have in common—the "tache blanche" or blank spot they share the way humans and falcons share the city of Paris (or Hocquard and Michael Palmer share the terrain opened up by translation). Nudity names the no-man's-land they cohabit without any connection whatsoever. Nakedness is the milieu, the medium—it is the "distance"—of this relation.

Fuzzy

We have observed how Roubaud sometimes seems to dwell on one or the other of two opposite dilemmas that plague his conception of poetry. On the one hand, there is his conviction that poetry is form: not the form of this or that, just form, its own. (It doesn't say anything; it doesn't say this, or that, it just says, by saying.) Its form—its sheer identicalness—is that of the self-enigma, mute question, riddleless riddle, which falls. We thought we recognized this poetry-form, moreover, in the thought that that same thought is true, or false. In order to be a thought at all, as we saw, that thought must be the thought, on some particular occasion, of something *else* that's true, or not. But it baulks. It just wants to be the true thought of itself. Impossible.

This implies that form can only be apprehended via some regrettable adulteration: some mode or manner that it happens to assume on some specific occasion, when it is the form of this, or of that. Apparently—as I suggested earlier—it can never be perceived at all save thanks to a lingering remnant of something *else* still clinging to it. "Whether it be truly infinite," we encountered Roubaud saying of "form"—in "Idée de la forme"—"whether it be truly infinite or simply beyond my reach, I cannot behold it but asquint, upon a vestige, a delayed effect, a garment, a reversal, a mirror . . ." (*The Plurality of Worlds*, 69/*La pluralité*, 69). Wherever form is perceptible it is impure; it always brings with it some extrinsic effect, the random quirk or smudge of something else—some stray, accidental formless element improper to it.

Sometimes, on the other hand, Roubaud describes a kind of visionary experience, as in "Jusque dans la nuit" (*La pluralité des mondes*, 63-68/*The Plurality*, 63-68), where we have already watched daylight receding, objects gradually shedding their attributes, putting aside their daytime robes, those singular features of their particularity, their being this thing or that ("parfum de leur *haeccéité*"), and appearing nude, in their pure, unqualified essence. They are revealed, I imagine, to themselves by themselves alone, or almost—with barely tolerable dread hovering over them, horrid premonition of their brutal disappearance. They are going to black.

In pages from *The Coming Community* that Roubaud borrows in his own way, Agamben speaks of beings he calls "whatever beings," which rather than *having* qualities—rather than possessing attributes, particular properties—*are* their attributes, their manner of being.[1] They *are* their *thus*, Agamben writes; they are the *way* they are.[2] This means they have no essence that would undergo qualifications, for they *are* their qualities. They have no ideal form that particular features would modify. They *are* modes, dispositions. But this is not to say that their singular characteristics, their manners of being are proper to them, not if by this one means that these characteristics are traits serving to identify them. No. "Whatever beings" have no identity. Rather, the way they are is the improperness proper to them: they are the improper ways they are; indeed, they are the impropriety of their being—the unseemliness, if you will, of their existing at all.

So Roubaud's painful *either/or* gives way, thanks partly to Agamben, to a different kind of distinction. Roubaud seems to fear that either form's sole appearance is adulterated, *or else* that it approaches the self-illumination that quits the world and gives itself to invisibility. However, if form cannot declare itself without also declaring *l'informe*, the two are not separate, he writes, in "Idée de la forme." Nor are they quite the same, quite indistinct. For form—I believe he is thinking—form, like Agamben's "whatever being," *is* its way of appearing, its improper way: form is its adulterated manner of taking place in the world. And when it does, it shows that it does, which is to say it shows that to show is its way: that to appear in this world is its secret, inner determination. Taking place here—"[dans] ce monde flottant, ce monde faillible, ce monde planche pourrie," as Roubaud writes elsewhere[3]—taking place in this lousy world, and showing that it does, form exposes its interior law of outwardness, its inner exteriority. Its private publicness, if you will. Let me quote the passage I have in mind.

> Car la forme ne peut se déclarer elle-même sans déclarer aussi l'informe, qui pourtant n'est pas séparé d'elle ni renvoyé à un autre lieu: au contraire, la forme ne peut que donner lieu à l'informe, qu'exposer, secrète, intérieure, son impropriété.
>
> ("Idée de la forme," in *La pluralité des mondes*, 69)

> For form cannot declare itself without also declaring the formless, which, however, is not separate from it nor relegated to another place: on the contrary, form cannot but give rise to the formless, cannot but expose its secret inner impropriety.
>
> ("The Idea of Form," in *The Plurality of Worlds*, 69)

This exposure by form of its inner outwardness is one of several ways Roubaud has of suggesting a tiny movement by form apart from itself. Form stirs, he sometimes writes. "Bouge." Which also means—especially in a photography context—*blurs*. Form vacillates ever so slightly, and *is* this thin fringe of doubtfulness, a haze. The dissolving borders of the cypress trees in Alix Roubaud's photograph.

It happens that just after "C'est à-dire non autre," in the small text beginning "Possibilité de ne pas être," which I have been picturing as a poem about *li non Aliud*, Hocquard writes: "Arroser les fèves / avant la pluie." "Water the beans / before the rain." This useless bit of gardening contributed to my associating the not-other and the "tache blanche," white patch, because unsuitability for use or development of any kind is one of the virtues of Hocquard's blank spots. Of his in-between margins. "Fausses propriétés." Moreover he writes elsewhere, "nudity serves no purpose. That is its utility" (*Méditations*, 46). Nudity's utility lies in floating "à part," a nonlieu, grounds for nothing. Not for a trial, a judgment or for any development at all, just a fog of breath off to the side, a cloudy margin along the edge of being. Here is the entire "elegy" :

> Possibilité de ne pas être
> comme tu n'es pas   C'est-à-dire
> non autre   Arroser les fèves
> avant la pluie
>   Respiration à part   (*Conditions de lumière*, 174).
>
> The possibility of not being
> as you are not   That is
> none other   Water the beans
> before the rain
>   Breathing aside   (*Conditions of Light*, 174)

Beispiel

Agamben associates the fuzzy margin where, for Roubaud, form stirs, with a small "gap" between the general and the particular, the common and the proper noun, where exemplary being, as he puts it, lives its purely linguistic life. "Exemplary being" means a being that is one in particular among all the other particular beings for which it *also* stands in general. I picture "exemplary being" relieving thought of a familiar burden. Just as "whatever being" mercifully removes the weight of the seemingly inescapable opposition between essence and accident (between form and mode or disposition), so "exemplary being" lightens the opposition between general and particular, universal and singular.

For "exemplary being" lives in between, on the border. At the wavering, intermediate edge. *Beispiel*, German for *example*, means a bit of slack or give, Agamben reminds us: some *play*, just off to the side. At the frontier, we might think, between the general and the particular. This *spiel* may have suggested to Roubaud a hesitant, shuttling motion, a vacillating margin where, as he writes in "Idée de la forme," the "demarcation" between "the assembled tribe of cypresses," contemplated at dusk, and the "singular line of each tree's presence" recedes, and lets the "passage" show instead: the passage back and forth between general and particular, "la tribu commune" and the specific traits of every single tree.

Relations between distinct specificity, fixed within exact contours and, on the other hand, a certain indefiniteness, preoccupy Roubaud, as we have observed. The seven separate black hats, for example, on the heads of seven small figures fishing on a riverbank by a mill in a landscape by Constable—and, on the other hand, the wide, cloudy sky above in the same painting, or the mottled, shapeless clouds in Constable's cloud studies. How to draw distinct, fixed specificity and shapeless, mutating vapor into a *composition*? Similarly, how to combine the ever-moving variability of clouds with the formal distinctions among them articulated by Luke Howard? These are among the questions in Roubaud's *Ciel et terre et ciel et terre et ciel*, which features Mr. Goodman in middle age when—a recent widower paralyzed by grief, but also moved by unexpected stirrings of his memory—he turns his attention from the study of crystals (his professional specialty) to the study of clouds.

Goodman's fellow photographer in *Eros mélancolique* comes to mind in this connection too: I mean the image-maker only very briefly present in the novel who seems to glimpse at last his heart's desire, the face of his beloved, when he contemplates the many photographic images he has taken of her—distractedly, arbitrarily, simply pushing the button on the camera again and again—as they float and fade, one after another after another, drifting by across his computer screen. He never could remember her face distinctly enough when she was absent nor could he even quite see it when he was with her (she was too flighty, changeable). He suffered from this. But perhaps the glide across his screen of multiple images (echos, repeats, with slight variations, of each other) allowed him to perceive the shifting modes and moods whereby a singular existence is "individuated." For the passage, according to Agamben, from the general conformation of a human face, say, to *this* beloved countenance, doesn't happen punctually, but in a shuttling, weaving movement—in a manner we might compare to the way clouds approach and diverge from the forms (cumulus, cirrus . . .) with which they never coincide exactly but whose movement they are.

The life of "exemplary being" is linguistic for Agamben (it is "a life lived in language") because it is the life of any being bearing a name. For what is a name if not just this continuous weaving between common and singular, between what Roubaud calls "l'indication intellectuelle" and "l'absorption stupéfaite, gourde." The name is a sort of hesitation between common and singular, between the concept of a thing—an abstraction, a category—and, on the other hand, the thing's absolute singularity: incomparable, identical, swallowed up into itself, numb, dumb. Note that what matters here, in the quivering blur—where Agamben says "exemplary being" lives its life as a being that is named—is not any given name. It is by no means a matter here of a being that is identified with its own proper name. What counts is just the condition of being named: just the fact of having some name or another, having a life in language. Beings that dwell and communicate in "the empty space of the example" belong to no class, no set; they are tied to no common property. They are "expropriated," Agamben writes, of all identity, "so as to appropriate belonging itself, the sign ∈" (*The Coming Community*, 10.1).[4]

"Le maintenant de la poésie"

"Poems stand or fall as they are," Roubaud writes, using the English expression and underlining it (*Poetry etcetera*, 117/*Poésie etcetera*, 115). This is the sense of the axiom "Poetry is NOW": every poem is *as* it is; each is just *the way* it is, at "every now that occurs."

It is not especially important to know when a given poem was composed, whether it belongs to an ancient tradition or is an avant-garde experiment. The *Odyssey*, the *Divine Comedy*, Mallarmé's famous sonnet beginning "Le vierge le vivace et le bel aujourd'hui," Queneau's *Petite Cosmogonie Portative* and ÉTAT by Anne-Marie Albiach are all "now": they are all "poems of now" (*Poetry, etcetera*, 117/*Poésie, etcetera*, 115). There is no need to bring them closer to us via commentary, translation, or modernized spelling. No such operations are likely to make them more successful or less; they stand or fall *as they are* whenever they are read or spoken. In silence by a shepherd alone with his sheep, or out loud at a poetry reading in Binghamton, New York. They are the *way* they are on each particular occasion, at every single *now* that occurs. (*Poetry etcetera*, 117/*Poésie etcetera*, 115).

Form, we read in "The Idea of Form," has no past and no future; it is, rather, poetry's *thus*: form is the *way* poetry is in *this* poem, now. On this particular reading.

> Il ne lui est pas arrivé d'être ainsi (il n'y a pas de forme ancienne); il ne lui arrivera pas d'être ainsi (il n'y a pas de forme future): elle est ' ainsi, maintenant '; ' maintenant ' est la poésie.
>
> ("Idée de la forme," in *La pluralité des mondes*, 72)

> It has not happened to be thus (it has no anterior form); it will not happen to be thus (it has no future form); it is ' thus, now '; ' now ' is poetry.
>
> ("The Idea of Form," in *The Plurality of Worlds*, 72)

Form is the way poetry shows in the world—poetry that is worldless. Form stirs (*elle bouge*), the better to install, in its own minute discrepancy with itself, the now of poetry.

Again, form shifts a little to the side, and in the gap that Roubaud calls the "infinitely slim present," it lodges poetry's "maintenant."

> Dans le présent infiniment mince bouge la forme, pour mettre en place le ' maintenant ' de la poésie
>
> (*La pluralité*, 72)

> In the infinitely tenuous present, form moves to set up the ' now ' of poetry.
>
> (*The Plurality*, 72)

Remember "le deuil du présent." And "le mur du deuil." "Le présent, j'en suis persuadé," Roubaud wrote, "n'a pas de réalité."

But, one might think: there is a blur, where form shifts and clouds up, the better to set in place, in this shaded margin, poetry's "bel aujourd'hui." Beings having the possibility of privation can perceive this. For, able not only to see but also to not see, they can see shadows.

And yet, even as form hesitates, sliding ever so slightly apart from itself, and even while being passes its oscillating, fluctuating life in the word (belonging, but not to anything), the mute stupefaction of the absolutely singular, perfectly identical persists nearby. The demon of silence, Roubaud says, after Pseudo

Dionysius. I doubt he forgets the "à quoi bon?" demon either. The "formal angel" itself ("l'ange du noir") is a merchant of silence, "colporteur du silence." For form brings a dumb, impossible language up very close: "parole d'identité voulue abolie." "Here is its infernal inference: to come as near as possible to the demon of silence who *implores our help.* (Hence, in the guise of indifference, the modern terror of, and recoil from, poetry.)"

It does not say anything. It ' would prefer not to .'
(*La pluralité des mondes*, 72/*The Plurality*, 72)

There is no particular comfort in Roubaud's preserving form's tiny discrepancy, "infime écart" (*Le grand incendie*, 405/*The Great Fire*, 315) where "le 'maintenant' de la poésie" lodges. Nor is it especially edifying, but it is the only way, as he puts it, "la seule manière."

Donner des mondes en même temps et l'indication intellectuelle et l'absorption stupéfaite, gourde ne promet à la vue aucune avenue morale, à la descendance aucun ombrage, aux sentiments aucun secours étymologique.

Il n'en est pas moins vrai qu'elle [la forme] est la seule manière; et seul produit les exemplaires des choses, non leurs essences; par où elle évite les mômeries du sens, les catastrophes du message, comme les jongleries de la substitution. " *La manière est le nombre et l'état des choses, où chacune demeure telle qu'elle est.* "

(*La pluralité des mondes*, 71; the italicized quotation is from Agamben.)

To show, at the same time, both an intellectual awareness and a stupefied, dumb absorption of worlds does not promise moral avenues to sight, umbrage to descendants, or etymological support to sentiment.

For all that it is true that form is the only manner and alone produces samples of things, not essences; whereby it avoids the simpering of sense, the catastrophes of message, as well as the juggling of substitutions. " Manner is the number and state of things where each remains as it is. "

(*The Plurality*, 71)

Among the various "ways" that Roubaud has of being a poet, one follows the diaphanous edge of forms wherein everything has just room to be as is. At this hazy border winter silence always brushes up against song, and a dumbfounded language cannot be relegated to some other place. A verdant Mount Cicada points faithfully to its dismal brother mountain, and the season of love arrives in an inverse flower with petals of ice. *Le dreit nien* comes up close and stays. But it does not quite swallow up the song, for the opposites that infringe and intrude on each other and overlap and interweave are never reduced to the same. Indistinction never takes over for good. In this way Roubaud holds out against le fol amour, love itself-self, gouffre pur, le tout-rien. The possibility of privation just barely preserves, in the pale light of a snow-white sun, a margin that neither quite separates nor completely joins possible and impossible. Roubaud is an admirer of the troubadours who staked everything on keeping love unshadowed by death, its contrary. But for him the principle of noncontradiction does not really apply to poetry, and the close kinship he feels with medieval lyric is not quite so much with the poets of the "trobar leu," as with the harsher "trobar clu." His praise of light is dark, "un éloge inverse."

9

Entre Deux

Nueté

Let me recall the third term in between two others that Hocquard speaks of: the one in the middle of tautologies, which he compares to the inexpressible element at the midpoint of a bridge—or again the "moyen terme" required to spark a relation of indifference between two such that each takes the other by surprise. Each is unforeseeably discovered by the other. This happens now, you may recall, which is to say it hasn't happened, and it won't. It occurs in the instant that lacks, the blank spot in chronology, the cut or the hole. Now. Nudity is this accident. It's the good, or bad stroke of luck—the necessary "moyen terme," in any event—for the instantaneous, reciprocal exchange between two. Nakedness is the medium, "le médium neutre," of a relation of sheer astonishment. Amazement's neutral element—rapture's bath, you might think, remembering Anne Portugal and Susannah. And indeed, it is while writing about those two (Portugal and Susannah) that Pierre Alferi says poetry is neither high nor low and bears neither on first things nor last: it is just medium. "Un médium plus diaphane que tous les médias."[1] The most diaphanous of all media.

Vaporous, Hocquard says: nudity is vaporous, a cloud. "Une nue," in French. These words form a recurring anagram on his pages. Almost a palindrome ("une/nue"), whose letters "neuter" recombines. His friend Claude Royet-

Journoud must have noticed this, for he suggested to Hocquard the old French word "nueté" for "nudité."

"Plus neutre," m'écrit Claude, "moins sonore aussi" (*Méditations sur l'idée simple*, 87).

"Nueté" makes "nudité" more featureless, it seems: more "nue": "nueté" bares nudity even of its bareness ("déshabille la nudité").

Too plain even to be plain, nakedness makes a gap in the world and this void is misty, Hocquard writes. Cloudlike:

> Ta nudité fait un trou dans ce qui
> t'entoure. Ce vide est vaporeux. Il n'a pas
> de bord. (*Méditations photographiques*, 14)

> Your nakedness makes a hole in what
> surrounds you. This void is vaporous. It has no
> edge. (My translation)

This void with haze instead of edges, opened in the middle of things, can also refer in Hocquard's books to the instantaneous whirligig we have glimpsed, where two, let us say Susannah and some old spy—or just any subject of a verb, such as *see*, and any object—switch places "par surprise." It is a blur: you cannot tell the seer from the seen, the discoverer from the one exposed; the scene reverses too fast. "Entre deux il y a un champ dont la forme *tourne*...," Hocquard writes (my emphasis).

Between two there is a field, then, a blurry patch, a cloud of indifference. And it is *between us*: it is the medium of our relation—I mean, it is the element of the relation between some one and some other one. It is between us, in that sense, and also it is a confidential matter, as we saw earlier, concerning two people only (just between us, *entre nous*).

> Entre deux il y a un champ dont la forme tourne
> *entre nous*. (*Un test*, Livre II, XXV)

> Between two there is a field whose form turns
> *between us*. (*A Test*, Book II, XXV)

Public Gardens

Earlier we caught a hint of "entre nous" in the spirited mode of Jacques Jouet, and a glimpse of his poetry's "moyenneté": its in-between or mediumness. In Anne Portugal's books, too, there is an *entre deux*, an in-between setting. Poetry seeks its formula, she said. We have dwelt briefly on this "disposition placed at a midway point, mid-August," considering the thought that among the questions for poetry in her books is how to prepare this mi-lieu. How to design a setting for shared pleasures, how to lay out the plans for a "propriété commune." Her poems, I wanted to suggest, sometimes offer themselves as an experimental locale suitable for sociable life. A public garden, a pocket park, a playing field, a fairground. The turn of the "vers," where it lofts back again the question it cannot answer—what is going on here at the turning point?—seemed to me to sketch, on occasion, in its veering way, such an environment. Tentative, unstable, both frightful and happy.

"Voisinage" is a name for it in Anne Portugal's poems: neighborhood, environs, general vicinity. "Voisiner" means to be in proximity. A neighborhood requires "approximation," which is to say, different tendencies and aims, moods or sensibilities entering each other's vicinity, such as pleasure and virtue, indolence and rigor ("l'approximation de l'aisance / et de la charité"[2]). It could be different people, too, that draw near each other, along a strip of green, say, a tree-lined margin, just in passing. Public gardens lend themselves well, Anne Portugal has observed, to passing by, passing through, without necessarily saying anything, or thinking, but passing, especially from the private to the public. Mi-lieux, halfway between public and private, city gardens could be approximations of the exclusive and the general, the common and the uncommon. That would account in part at least for their lending themselves to Anne Portugal for thinking about poetry space and for thinking of it as the milieu of no one's singularity. As the natural environment, if you will, of a nondescript beauty. Its medium. Its bath.

"Approximate" is like "adjoining." "[A]h l'amour mitoyen / l'amour mitoyen ah."[3]

"Adjoining love." Love along an edge of some kind, perhaps. On either side of a border, or a party wall. Love as a sort of colocation, in a semidetached house, or a neighborhood of duplexes. All these associations are suggested by "mitoyen." Approximation is, I daresay, the program, or at least part of it, in *Le plus simple appareil*. For among the concerns of this poetry book is the "appareillage" of a milieu. The equipping, the fitting out of an in-between locale. Its installation.

"La notion la plus utile ici est celle du *voisinage*," we read, in a poem from that book. It features an exchange of gazes over a garden wall, and a road lined by lime trees, passing along beside the wall, adjoining it. Such, I gather, is exactly approximation's design. "La figure elle-même / la figure que nous avons posée au début de notre / histoire" (*Le plus simple*, 29/*Nude* 24).

This poem, with the help of another not too distant from it in *Le plus simple*, leads us to picture a rose garden known to Apollinaire, located at a midpoint, halfway between Mobile and Galveston on the coast of Texas. Apollinaire wrote, in a poem called "Annie,"

> Sur la côte du Texas
> Entre Mobile et Galveston il y a
> Un grand jardin tout plein de roses
> Il contient aussi une villa
> Qui est une grande rose
>
> Une femme se promène souvent
> Dans le jardin toute seule
> Et quand je passe sur la route bordée de tilleuls
> Nous nous regardons   ("Annie," in Apollinaire's *Alcools*)
>
> On the coast of Texas
> Between Mobile and Galveston there is
> A big garden all full of roses
> Inside there is also a villa
> Which is a huge rose
>
> A woman often walks
> All alone in the garden
> And when I pass by on the road bordered with lime trees
> We gaze at each other   (My translation)

Portugal wrote,

> la notion la plus utile ici est celle du voisinage
> le regard par-dessus le mur
> la route bordée de tilleuls

> Annie et le poète
> à l'heure exacte
> exactement
> c'est la figure elle-même
> c'est la figure que nous avons posée au début de notre
> > histoire   (*Le plus simple appareil*, 29)

> the most useful notion here is that of proximity
> the gaze beyond the wall [across the top of the wall]
> the road lined with lime trees
> Annie and the poet
> right on time
> right
> it's the very figure
> it's the figure we posed at the beginning of our story
> > (*Nude*, 24, with my slight modification)

The most useful idea, then, is the idea of proximity—an in-between setting, the scene of a silent colloquy, reciprocating gazes. This is my emphasis, my focus.

> maintenant
> nous avons un vértitable foyer
>
> entre Mobile et Galveston
>
> est-ce que le jardin de Suzanne peut contenir autant de roses
> que le jardin d'Annie ?   (*Le plus simple appareil*, 33)

> now
> we have a veritable hearth
>
> between Mobile and Galveston
>
> can Susannah's garden hold as many roses
> as Annie's garden   (*Nude*, 28)

Norma Cole's translation reminds us that the real focus ("véritable foyer") is also a "veritable hearth"—something like a home or household? Because of the rose garden, I tend to picture (not wishing to insist) a hostel inside a small park, or a "résidence": essentially just "a place to stay," for a while. Nothing to make a fuss over, only an in-between area shared by adjoining terrains, a little

Entre Deux / 179

stretch of mediocrity, where the incomparable could drift into the vicinity of the nondescript. A neutral medium (a third term) installed in the middle of our affairs (like a pocket park in a city), where the straight backbone of Hocquard, or Royet-Journoud, and the poor posture that Portugal loves in Apollinaire, in Verlaine, might cohabit distantly. Indolence and virtue, "aise" and "charité." A favorable venue for a nondescript beauty; the readying of its medium.

Anne Portugal has suggested that in such an element (such a poetry bath) it might be possible to show oneself, or cause someone else to recognize themselves—"as self," she emphasized—"in the greatest indifference" ("The Garden," 40). I take the liberty of interpreting "self," with its stress, as "the one no other one is"; and "indifference" as a state of indifferentiation. By which I mean that the self in question would be un- or dis-impersonated: not any one (of the three different persons of the verb), but rather, simple. And bare: unmasked. This exposure (of indifference) is directed, Portugal said—again in her text for Gavronsky—not toward any "collectivity," but rather toward "the state of anonymity." So one might think the gardener poet looks after a grassy patch in between no one and anyone at all where the bare state or condition of being—of being the same as no one, just like anyone—might communicate.

Vigilance, she said, is essential in this garden—to guard against temptation. Distinction is a temptation. It is tempting to want recognition (recognition of oneself, say, as self) to hinge on a distinguishing attribute. Portugal once stated that "one's own pitiful excellence" must be excluded at all costs from poetry ("The Garden," 40). In poetry's vicinity recognition is reserved for the simplest distinction, which is none. "Secret le plus simple," Pierre Alferi says (*Brefs*, 50), tacitly citing Portugal; "secret sans mystère . . ." *Mystère*, repellent word, Blanchot wrote. And "Mysterious, that which is laid bare without being uncovered" (*Awaiting Oblivion*, 56[4]).

Mysterious, if you will, the secret too plain even to be plain. Anne Portugal's writing prepares an environment suitable for that "évidence." A milieu, I mean, favorable to that "mystère," and its unlikely recognition.

"What secret, Helena?" "It's a secret" (*Cette histoire est la mienne, ma haie*, 486). I have been suggesting, reading Hocquard, that this mysteriously self-evident, secret secret resides between us and is our secret common place. "Ce trou est sans mesures," Hocquard writes. What state, he asks in another sonnet from *Un test de solitude*—what state is figured by this hole?

Quel *É*TAT

"ÉTAT" is an Albiach word, the title of her first poetry book. In the sonnet from *Un test de solitude* that I am referring to, Hocquard prints it just as she does, in all caps, with the initial letter unaccountably italicized.

Elsewhere in *Un test de solitude* Hocquard proposes to consider all verbs "verbes d'état," (with "état," printed this time entirely in lowercase roman characters). He proposes to consider all verbs to be "verbes d'état," including the ones usually understood to be action verbs, and this proposal suggests that we take "state," "état," to mean a condition, a state of being. A sentence from a prose text by Hocquard that I cited earlier suggests the state of innocence. "They poisoned me in the garden in order to take over my state." They made it into property. Their way of taking it over was to foist it on me as a thing that belongs to me. An attribute, or a name. Or as a thing I belong to (my fate, let us say, the fate of all those like me; or again my country, my class, with which I am identified). Thus, I imagine, did they poison what I'd venture to call (thinking of Agamben) "belonging itself," and corrupt what Hocquard names "fausse propriété," which is the simplest state, the common one, the state of being.

Indeed, by way of an answer to the question What STATE is figured by the measureless hole between us, Hocquard writes that "is" figures this state. "Is," the middle of a tautology. How to account for blank areas, he inquires, "régions blanches," or vacant lots, "terre[s] vague[s]" lying in between one voice and another, separating every solitude (each "une") from every other one. What ÉTAT is mapped by these featureless margins, the discontinuous no-man's-land that we share, according to my reading, like no one's secret. "Is" figures this ÉTAT, Hocquard responds.

> Que faire des régions blanches.
> Quel ÉTAT figurent ces régions.
> Dans Viviane est Viviane, est figure cet ÉTAT.
> (*Un test de solitude*, Book II, VI)

What to do with the blank regions.
What STATE, what ÉTAT do these regions figure.
In Viviane is Viviane, this ÉTAT figures
> (*A Test of Solitude*, 52: Jean-Jacques Poucel's translation does not quite coincide with my reading of the French, though I suspect my reading may echo the tacit implication of his translation.)

Our state is simply our being, alive, and "is" figures this state by leaving a blank in its place, or a pit.

Veiller

Anne Portugal stresses vigilance, as I noted earlier. "We will keep watch in the garden," she wrote. We will keep watch, I thought I understood her to mean, over indifference, the distinction proper to no one. Over simplicity too plain to be plain. Since I have already introduced the word *innocence* (associating it with the common state), I might repeat it here: we will keep watch over innocence, which has no claim on its name, as Blanchot writes, in *Le pas au-delà* —which is innocent first off of that.

> "... innocent, you alone have the right to call yourself innocent."
> —"If I have the right, as I believe, I am not innocent, innocence is without right."
>
> (*The Step Not Beyond*, 87/*Le Pas au-delà*, 121)[5]

Nothing substantiates innocence. It is not a quality that could be attributed to anyone, nor can it be vindicated. It is nothing like a side one could defend. I suspect that Hocquard reserves pejorative expressions for it, like "fausse propriété," or "naked lie," lest it appear to have anything to recommend it. It does not. It *is* not innocent, or innocence—it *is* not itself (it *can't* be, lest it *not*). Rather, it just endures this condition (suffers this state) of secrecy.

Suffering suffers, is how Blanchot really puts it, in *The Writing of the Disaster*, from being innocent, and would even like to become guilty in order to subside. It would like, I suppose, to activate its being (take over its state). Claim its name, its meaning. That way it would suffer less. But the passivity in it shrinks from such a lapse. It is safe from the thought of salvation (*L'écriture du désastre*, 70/*The Writing of the Disaster*, 41).[6]

We will not save anything, Anne Portugal said; "we will keep watch in the garden"—of Gethsemene, it seems, not of Eden, as in Hocquard—"we will keep watch, but we will fall asleep at the crucial moment. We will not save anything" (The Garden," 40).

Fin

It is our common state that requires vigilance—countless different kinds, no doubt, and actions too, of course—but also the feeble kind of watchfulness that protects it from salvation. I would like my book to join in that unjustifiable kind.

By common state I mean the one that has no claim even to its own name, and whose proper mode is to be stripped of its proper features—*effaced*, exposed.

I suspect that our state—no one's secret shared among us—suffers in Hocquard's writing, and in his mind, the way suffering does in Blanchot's, and that it would almost like to shoulder guilt in order to suffer less. Hocquard might well think he risks complicity with this yen for shame—with a fearful, guilt-ridden inclination to be saved or covered up, and he may be determined to be on his guard against it. For once, half in jest I suppose, he took the Fifth when asked, by a very perceptive and sympathetic interviewer if he wouldn't agree there was something vibrating in his writing that could be named love. He politely refused to answer on the grounds he might incriminate himself, adding only that there was still some music in his work that he hoped eventually to get rid of (*ma haie*, 292). He is leery of music, as I've mentioned, because he thinks it puts vigilance to sleep. He might have thought, on the occasion of the interview I am referring to, that by acquiescing to the interviewer and giving the vibration in his work its lovely name, he would be surrendering to an impulse, like Adam's after he is poisoned, to mask nakedness. To cover up a "naked lie."

Certainly *I* risk this surrender, with all the emphasis I have placed on the rainbow colors of inert, gray stone showing briefly at midday—and on the smile, too, of expressionless rock, that diffuses consolation and desolation both, indifferently, before dissolving. I have probably elicited a sweet swell of the lingering music whose complete disappearance Hocquard thought he still hadn't managed to effect in his writing. Probably those dim, stony hues to which I have been so attached, and that smiling indifference lend too much distinctiveness to what I've called the special accent of indistinction (*l'accent du neutre*), and risk substituting for it some rare yet after all identifiable quality: some "influence from the outside." So, instead of helping Hocquard's writing, I may have contributed to stopping it from exposing beauty, unmasking music sufficiently. From watching well enough, I mean, over its secrecy.

Of course, Hocquard does not invariably insist on the indistinguishable. On the contrary, you may recall how the unheard on his pages is, in a slightly altered intonation, "l'inouï!" and you may not have forgotten the mutual discovery that is love at first sight, *le coup de foudre*, "la rencontre ineffable." But this immediate reciprocity, this sudden birth—this instantaneous recognition—is a faceless affair. Of the sort, perhaps, suggested by Anne Portugal when she speaks of a communication apt to pass, in a public garden or a poem, between the greatest indifference and the state of anonymity.

So, when I think I sense the rose tonality of no one's beauty, one among the various timbres of indifference, I should recall Anne Portugal's pruning shears of laughter. And try to learn from her, who said once that poetry was a way of learning more about nothing, how, in words, to stick closer to simplicity. It wants no one's recognition.

Roubaud—responding to a somewhat different dilemma: how to hold out against the mad love of pitch-black's unknowable beauty (of light itself drawn back into itself and out of all worlds); how to withstand the fatal attraction of the black sun and yet not, for all that, settle for adulterated beauty, perceptible thanks to some slackening of its absolute, blacked-out distinction, some extraneous coloring or reflection)—Roubaud might say, in answer to *this* question, that the only way lies with unknowable beings' unseemly, outward way of being unreachably inward. With their diaphanous way of blacking. For he says—at least sometimes—that poetry's way lies along the gray blur around the edges of beings which, released from their identity, just *are* their multifarious, their capricious modes and moods and manners of showing. They *are* the sheer impropriety of their appearance in this lousy world. Poetry—the *now* of poetry—lodges in the margin of haze where things (trees, clouds, faces) shift a little and deviate from themselves, the better to be, not they, but not other, either. Their own fantastical memory, perhaps—perceptible by senses capable of impotence.

NOTES

Introduction

1. Emmanuel Hocquard, *Théorie des tables* (Paris: P.O.L, 1993); trans. Michael Palmer as *Theory of Tables* (Providence, RI: o-blek editions, 1994).

    Both the original and the translation are unpaginated. The number 34 is the number of the thirty-fourth poem in the sequence of fifty-one. Hocquard was fifty-one years old when he finished writing *Théorie des tables*, in New York. At the end of it he adds an *Afterword*, translated by Norma Cole at the end of Palmer's translation of the poems. This *Afterword* is called "Un Malaise grammatical," "Grammatical Unrest." In it Hocquard describes how "impressed" he was by Michael Palmer's poetry volume *Sun*, which he went on to translate into French. Thus, an exchange. Hocquard notes in "Grammatical Unrest" that "impressed" (*impressionné*) is to be understood as a term in photography: "exposed." Further along in *The Play of Light* it will be interesting to remember that Hocquard felt exposed by Palmer's poems.

2. Emmanuel Hocquard, *Aerea dans les forêts de Manhattan* (Paris: P.O.L, 1985); trans. Lydia Davis as *Aerea in the Forests of Manhattan* (Evanston, IL: Marlboro Press, 1992).

    My general plan for the French texts that I cite is to give only the English translation if the text is in prose. But I will give the page reference to the original text as well, and occasionally I do cite the French original. If no English translation has been published, I will provide my own rough version. However, for poems that I cite I will practically always give both the original and the English translation (providing my own, if necessary).

3   Anne-Marie Albiach, *É*TAT(Paris: Mercure de France, 1971), 14; trans. Keith Waldrop as *É*TAT (Windsor, VT: Awede, 1989), 16.

Hocquard quotes this phrase of Albiach's as an epigraph to "La Bibliothèque de Trieste," in *ma haie* (P.O.L, 2001), 16. The other epigraphs to that text are from Wittgenstein ("Une oeuvre [poétique] consiste essentiellement en élucidations"), and Louis Zukofsky ("Toute la poésie, c'est cela. Soudain, on voit quelque chose." In my translation, "The whole point of poetry is just that: suddenly you see something").

The title of Albiach's book *É*TAT always appears in all uppercase letters, and features an italicized initial letter. My guess as to the reason for this irregularity is that Albiach wishes one to sense *est* ("is") in the word *É*TAT ("state"). I will return to this intuition at the end of *The Play of Light*. It is sometimes said that the typographical irregularity in *É*TAT is meant to suggest a difference that is inaudible—perceptible only in writing. Albiach herself said it is meant to render the word impenetrable.

4   See, in Roubaud's *The Great Fire of London*, trans. Dominic Di Bernardi (Champaign and London: Dalkey Archive Press, 1991) 148, where Roubaud writes, of the enigma in his life-work, that "it was a very special kind of enigma: the auto-engima. The question [...] was not 'What is it?,' but 'What am I?' " See page 196 in the original, *Le grand incendie de Londres. Récit, avec incises et bifurcations (1985–87)*, "Fiction & Cie," © Éditions du Seuil, 1989, n. e., 2009 (Paris: Seuil, 1989).

Dominic Di Bernardi provides an excellent "Afterword" at the end of his translation. And Peter Consenstein is the editor of a *Casebook on Jacques Roubaud's The Great Fire of London* (Champaign, IL and London: Dalkey Archive Press, 2002).

For the allusion to Percival, see *The Great Fire*, 140–41 (*Le grand incendie*, 186–87), as well as Roubaud's *La Fleur inverse* (Les Belles Lettres, 2009), 35–37, and *Graal fiction* (Paris: Gallimard, 1978), 183. We will return to these matters further on.

5   See Roubaud's essay "Première digression sur les débuts de la photographie," in *Du Visible a l'invisible. Pour Max Milner, Tome II, "La Nuit transparente,"* ed. Stéphane Michaud (Paris: José Corti, 1988), 29. Several of the ideas developed in this essay reappear in Roubaud's novel, *Eros mélancolique*, written with Anne Garréta (Paris: Bernard Grasset, 2009).

6   *Some Thing Black* is the title of one of Roubaud's poetry books. Trans. Rosmarie Waldrop (Champaign, IL and London: Dalkey Archive Press, 1990). The original is *Quelque chose noir* (Paris: © Éditions Gallimard, 1986).

7   Jacques Roubaud, *Poésie: (Récit)* (Paris: "Fiction & Cie," © Éditions du Seuil, 2000), 13.

8   Emmanuel Hocquard, "Tum color ...," in *Un privé à Tanger* (Paris: P.O.L, 1987), 83.

9   Emmanuel Hocquard, *Ce qui n'advint pas* [That which Did Not Occur] (centre international de poésie *Marseille*/Spectres Familiers, 2016).
10 Emmanuel Hocquard, *L'Invention du verre* (Paris: P.O.L 2003); trans. Cole Swensen and Rod Smith as *The Invention of Glass* (Marfa, TX: Canarium Books, 2012).
11 Emmanuel Hocquard, *Conditions de lumière* (Paris: P.O.L, 2007); trans. Jean-Jacques Poucel as *Conditions of Light* (Iowa City and Paris: La Presse, 2012).
12 Jacques Roubaud, "Colors Worn," in *The Plurality of Worlds of Lewis*, trans. Rosmarie Waldrop (Champaign, IL and London: Dalkey Archive Press, 1995), 89. The original is "Couleurs portées," in *La pluralité des mondes de Lewis* (Paris: © Éditions Gallimard, 1991), 88-89.
13 Anne Portugal, "The Garden," in *Six Contemporary French Women Poets: Theory, Practice, and Pleasures*, Introduction and Translations by Serge Gavronsky (Carbondale, IL: Southern Illinois University Press, 1997), 39-43. "The Garden" is Portugal's response to a questionnaire provided by Gavronsky, who encouraged the six women poets in the anthology to answer it in whatever form and order they liked.
14 See the epigraphs to "La Bibliothèque de Trieste," in *ma haie* (P.O.L, 2001), 16. The Wittgenstein sentence is from the *Tractatus*, 4.112.
15 See the *Tractatus*, 1; 5.632; 5.64.
16 *The Great Fire of London*, 156. Translation slightly modified.
17 "The Phantoms of Eros" is the title of the first chapter of Agamben's *Stanzas* (Minneapolis and London: University of Minnesota Press, 1993).
18 Giorgio Agamben, *The Coming Community*, trans. Michael Hardt (Minneapolis and London: University of Minnesota Press, 1993).
19 Werner Hamacher, *95 Theses on Philology*, theses 8 and 64. See, in *Give the Word. Responses to Werner Hamacher's 95 Theses on Philology*, ed. Gerhard Richter and Ann Smock (Lincoln: University of Nebraska Press, 2019), xiii-xiv and xxxix.
20 *The Problem of Distraction* (Stanford, CA: Stanford University Press, 2012). See page 44 for the sentence "No one is distracted."
21 I have often thought, when bumping in my own way into no one, of Daniel Heller-Roazen's book *No One's Ways: An Essay on Infinite Naming* (New York: Zone Books, 2017). This work bears on the particle "non" which—it turns out—philosophers from Aristotle to Kant, Hegel and beyond have persistently tried adding to names. Thus, Aristotle spoke of "non-man." The results of such experiments preoccupy Heller-Roazen in a book whose scope (and depth) exceeds that of *The Play of Light* too far for there to be any real connection between the two. *No One's Ways* begins, though, with an "anecdote" from Homer which Emmanuel Hocquard

particularly values: Ulysses saved his own life once by altering his name and calling himself "No One," or "Non-one."

22 Jacques Khalip, *Anonymous Life: Romanticism and Dispossession* (Stanford, CA: Stanford University Press, 2009).

23 I do not doubt that the terms I emphasize (*singulier*, *pluriel*, etc.) have shown, in the course of the work they have inspired, some limits along with the invaluable challenges they offer. See Gayatri Spivak's "Response to Jean-Luc Nancy," in *Thinking Bodies*, ed. Juliet Flower MacCannell and Laura Zakarin (Stanford, CA: Stanford University Press, 1994), 33-51, for a stimulating critique of Nancy's thought, by a sympathetic and attentive reader.

24 Jean-Luc Nancy, *The Inoperable Community*, trans. Peter Connor et al., Foreword by Christopher Fynsk (Minneapolis and London: University of Minnesota Press, 1991).

25 Maurice Blanchot, *The Unavowable Community*, trans. Pierre Joris (Barrytown, NY: Station Hill Press, 1988).

26 I recognized, when reading Michael Lucey's remarkable book, *Someone: The Pragmatics of Misfit Sexualities, from Colette to Hervé Guibert* (Chicago and London: University of Chicago Press, 2019), that Hocquard's change of mood, as it were, with regard to Blanchot would be interesting to consider from a Bourdieuvian perspective like Michael Lucey's. In the fifth chapter of *Someone* Lucey examines the "literary field" of the 1970s and '80s in France, and various writers' maneuvers within it. Blanchot's prestige, which is to say the prestige of "écriture," contributed to making that field practically unlivable for the writers who count for Lucey. The subject of chapter 7 in *Someone* is "intonation" in the work of Robert Pinget. "Intonation," as I've suggested, is a key question for Hocquard. While *Someone* is a book of a different species from *The Play of Light*, I would like to imagine that some reader might think of the second chapter of my book when reading the fifth and seventh of Michael Lucey's.

27 "Ode contre un rossignol," in *Un privé à Tanger*, 181-84.

28 *Poésie*, 152.

29 *Poésie*, 155.

30 *Poésie*, 164.

31 *Le grand incendie de Londres—Récit, avec incises et bifurcations, 1985-1987—* is the title of the first volume, or "branch" of a six-branch autobiographical prose work whose title is also *Le grand incendie de Londres*. *The Great Fire of London* is the title of the English translation by Dominic Di Bernardi of the first branch. Inside the cover of this initial volume, the title is given again, but this time like this: 'Le grand incendie de Londres'—as if the work we are about to begin were not quite the real thing. Then, past the title page and a preface, we come upon the following:

> Branche Un
> Destruction.

So, *Destruction* is the title of the first branch of a six-volume work that would have been, as the preface explains, *Le Grand Incendie de Londres*. This novel, we learn, was to have accompanied a Project, a poetry Project conceived by Roubaud in 1961, as his "alternative to voluntary death." This Project, and its double, the novel, failed, however—inevitably, in Roubaud's understanding (because of the "auto-enigme"). Parts of the Project were constructed, however; they can "offer the illusion" of a whole something like the one initially planned. The accompanying novel, however, came to nothing. Roubaud is starting over—more modestly, he says—at the beginning of *branche un*. But in order to explain what this current prose work will be, he must begin by saying what might have been.

We will return to the history of the poetry Project and the accompanying novel further on, but for the moment let me just indicate that when I refer to *Le grand incendie de Londres* (*The Great Fire of London*) I will always mean the first volume of the long work, now six volumes in all. I never use the title *Destruction* for this initial "branch."

It is called *Destruction* by Roubaud because of his conviction that prose, unlike poetry (where reference and meaning are arrested), makes memories explicit, transmissible—public, if you will—and in this way destroys them. Martin Klebes explains this in "Jacques Roubaud: Projecting Memory," *Wittgenstein's Novels* (London and New York: Routledge, 2006), 142-43. Indeed, in the early pages of "branch one," Roubaud refers to his memories fading as he writes, in "a haze of lines, in lines, in black lines, in desolation" (*The Great Fire*, 30/*Le grand incendie*, 45-46).

The titles of the six branches of the whole prose work are: *Destruction* (Paris: Seuil, 1989); *La Boucle* (Paris: Seuil, 1993); English translation by Jeff Fort as *The Loop* (Champaign, IL and London: Dalkey Archive Press, 2009); *Mathématique: (récit)* (Paris: Seuil, 1997); *Poésie:(récit)* (Paris: Seuil, 2000); *La Bibliothèque de Warburg* (Paris: Seuil, 2002); *Impératif catégorique* (Paris: Seuil, 2008). The six branches were published together by Seuil in 2009, under the title *'le grand incendie de Londres,'* and it is this form of the title that Roubaud himself always uses to refer to the shadow of the entire work that he initially conceived. It—the complete work as originally conceived—does not exist. I will follow Roubaud's practice, referring to the six branches taken all together as *'le grand incendie de Londres,'* and to the first volume as *Le grand incendie de Londres*. This small typographical distinction, significant for Roubaud, will have its importance in my discussions, but only at a few particular junctures. For I quite rarely refer to the six branches taken all together (*'le grand incendie'*), or to the entire nonexistant work, *Le Grand Incendie de Londres*. Whereas I regularly refer to "branch one," *Le grand incendie de Londres*. Please see the bibliography of the present book for the complete annotation of the edition of this volume by Éditions du Seuil, which I cite.

I should add that I capitalize the initial letter in the word *Project*, when referring to Roubaud's poetry Project—which was to be accompanied by a novel. And I refer to the entire double project (poetry *and* novel) as Roubaud's project (without a capital *p*). It was conceived as a lifetime undertaking, as we will see.

32 Jacques Roubaud, *Dire la poésie*, in *Dors précédé de Dire la poésie* (Paris: Gallimard, 1981), 25. This volume has been translated by Matthew Smith as *Sleep Preceded by Saying Poetry* (Providence, RI and Paris: La Presse, 2019). See pages 19-20 of Smith's translation for Roubaud's description of the diversifying, intertwining paths of the thought in speaking, or in saying.

33 For further discussion of this diversifying, criss-crossing character of Roubaud's writing (as well as a brief introduction to his work in general), see my "Cloudy Roubaud," in *Representations* 86 (Spring 2004): 141-74, especially the beginning. For a far fuller account of the interrelations among different parts of Roubaud's life work, see Elisabeth Cardonne-Arlyck's "Jacques Roubaud: 'Je redeviens guetteur, guetteur mélancolique,' " in her stunning book *Véracités* (Paris: Editions Belin, 2009), 167-265.

34 Jacques Roubaud, *Poésie, etcetera: ménage* (Paris: Editions Stock, 1995); trans. Guy Bennett as *Poetry, etcetera: Cleaning House* (Los Angeles: Green Integer, 2006). See sections B and C for elaborations on this "axiom": "La poésie ne dit rien. La poésie dit."

35 Jacques Roubaud, *La pluralité des mondes de Lewis* (Paris: © Éditions Gallimard, 1991); trans. Rosmarie Waldrop as *The Plurality of Worlds of Lewis* (Champaign and London: Dalkey Archive Press, 1995). The words I cite are from the long prose poem in this volume (69-74 in both the original and the translation) called "Idée de la forme," "The Idea of Form."

36 Danielle Collobert, *Dire II*, in *Oeuvres I* (Paris: P.O.L, 2004), 253.

37 Jacques Roubaud, "Danielle Collobert. 'Cri ou comme brûle jamais dit,' " in *Danielle Collobert* (Marseille: centre international de poésie Marseille, 2006), 35-37. This small volume contains the papers presented at a Round Table on June 2, 2006, plus an interview by Jean Daive with Danielle Collobert's mother, Francine Collobert, a bio-bibliography and some photographs, notably of the Breton town Rostrenen where Danielle Collobert grew up. Roubaud's text also appeared in *Critique* 385-86, "Trente ans de poésie française," 1979. The English translations of phrases from Roubaud's text are my own.

38 That was just two years before he took on Roubaud's first poetry book, whose title is the sign for belonging in set theory, ϵ .

39 English translation by Nathanaël (Brooklyn, NY: Litmus Press, 2013).

40 English translation by Norma Cole: *It then* (Oakland, CA: O Books, 1989).

41 Roubaud alludes more than once to Lewis Carroll's *The Hunting for the Snark*, as we will see further along.

42   Roubaud develops his own concept of autobiography, some aspects of which we will examine further on in this book. And the reader may wish to see his *Autobiographie, chapitre dix. Poèmes avec des moments de repos en prose* (Paris: Gallimard, 1973), which we will not approach here. It is still perfectly reasonable to see in the six-volume prose work called *'le grand incendie de Londres'* a story of Roubaud's life—with one volume on childhood memories (*La Boucle*), one on his formation as a mathematician (*Mathématique*), one on his apprenticeship in poetry (*Poésie*), and so on. However, that these volumes also form the story of *'le grand incendie de Londres'*—its conception, the calculations involved in planning it out, the conditions of its various setbacks and revivals, its inevitable failure—begins to suggest that for Roubaud, a *book* tells its story in an autobiography. A book recounts its own life. Without, for all that, having existed in advance. So, perhaps it is better to say it recounts the life of its title—the title of the book it was to have been. And it might be thought that for content this autobiography of a title has only, in various forms, this question: why is this my name? what am I? Martin Klebes's "Jacques Roubaud: Projected Memory" (in *Wittgenstein's Novels*) discusses this riddle in a very interesting, instructive manner; see, esp., 164.

Just as I was finishing my work on this book, Roubaud published a tentative account of his own life—an autobiography in the ordinary sense of the term. He called it *Peut-être* (Perhaps). The full title is *Peut-être ou La nuit du dimanche* (Paris: Seuil, 2018). Perhaps or Sunday Night.

43   See Roubaud's text in *Danielle Collobert*, 37.

44   *Quelque chose noir*, 15/*Some Thing Black*, 14. The title of this volume of poems (*Quelque chose noir*) echoes, incompletely, a phrase of Alix Cléo Roubaud's, which is also the title of a series of seventeen of her photos accompanied by twelve poems by Jacques Roubaud: *Si Quelque Chose Noir* (*La Licorne*, "Roubaud," UFR de langues et littératures de l'Université de Poitiers, 1997). "C'est impossible," Roubaud writes there, "si quelque chose noir, que cela s'éclaire." It is impossible, if some thing black, that it should become clear.

45   Danielle Collobert, *Survie*, in *Oeuvres I*, 416. Trans. Norma Cole as *Survival*, in *Crosscut Universe: Writing on Writing from France*, ed. Norma Cole (Providence, RI: Burning Deck, 2000), 42.

46   Emmanuel Hocquard, *Tout le monde se ressemble: Une anthologie de poésie contemporaine* (Paris: P.O.L, 1995), 61.

47   The first volume of Collobert's *Oeuvres* contains *Meurtre*, *Dire I* and *II*, *Il donc*, and *Survie*, plus a brief bio-bibliography. *Oeuvres II* (Paris: P.O.L, 2005), edited by Françoise Morvan, contains material unpublished during Collobert's lifetime, as well as collaborative projects (radio plays) presented by Uccio Esposito-Torrigiani, an actor and writer, and Collobert's longtime friend.

See Norma Cole's *Crosscut Universe* for her translation of Collobert's *Survie* (*Survival*), and of Roubaud's text on Collobert (which I cite), *scream or like burns never said.*

On Collobert, see John C. Stout's article, "Writing (at) the Limits of Genre: Danielle Collobert's Poetics of Transgression," in *Symposium* 53, no. 4 (winter 2002): 299-309.

48   For an interesting discussion of Hocquard's and Roubaud's activities as translators of American poetry and as editors of anthologies of twentieth-century American poetry in French translation, see Marjorie Perloff, "Traduit de l'américain," in *Poetic License: Essays on Modernist and Postmodernist Lyric* (Evanston, IL: Northwestern University Press, 1990), 53-69. Perloff comments on several special issues devoted to American poets in the 1970s, in the journals *Change* and *Poé&sie* where Roubaud collaborated with Jean Pierre Faye and Michel Deguy. She also briefly discusses Deguy and Roubaud's 1980 anthology *Vingt poètes américains*, as well as Hocquard and Claude Royet-Journoud's 1986 *21 + 1: Poètes américains d'aujourd'hui*. She brings out a striking contrast between the picture these French writers presented of contemporary American poetry—where language, as they saw it, was "the arena of production rather than representation," and Gertrude Stein was the "presiding deity"—and, on the other hand, the picture presented in the US by Helen Vendler, in *The Harvard Book of Contemporary American Poetry* (1984), and by Dave Smith and David Bottoms in *The Morrow Anthology of Younger American Poets* (1985). In these US anthologies, Wallace Stevens presides, and representations of "Romantic selfhood" prevail, Perloff observes.

49   For Hocquard's intellectual biography see, in *ma haie*, "La Bibliothèque de Trieste" (15-32), "Entretien avec Stéphane Baquey" (273-92), " 'Vaut-il la peine de voir un ours blanc?' " (136-48), "Comment en suis-je arrivé là?" (443-60).

To Hocquard's activities as editor, translator, unassuming and friendly promoter of many different projects, exchanges, and collaborations, one should certainly add his work from 1993 to 2005 as a teacher at the Ecole des Beaux-Arts in Bordeaux. Just as I was finishing this book, David Lespiau produced an edition of all the texts Hocquard produced in connection with the workshop ("atelier de recherche et de création"), which he ran in Bordeaux and called Procédure, Image, Son, Ecriture (P.I.S.E.). The volume is titled *Le cours de Pise* (Paris: P.O.L, 2018).

For a fine selective bibliography of Hocquard's work, see *Hippocampe* 14 (summer 2017): 112.

In 2004, Glenn W. Fetzer published the very useful *Emmanuel Hocquard and the Poetics of Negative Modernity* (Birmingham, AL: Summa Publications). More recently, Gilles Tiberghien published a stimulating account of Hocquard's work: *Emmanuel Hocquard* (Paris: Seuil, 2006).

For Roubaud's various *partis pris* and alliances on the cultural scene, see his *Description du Projet* (Caen: Nous, 2014), with its helpful "Foreword" by Jean-Jacques Poucel.

For a good selective bibliography, see Yves di Manno and Isabelle Garron, *Un nouveau monde: Poésies en France 1960-2010* (Paris: Editions Flammarion, 2017), 296-98.

The book that Jean-Francois Puff composed with Roubaud—*Rencontre avec Jean-François Puff* (Paris: Argol, 2008)—is a rich resource on the author's life and work. Puff is also the author of a very substantial critical work on Roubaud: *Mémoire de la mémoire: Jacques Roubaud et la lyrique médiévale* (Paris: Editions Classiques Garnier, 2009).

50 Quoted on the back cover of the centre international de poésie *Marseille*'s publication, *Danielle Collobert*.

Chapter One

1 Jacques Roubaud, *Echanges de la lumière* (Paris: Editions A. M. Métailié, 1990); trans. Eleni Sikelianos as *Exchanges on Light* (Iowa City and Paris: La Presse, 2009).

2 Roubaud recounts in *La Boucle*—the second volume or "branch" of his long prose work (his own particular kind of "autobiography," *'le grand incendie de Londres'*)—how in 1982 he came upon Goodman's Paradox, a paradox of induction, named after the logician Nelson Goodman who proposed it. He says that at that point he made Goodman's name the name of a character in his own work, "a character in prose, and a temporal character" (*La Boucle*, 233ff/ *The Loop*, 216ff).

Goodman has accompanied Roubaud ever since 1982. He is Mr. Goodman in *Exchanges on Light*; we find him in middle age in *Ciel et terre et ciel et terre et ciel* (first published by Les Flohic éditeurs, 1997, then by Argol in 2009). Goodman is a professor in *Ciel et terre*—a professor of crystallography at St. Andrews University in Scotland. But he has taken, after the death of his wife, to studying clouds. In *Eros mélancolique* he is James Goodman, a graduate student studying the chemistry of early photography on a research grant in Paris. This is in the 1960s. In the '40s—in *Parc sauvage* (Paris: Seuil, 2008)—he is only a child, hiding with his mother in Provence, near Carcassonne, in the landscape of Roubaud's childhood (*garrigue, cyprès, touffes de thym, nuages*). I take him to be Roubaud's alter ego, as it were, or double: the person Roubaud would be if he were English, or a German Jew brought up in the UK. Roubaud's mother was an "angliciste," so English was, in a way, his mother tongue; his family was active in the Resistance, and Churchill loomed large in his childhood imagination (*Churchill 40* is the title of one of his poetry books [Paris: Gallimard, 2004]). A reader of Roubaud soon becomes familiar with his favorite neighborhoods in London, favorite English authors, English ale, and so on. On the topic of Roubaud's English side, see Michael Sheringham, "Les Vies anglaises de Jacques Roubaud" in "*compositeur de mathématique et de poésie*," ed. Agnès Disson and Véronique Montémont (Nancy: Editions Absalon, 2010): 235-47.

3   At the end of the *Exchanges*, Goodman thanks each of the participants. "They modestly did not wish their names to be revealed," he says, "except as abbreviations [Basil of C., Dennis Ps., Lewis de B., John Ph., William H.] from which, nonetheless, their identities are easily decipherable." And Goodman goes on to name and thank a few of the many others who, without taking part directly in the *Exchanges* nevertheless, in one way or another, contributed to enriching them: M. et Mme. Procusk Jambique, for example; Ibn Ishaq, Cavalcanti, Guy Le Fèvre de La Broderie, Héron d'Alexandrie . . . (*Exchanges*, 77/*Echanges*, 85).

4   For the whole poem that contains these lines, see *Le grand incendie de Londres* 405, under the rubric *Beauté du noir*. Immediately following, under the rubric "*Of black itself*," are Roubaud's French translations of two sonnets by Edward Herbert, lord of Cherbury: *Beauté du noir*, and *Au noir lui-même*. In Di Bernardi's translation, *The Great Fire of London*, see 315-17.

5   Roubaud once suggested, in an oral discussion of his work, that *black*, *noir*, in the title *Quelque chose noir*, may be a verb. Some thing blacks. See the transcription of the round table discussion at the end of *Pour éclairer Quelque chose noir / textes réunis par Francis Marmande et Sylvie Patron* (Paris: Université de Paris Diderot, 2008), 182. Roubaud said: "Alors, pour *Quelque chose noir*, on pourrait presque dire que *noir* est un verbe. Quelque chose comme ça."

6   On Raquel Levy and her art, see *Raquel. Peinture. Poésie* (éditions Sponte sua forte, 2018). It is a monograph presenting Raquel's life's work: diptychs and triptychs, notably, but including other works too, such as many painted pages that she contributed to books by writer friends. Among the poets whose tributes to her appear in this handsome volume are Emmanuel Hocquard, Anne-Marie Albiach, Claude Royet-Journoud, Pascal Quignard, Jean Daive, Edmond Jabès, and Yves Bonnefoy. Raquel died in 2014.

7   See Emmanuel Hocquard, *Méditations photographiques sur l'idée simple de nudité* (Paris: P.O.L, 2009), 11.

8   Emmanuel Hocquard, *Un test de solitude* (Paris: P.O.L, 1998); trans. Rosmarie Waldrop as *A Test of Solitude* (Providence, RI: Burning Deck, 2000). In the original volume, the pages are not numbered, but each poem is: I-XXXIII in Book I; I-XXV in Book II. I will indicate which poems among those I cite are from Book II; otherwise it should be understood the poems are from Book I.

9   *Conditions de lumière*, 87/*Conditions of Light*, 87.
10 This is the first statement in the *Tractatus Logico-Philosophicus*.
11 "Conversation du 8 février 1982," in *Un privé*, 154-70.
12 Jacques Roubaud, *la fenêtre veuve* (Courbevoie: Théâtre Typographique, 1996). This "Prose Orale" is unpaginated. It has not been translated, so the rough translations here are my own. Roubaud also published this text in the review *Poé&sie* 22 (1982). "Mount Cicada" must be Mount Cicala, a hill from which Vesuvius is visible and where Castel Cicala, home of Giordano Bruno, is located.
13 See *Poésie etcetera*, 79/*Poetry etcetera*, 78), where Roubaud suggests that if poetry could be thought to say anything at all when it just says, then the "kekchose" it would say ("un je ne sais quoi") would be "l'ombre intérieure de la poésie prise dans les poèmes." "The inner shadow of poetry caught in poems."
14 E. Cardonne-Arlyck, however, quotes Roubaud in *La Bibliothèque de Warbourg*, speaking of "a possible world of poetry." His work composing the sonnet book whose title is the sign of belonging in Set Theory, and the later volume *Trente et un au cube* (1973), had made poetry strange to its French habitat, and by the same token rendered Roubaud a stranger to his own life. "I had made myself a stranger to the world via poetry," he wrote. "I had begun to inhabit a possible world of poetry, which I maintained firmly separate from the real world by means of an invisible and uncrossable wall" (*La Bibliothèque de Warbourg*, 146; cited by Cardonne-Arlyck, 208. My English).

I mention this ("un monde possible de poésie") not because I wish to oppose the idea (insisting on *no* possible world for poetry and on the "voie de l'impossible" exclusively); I would just locate the determination, to reside entirely within an intricately constructed formal system, having its own exacting demands and marvelous potential, along a different "*voie*" among the many intertwining ones in Roubaud's oeuvre. Or I would consider it to emerge from a different mood among his several, or to reflect a different period in his lifetime's undertaking.
15 I cite this phrase from Roubaud's book on the art of the troubadours, *La Fleur inverse*, 14.
16 *Apatride* (*apatriate*) is another word Roubaud employs, borrowing it from the Austrian philosopher Alexius Meinong, to refer to worldless beings: paradoxical ones, Roubaud says, after Meinong, that do not conform to the law of noncontradiction and find themselves therefore excluded from any universe. *Apatride* is the title of the poem I cite below, from *Quelque chose noir*. It says (in its paraphrasable, nonessential dimension) that beings that are past and gone, yet spoken to—beings that are addressed, in the present, and affirmed as present by the address though they are gone—are without any possible world. The poem says something more:

it suggests, I believe, another "*voie*," "la voie de la double négation," and the thought of a *not not-you*. Toward the end of *The Play of Light*, we will think again of this "double negation" path, suggested to Roubaud by Nicholas of Cusa.

In *Apatride* we learn that there is a kind of negation, which is the opposite not of an affirmation, but of another negation. It is not that other *not*.

When I name you, the poem says, negation does not oppose the affirmation "you are," but rather the "not" that precedes my words. It opposes your *not being* before I name you. Naming you, I say you are not that not-being. You are not not. You are not not-you.

The poem says that this naming makes a presence anterior to disappearance shine, and by the same token gives disappearance a different status from that of absence pure and simple. I expect disappearance gets the status of a privation, which, in Roubaud's vocabulary is different, as we will see in other contexts, from pure and simple dereliction. Privation is loss, irrecoverable, but of something, someone who was once—who once was not not. So, I suspect that "ton nom," "trace irréductible," is the memory of you. It cannot be annihilated. But neither can it be described. Your memory, then—your name: an absolutely minimal, perhaps unknowable, but indestructible trace.

For a presentation of the "Way of Double Negation," see *La Boucle*, 229-30/*The Loop*, 212-13.

Here is the poem, *Apatride* (*Quelque chose noir*, 87). In Rosmarie Waldrop's translation, *Some Thing Black*, see page 84.

Apatride

Les êtres paradoxaux, apatrides (*heimatlos*) de Meinong,
qui échappent au principe de non-contradiction ne sont
pas les seuls êtres sans univers

Les êtres passés et révolus, parlés présents, affirmés présents par l'adresse, ne sont pas plus quelque part (je veux
dire en quelque construction) possibles

Et pourtant il ne m'est pas envisageable de me passer
de dire "toi"

En te nommant je voudrais te donner une stabilité hors
de tout atteinte

La négation de toi alors s'opposera non à l'affirmation
(tu n'es pas) mais au néant qui est avant ma parole

Te nommer c'est faire briller la présence d'un être antérieur à la disparition

> Donner au même moment à cette disparition un statut
> autre et plus que la pure, que la simple absence, un statut
> second
>
> Ton nom est trace irréductible. Il n'y a pas de négation
> possible de ton nom.
>
> Ton nom ne se supprime pas (mais il restera sans description, qui viendrait briser cette solidité pour en faire un énoncé malléable, moins exigeant, veule, dérisoire, et, pour tout dire, faux).

17 See *The Invention of Glass*, 109 (same page in the original). Hocquard cites a book by Claude Richard, *Lettres américaines* (Aix-en-Provence: Editions Alinéa, 1987). He introduces the quotation with the words "Lettres blanches": white, or blank letters. Here are the lines by Richard that he cites, in Carol Mastrangelo Bové's translation (*American Letters* [Philadelphia: University of Pennsylvania Press, 1998], 132).

"In *The Music Lesson* there is a blank letter in the young girl's hands. At the center of the painting *Man and Woman with a Glass of Wine* are white leaves from a book on the table. In *Woman Reading a Letter*, no signs appear in the shining, virginal place between two clenched hands. *The Concert* has the shiny white of musical scores. Most significantly, at the end of Vermeer's life, *The Love Letter* closes on the mystery and blinding light of the letter, which appears once more in *The Message*, where the servant gives it to the mistress."

18 See chapter 4, "Jacques Roubaud: Projecting Memory," in *Wittgenstein's Novels* by Martin Klebes. This is a valuable essay on Wittgenstein's presence in Roubaud's writing. Or rather, on a "pseudo-Wittgenstein" in Roubaud, an adaptation of Wittgenstein like Roubaud's other "fictionalizations" of philosophers and their texts—his "conscious misappropriations" of David Lewis and others. Roubaud is perfectly frank about this. See Klebes, 142. On the subject of private language, Klebes mentions poetry as a private language, and cites Roubaud saying that poetry escapes the Wittgensteinian condemnation of private language. See 141.

19 See *Méditations photographiques sur l'idée simple de nudité*, 31. We will return to this passage.

20 For example, see *ma haie*, 232-33.

21 This is the title of the anthology of contemporary French poetry that Hocquard edited (Paris: P.O.L, 1995). In English, Everyone is Alike. His introduction to the anthology, also called "Tout le monde se ressemble," appears in *ma haie*, 225-41.

22 See "La Mercury bleue pâle" in *Un privé à Tanger*, 17.

23 See "Ma vie privée," in *ma haie*, especially 258-61. For an appealing description of Hocquard and his irreverent "bande" (his crew or gang), see

Anne Maurel, "Une libre compagnie," in *Hippocampe* 14: 73. "They form a crew all their own, denouncing as illusory and deceptive the ambition (inherited from Romanticism but still in vogue) to possess a personal language without precedent. They write poetry for a few friends initially, before making it public; it's a poetry that uses everyday words. Flat language. [...] For sentences drag each other on. They impose their own links and sequences and their own automatisms, as if everything were always obvious. Their conventional articulations relate the unknown back to the known, annul what befalls. It is necessary to 'undo' language—its clichés and stereotypes, its erroneous, approximating or complaisant formulations—undo sentences the better to 'redo' them, arranging words differently on a page. Scatter, air them out. Study them." (My translation)

24 Jacques Roubaud, *La Fleur inverse: L'art des troubadours* (Paris: Société d'Edition Les Belles Lettres, 2009), 139-40. This is the second printing of the second edition, which first came out in 1994.

25 See *Cette histoire est la mienne (petit dictionnaire autobiographique de l'élégie)*, in *ma haie*, 487 in particular. *Cette histoire est la mienne* has been translated into English by Norma Cole: *This Story Is Mine: Little Autobiographical Dictionary of Elegy* (Saratoga, CA: Instress, 1999). The translation, a pamphlet-like booklet, is unpaginated. But the brief sections in it are ordered alphabetically, by title, like entries in a dictionary.

26 See *Tratatus* §5.63-5.641.

27 In Norma Cole's translation, the lines quoted here are in the section called "Identity."

28 *Théorie des tables*, 3.

29 In Norma Cole's translation, see the section called "Robinson Method."

30 I mean to remind the reader here, of the Albiach sentence Hocquard is fond of, and which I quoted earlier (it is the inverse of the phrase I've just written): "Toutes les évidences lui sont mystère." Everything obvious is to him an enigma, or—in Keith Waldrop's translation—"all the clues are mystery to him."

This would be a good place to mention a book, which I do not believe Hocquard ever cites but which I am sure he must know and like very much (being a classicist by training): *Les ruses de l'intelligence: la mètis des Grecs*, by Marcel Detienne and Jean-Pierre Vernant (Paris: Flammarion, 1974); trans. Janet Lloyd as *Cunning Intelligence in Greek Culture and Society* (Atlantic Highlands, NJ: Humanities Press, 1978). Part 2 of chapter 1, "The Fox and the Octopus," is especially pleasurable to read while reading Hocquard and sensing the relation, in his writing, between a problem and its solution, which can suddenly prove to be like the relation between some object and its copy: they are the same, but sound a little different. Or they are the same, but reversed, inverted. A "being of metis," Detienne and Vernant write—a being with a cunning intelligence—"is the opposite of what it seems to be; it is ambiguous, inverted, and operates through a process of reversal" (44). Its ruses are those of its antagonist, reversed, turned back against the threat. Thus the Greeks' special type of fishing net called a cloud—an invisible mesh of bonds—answers the cuttlefish's inky cloud; and the fox *becomes* a trap in the image of the one threatening to capture it when it turns round on itself so that its front becomes its rear and vice versa. Shapeless, no beginning or end, "a deep night, pure aporia" (42)—or sheer tautology. Sophists, Détienne and Vernant observe, were considered by the Greeks to be good at the twisting, interweaving, and coiling skills important in the fashioning of snares and traps, for Sophists are masters at bending and entangling two contrary theses. They are "able to convince the audience that the same things are now similar to each other, now dissimilar, now single, now multiple." In Hocquard's novel, a certain fondness for sophism is noticeable—in the remark, for example, that sophists were fishermen, whereas Socrates was a midwife, and in the motif of hunting and fishing generally. It would be interesting to pursue this aspect of Hocquard's work, investigating the stags and stag hunting in *Aerea dans les forêts de Manhattan*, and the link between Aerea herself and Diana the huntress.

31   Introduction to *Tout le monde se ressemble*, in *ma haie*, 229.
32   "Je ne sais pas si Fernando Pessoa a vraiment existé," in *Un privé*, 90-93.
33   See *Méditations photographiques sur l'idée simple de nudité*. A single example:

>   la nudité est sans objet. Elle n'entre pas
>   dans une histoire, même si elle traverse
>   bien des histoires. Elle n'appartient pas à.
>
>   Comme respirer, la nudité n'est pas
>   personnelle. Il 'existe même pas de verbe.
>
>   nudité est l'idée la plus simple   (*Méditations* 18)
>
>   nudity has no object. It does not enter
>   into a story, even if it crosses
>   through many stories. It does not belong to.
>
>   Like breathing, nudity is not
>   personal. There is not even a verb.
>
>   nudity is the simplest idea   (my translation)

34   In *L'Invention du verre*, see 27 and 98. In *The Invention of Glass*, see 27 and 97.
35   See "Le bouclier de Persée," in *Un privé*, 82.

36 This poem is "Une," in *Album d'images de la villa Harris* (Paris: Hachette, 1978), 46-59. The essay "Comment j'ai écrit *Une*" is found in *Un privé*, 41-45.

Chapter Two

1. Maurice Blanchot, *L'espace littéraire* (Paris: Gallimard, 1955); trans. Ann Smock as *The Space of Literature* (Lincoln, London: University of Nebraska Press, 1982).
2. Maurice Blanchot, *L'écriture du désastre* (Paris: Gallimard, 1980); trans. Ann Smock as *The Writing of the Disaster* (Lincoln, London: University of Nebraska Press, 1995).
3. I thank Claire Nancy for confirming—based on her own lively recollection—my intuition about Hocquard's and Lacoue-Labarthe's close intellectual connection during the 1970s, and notably about the admiration they shared for Blanchot.
4. Philippe Lacoue-Labarthe, *Phrase* (Paris: Christian Bourgois, 2000), 51, 63, 69. The English translation of *Phrase* is by Leslie Hill (Albany: SUNY Press, 2018). The title is the same in the original and the translation. It is Leslie Hill's English that I cite: see 34, 42, 45 in his translation.
5. See Pascal Quignard, *Inter* (Paris: Argol, 2011), 23. This volume contains the poem Quignard composed in Latin in 1976, "Inter aerias fagos," and its first French translation by Hocquard, done in 1979, "Dans l'air entre les branches de l'hêtre"—plus a letter dated 2009 from Quignard to Benedicte Gorrillot, who, in that year, proposed to organize a collection of new translations of the poem. In his letter to Gorrillot, Quignard reflects on his poem "Inter aerias fagos," and its importance to him in the decades since he wrote it. Besides this letter, the original poem and Hocquard's 1979 translation, *Inter* contains the new translations that Gorrillot gathered, by Pierre Alferi, Eric Clémens, Michel Deguy, B. Gorrillot, E. Hocquard, Christian Prigent, Jude Stéfan. "Inter aerias fagos" itself appears on unnumbered pages in *Inter*, between pages 41 and 59.
6. Jean-Marie Gleize, *Le livre des cabanes* (Paris: Seuil, 2011), 18. The first section of this book is called *Dire être né*. "To say having been born." The lines I have cited are underlined in the original.
7. Jacques Roubaud, *La forme d'une ville change plus vite, hélas, que le coeur des humains* (Paris: © Éditions Gallimard, 1999), 93, 146; trans. Rosmarie and Keith Waldrop as *The Form of a City Changes Faster, Alas, Than the Human Heart* (Champaign and London: Dalkey Archive Press, 2006), 80, 131.
8. Philippe Lacoue-Labarthe, *La poésie comme expérience* (Paris: Christian Bourgois, 1986), 66.

9   *Conditions of Light*, 184/*Conditions de lumière*, 184.
10 "L'Émoi" appears in *Phrase*, 43-48.
    It also appears in *Agonie terminée, agonie interminable*, edited and with an Introduction by Aristide Bianchi and Leonid Khalamov (Paris: Editions Galilée, 2011), 153-59; trans. Hannes Opelz as *Ending and Unending Agony: On Maurice Blanchot* (New York: Fordham University Press, 2015), 111-14. This volume gathers all the texts that Lacoue-Labarthe devoted to Blanchot. "Dismay" is the title of Opelz's translation of "L'Émoi."
11 Maurice Blanchot published this fragment more than once. I quote here part of my own translation of it, which appears in *The Writing of the Disaster*, 72/*L'écriture du désastre*, 117.
12 See "Tout le monde se ressemble," in *ma haie*, 237.
13 Pascal Quignard, *Le voeu de silence* (Montpellier: Fata Morgana, 1985). This text was first composed in 1977.
14 Louis-René des Forêts, *Les mégères de la mer* (Paris: Mercure de France, 1995), 26.
15 Norma Cole's English translation is unpaginated, as indicated above; the passage cited can be found in the entry called "Childhood."
16 Liesl Yamaguchi suggested this to me.
17 Recall *A Test of Solitude*, XXXI, where the reader is instructed to consider "the missing word is this name" as a tautology. Here is the whole sonnet, in Rosmarie Waldrop's translation.

> *People can as it were come into being through their*
> *name*
> is a sentence.
> What name to give to the space between the
> *canale* and the burnt stump,
> a question.
> The missing word is this name,
> an answer.
> This name the missing word.
> Look at the missing word is this name as a
> tautology.
> A tautology is not a sentence.
> Is utterance [énoncé] par excellence.
> An utterance is not a sentence.

18 *Un test de solitude*, XXIV Livre II.
19 Pierre Alferi, "Un accent de vérité.—James et Blanchot—," in *Brefs* (Paris: P.O.L, 2016), 125-56.
20 I am referring to the essay "Prenez-le vivant," in *Un privé*, 61-66.

Chapter Three

1. For another description of Roubaud's 1961 dream, its decisiveness, and the vast writing program it implied, see *Poésie*, 36.
2. Di Bernardi translates: "at this point it [the novel] is touched by the dream's twofold nature, by the double language drawing it along" (*The Great Fire*, 130).
3. *Le grand incendie*, 170; 331-32/*The Great Fire*, 128; 255-56.
4. One of the three "styles" that Roubaud says he borrows from the Japanese poet Kamo no Chomei is the "style du double." It seems that *Le Grand Incendie de Londres*, as initially conceived, was to use this style constantly, and that something of it remains in 'le grand incendie de Londres,' the ruins of that projected novel. Cardonne-Arlyck discusses this, as well as the "*biipsism*," and the "rhythmic composition" *La Lampe* (a palindromic text, in its way, which I will come to) in "Jacques Roubaud: 'je deviens guetteur …'" 255, 258-59.
5. One imagines a virtual encounter like this for Roubaud and Alix Roubaud upon reading his solution to a riddle in *Le grand incendie*: there is a hermit who rises with the sun and climbs the dusty road to the top of the hill, arriving there as the sun goes down. He spends the night in prayer and the next day, rising again with the sun, goes back down the hill, arriving at evening where he began. Show, the riddle demands, that there is a spot on his path which he passes through at the same hour on the way up and on the way back down. To solve this puzzle it suffices to invent, Roubaud says, a phantom hermit (the real one's double), who gets up at dawn on the second day, at the bottom of the hill, just as the first hermit begins his descent. Then you must suppose that the phantom hermit follows the real one's path of the day before (step by step, at the exact same speed). Since the dusty road is the same, the two are bound to meet somewhere on it, and that spot, "le lieu de leur rencontre," is the solution to the riddle. *You* must think, Roubaud adds, addressing his reader, "that the phantom hermit is a memory hermit (un hermite de *mémoire*), and that in the declining evening light she, Alix, my wife accompanies my prose as slowly it advances along its paper path. If, a long time after reading the first branch of my narrative you read the last, you must think that somewhere along the way our two images coincide" (*Le grand incendie*, 32-33/*The Great Fire*, 20).
6. E. Hocquard, "Taches blanches," in *ma haie*, 403. For a remarkable discussion of Hocquard's blank spots, of related in-between spaces and edges (fringes, margins, lists)—and of Hocquard's work more generally—see James Petterson's fine essay, "Ni frontière, ni limite: *Ma haie* d'Emmanuel Hocquard," in *Ecritures Contemporaines* 7 (2003): 99-116. The title of this issue of *Ecritures Contemporaines* is *Effractions d'écriture*.
7. See *Méditations photographiques sur l'idée simple de nudité*—especially 24.

8   1,178 is the number of "moments" Roubaud foresaw—sometime around the year 2000, when he published *Poésie*—for his entire six-branch prose work. He counts his prose in moments, months, and years. The whole *Great Fire* was initially slated for six "years" (i.e., volumes or branches), of 196 "moments" each.6 x 196 = 1,176. Given the foreword and foreseeable afterword, though, it would come to 1,178 moments in all. "Cela fait beacoup, beaucoup de nombres," Roubaud observes in the course of the 589th moment of *'le grand incendie.'* This all makes for a great many numbers.

Five hundred and eighty-nine is half of 1,178. Which is to say, it is the midpoint of the whole long course, and the spot in the six-volume prose that corresponds on a related time-line to the date of Alix Cléo's death. "La nuit médiane." Something like the central axis of a palindrome. I've crossed it, Roubaud observes (*Poésie*, 238).

I offer these calculations as a very slight indication of Roubaud's "numerological obsession." I also mean the reader to notice how his compositions keep hinging on a night, a disappearance, something like *une absence médiane*.

9   *Tridents* (Caen: NOUS, 2019), 12. See, in chapter 6, note 8 for a brief description of this most recent—up to now—volume by Roubaud.

Chapter Four

1   Martin Klebes describes Bartlebooth's unfinishable project, and Roubaud's commentary on it, much as I have, but with somewhat different emphases, in "Jacques Roubaud: Projecting Memory," 136-37. His account of Roubaud's initial conception of the Project and accompanying novel, and of the novel's necessarily turning out to be the imitation of what it might have been, is also very useful. See 138-39.

2   Jean-Jacques Poucel, in his essay "Quelques remarques sur les tombeaux poétiques de Jacques Roubaud," provides references to several useful discussions of one crucial aspect of Roubaud's work: its destruction. See *Jacques Roubaud, 'compositeur en mathématique et poésie,'* 294-95, note 5.

3   Jacques Roubaud, *Sous le soleil: Vanité des vanités* (Paris: Bayard, 2004).

The wreckage of forms in Roubaud's work is absorbing—the planned structures left half complete, the projects given up. In "Traces et abandons oulipiens dans *Quelque chose noir*," Olivier Salon discusses the ruination of one particular Roubaud work—*Quelque chose noir*—and the crumbling of its structuring constraints. See *Pour Eclairer* Quelque chose noir, 169-80. Salon writes, for example:

> L'auteur s'impose une structure, celle de neuf neuvines [a *neuvine* is a complex structure inaugurated by the troubadour Arnaut Daniel and revived by Raymond Queneau]. Chaque neuvine se compose de neuf

vers, et chaque vers est lui-même décomposé en neuf segments, que séparent des espaces. Mais rapidement, l'écho avec le *Journal d'Alix*, auquel *Quelque chose noir* répond, impose autre chose: la structure initiale est bouleversée, ou plutôt, selon les termes mêmes de l'auteur, "ruinée," "bombardée." A la ruine terrible de l'auteur, impuissant dans son malheur, répond une autre ruine, active celle-là: la ruine de l'architecture formelle d'origine. Ne subsisteront de la structure formelle initiale que des éléments épars, comme les mots-clefs, presque tous repérables dans le premier poème du receuil. [...] Ce qui reste de la structure initiale est une architecture qui a subi des dommages. (180)

My translation: "The author imposes upon himself a structure, that of nine neuvines [a "neuvine" is a complex structure inaugurated by the troubadour Arnaut Daniel and revived by Raymond Queneau]. Each neuvine is composed of nine lines, and each line is itself broken down into nine segments, which are separated by spaces. But very soon the echo with the *Journal of Alix*, to which *Some Thing Black* responds, imposes something different: the initial structure is overturned, or rather, in the author's own terms, "ruined," "bombed." To the terrible ruin of the author himself, powerless in his grief, corresponds another ruin. This one is active: the ruin of the initial formal architecture. Nothing of the original formal structure will subsist except scattered elements, such as the key words, which are almost all apparent in the first poem of the collection. [...] What remains of the initial structure is a damaged architecture."

4   See Jacques Roubaud, *La Fleur inverse*, 36.
5   Jacques Roubaud, *Graal fiction* (Paris: Gallimard, 1978), 220.
6   Lewis Carroll's *Hunt for the Snark* is among the quests that preoccupy Roubaud, and we will refer to it again, in connection with *Eros mélancolique*. There is a kind of Snark called Boojum that, if found, disappears along with its discoverer.
7   "Danielle Collobert, 'Cri ou comme brûle jamais dit,' " in *Danielle Collobert*, 37.
8   This poem is the first in the sixth group of nine (there are nine groups of nine in all, plus one more poem, all alone, under the heading *Rien*). The last poem in that sixth group is also called "Cette photographie, ta dernière"—like the first. Here are its first several lines.

> Cette photographie, ta dernière, je l'ai laissée sur le mur, entre les deux fenêtres, au-dessus,
>
> De la télévision désaffectée, et le soir, dans le golfe de toits à gauche de l'église, quand la lumière,
>
> Se concentre, qui en même temps, s'écoule, en deux estuaires obliques, et inchangeables, dans l'image,

> Je m'assieds, sur cette chaise, d'où l'on voit, à la fois,
> l'image intérieure la photographie, et autour d'elle, ce
> qu'elle montre,

9   Jacques Roubaud, *Ciel et terre et ciel et terre, et ciel*, 52.
    This book of Roubaud's is particularly beautiful in part because of the John Constable cloud studies reproduced within it. See Stéphane Baquey, "John Constable, Goodman et Jacques Roubaud: l'apprentissage d'un usage des signes," in *compositeur de mathématique et de poésie* 359-68. Dominique Moncond'huy notes, in "Du Journal au tombeau ou de 'quelque chose' à 'rien,' " (in *Pour Eclairer* Quelque chose noir, 38-48), that Roubaud's title, *Ciel et terre et ciel* ... refers to Queneau: to the last phrase of his last poetry collection, *Morale élémentaire* (Paris: Gallimard, 1975): "Pour en arriver là, il aura fallu remuer ciel et terre." "To reach that point, one will have had to move heaven and earth." Jacques Jouet takes up this phrase also, in "Ruminations du potentiel." It is as if it echoed softly throughout the Oulipian oeuvre. To get all the way from Rimbaud's "absolument moderne" to the Oulipo's "absolument potentiel," Jouet writes, "il aura fallu remuer cieux et terres" (22). Of course, Roubaud's title also refers to Constable's cloud studies and to his landscapes, and to Roubaud's understanding of the relation between them. But the thought of an exceedingly demanding goal—a practically impossible restorative task of memory—may well also color Roubaud's book about Constable and James Goodman. *Ciel et terre et ciel* can be felt as a small part of this gigantic work of remembering.

10 Here is the whole poem which I have been paraphrasing: "L'occasion," in *La Forme d'une ville* 140-41/ *The Form of a City*, 125-26.

> je n'avais pas pu penser
> en cette particulière occasion
> ni de manière erronée
> ni de manière correcte
>
> en cette particulière occasion
> je n'avais pas pu penser
> que j'étais dans l'erreur
> que quelque chose que j'avais pensé
> à cette occasion
> était faux
> à moins d'avoir pensé aussi
> qu'en cette particulière occasion
> quelque chose d'autre j'avais pensé
> qui était faux
>
> et je ne pouvais pas avoir eu peur

> en cette particulière occasion
> avec ou sans raison
> quand ce quelque chose dont j'avais eu peur
> en cette particulière occasion
> n'était pas quelque chose que de craindre
> il était raisonnable
>
> je ne pouvais pas avoir eu peur de cela qui m'avait effrayé
> si je n'avais pas eu en cette particulière occasion
> une crainte
> une tout autre crainte, une autre peur
> déraisonnable.
>
> j'aurais tant voulu
> n'avoir qu'une pensée et qu'une peur
> et qu'aucune occasion particulière et hasardeuse privation
> de ces possibilités ne m'en préserve
> qui viendrait m'en priver pour toujours
>
> peur
> peur
> peur

11 Martin Klebes writes, in a similar vein, "This 'some thing black' [...] would remain 'unaccomplished.' [...] Because in its 'purity' it would signify the unmitigated certainty of the interruption that is death" ("Jacques Roubaud: Projecting Memory," 160).

12 On the subject of the "Arthurian intertext" in Roubaud, see Florence Marsal, *Jacques Roubaud. Prose de la mémoire et errance chevaleresque* (Presses Universitaires de Rennes, 2010).

13 The aim of narrative, Roubaud writes at one point, is "its completion and the revelation of what it is" (*The Great Fire*, 242/*Le grand incendie*, 315). Or perhaps you could say, narrative aims to formulate, bit by bit, the question to which it is the answer: the question, I expect, that Percival could not ask as long as he did not know who he was (going to have been).

14 Let me note here that in the medieval tale, when Percival sees the mysterious gleaming objects, including the Grail, or book, and doesn't know how to ask the right question, Roubaud understands that he doesn't know how to read the book. And "who is he who remains mute in front of the book?" Roubaud asks. "He who doesn't know the language, and can't translate." The Grail book, he concludes, could only be a search for its own translation, whose impossibility is the cause of the cultural wasteland that keeps expanding every time some language, no longer understood, dies (*Graal fiction*, 183–84).

Roubaud is thinking here in particular of the language of the troubadours, "la langue d'oc." In *Graal fiction* he argues that the Arthurian romances and the "matière de Bretagne"—the Celtic legends they elaborate—entailed a strategy for preserving, via compromises, modifications, hidden references and allusions, something of the poetry of Provence, the art of Guillaume d'Aquitaine, Jaufre Rudel, Raimbaut d'Orange, and the others, their songs of love and the Occitan civilization they belonged to, in a world hostile to it, dominated by Normans and the orthodox Catholic Church. But Roubaud suggests as well, I believe, when he describes Percival mute, before an untranslatable language he doesn't know, that the Grail book is the story of a search for the story's own forgotten tongue. Or, for poetry.

15 Georges Perec, *Le voyage d'hiver*/Jacques Roubaud, *Le voyage d'hier* (Nantes: Le passeur, 1997). Still other Oulipians, notably Jacques Jouet, have contributed elaborate episodes to the ever-branching legend of Hugo Vernier and the lost book he composed, *Voyage d'hiver*, containing, apparently, the greatest lines of nineteenth-century French poetry before Baudelaire, Rimbaud, Verlaine, or Mallarmé ever wrote them. Jouet's contribution is *Hinterreise* (La Bibliothèque Oulipienne, no. 108 (1999).

16 The first section of *La forme d'une ville* is titled "Recourir les rues," an hommage to Queneau's book of Paris street poems, *Courir les rues* (Paris: Gallimard, 1967).

17 The poem I have been recounting, "La rue," is on pages 93 and 94 of *La forme d'une ville*; 80 and 81 in *The Form of a City*.

Chapter Five

1 Cloud passages abound in Roubaud's work. See especially *Ciel et terre et ciel et terre et ciel; La Boucle* (the section called "Des Nuages," 423–61/ *The Loop* 396–431); *La pluralité des mondes de Lewis* ("Fin de nuages," 93–98/"The End of Clouds," 93–98).

2 *Dors précédé de Dire la poésie*, 18. In *Sleep Preceded by Saying Poetry*, see 11, 12.

3 In *Dors précédé de Dire la Poésie* (Paris: © Éditions Gallimard 1981); see pages 47, 51, 58.

4 This rhythmic composition appears in *Echanges de la lumière*, too, spoken three times, in three of its phases, by William H., in the course of the second and third evening sessions of Mr. Goodman's seminar on light.

Chapter Six

1 On the OULIPO (l'Ouvroir de littérature potentielle—Workshop for Potential Literature), see, for example, Raymond Queneau, "Littérature potentielle," in *Batons, Chiffres et lettres* (Paris: Gallimard, 1965), 317–45; Jacques Roubaud, "Of Oulipo," in *Poetry, etcetera* 197–219 ("De l'Oulipo" *in*

Poésie etcetera, 197–218); *Atlas de littérature potentielle* (Paris: Gallimard, 1981); *A Primer of Potential Literature*, trans. and ed. Warren Motte (Lincoln, London: University of Nebraska Press, 1986); *OULIPO* (Paris: association pour la diffusion de la poésie française, 2005). And, by Jacques Jouet himself, *Ruminations de l'atelier oulipien, de l'improvisation et du potentiel* (La Bibliothèque Oulipienne, no. 203, 2014.)

The present Jouet intermezzo is based in part on an essay called "Everyday," which I published in *L'Esprit créateur* 49, no. 2 (Summer 2009): 62–76.

On Jacques Jouet, see the special issue of *SubStance* 96 (2001), edited by Warren Motte.

2   Jacques Jouet, *Ruminations de l'atelier oulipien, de l'improvisation et du potentiel*, 22.
3   Jacques Jouet, *Cantates de proximité* (Paris: P.O.L, 2005), 38
4   See Jacques Jouet, *A supposer*... (Caen: NOUS, 2007): a collection of thirty-six *A supposer* texts: each a single sentence or "phrase," in the musical as well as the verbal sense, I believe.
5   Jouet has written a potboiler of his own, a "roman-feuilleton" or serial novel about a truck driver who quits his job but holds on to his semi trailer, which he parks in a freeway rest area. There he establishes his own Republic: *La République de Mek-Oyes* (Paris: P.O.L, 2001). I quote here from Jouet's description of this work:

> Un roman-feuilleton
> en deux parties toujours à suivre
>   moderne et à l'ancienne
>   routier comme autoroutier
> […]
> rapportant les aventures gagnant à être connues
> aussi amusantes qu'inauthentiques et agréables à se rappeler
>   d'un personnage nommé Mek-Ouyes et de ses proches
>   avec ses amours et ses haines
>   avec leurs réussites et leurs infortunes
>   leurs coups de chance au milieu des adversités…
>
> A serial novel
> in two parts always to be continued
>   modern in the old style
>   as crafty as road-wise
> […]
> reporting the adventures which benefit from being known
> as entertaining as inauthentic and enjoyable to recall
>   of a character named Mek-Ouyes and his pals
>   with his loves and his hatreds

> with their successes and their woes
> their lucky breaks in the midst of adversity ...
>
> (My rough translation)

On Mek-Ouyes, see Jean-Didier Wagneur and Roxanne Lapidus, "Mek-Ouyes and Public Things," *SubStance* 96: 38–44.

6   Mallarmé might well appear to be Jouet's nemesis: the sterility of the white page, and so on. But Jouet, never one to be tiresomely consistent, or to fail in loving what he also disapproves of, explicitly stages his own "coup de dés," in his endless poetry journal, *Navet, linge, oeil-de-vieux* (see note 9, below), where the "linge" of the title (a fringed napkin, or a placemat or dishtowel) serves on occasion as a kind of stage or arena for a contest; and once the entire threesome (turnip, placemat, oeil-de-vieux or painter's aid) is said to form the site of the conflict between "hasard et coup de dés." Moreover the reader will surely have thought of Mallarmé's "disparition élocutoire du poète," who "leaves the initiative to words," whenever they encounter Jouet's aspiration to fade out of literature, leaving the forms he invents to function on their own. Jouet acknowledges this link to Mallarmé in *Poèmes de métro*, 107. See my "Everyday," in *L'Esprit créateur*, for other references by Jouet to Mallarmé.

7   Jacques Jouet, *Poèmes de métro* (Paris: P.O.L, 2000), 196.

8   See Jacques Roubaud, *Churchill 40* (Paris: Gallimard 2004), 51.

> La poésie, ai-je entendu, sort de la page
> Elle va sur écran, elle court dans la rue
> Jouet dans le métro transporte sa charrue
> De vers: un vers pour chaque station d'un voyage
>
> Le métro s'en allant prend les mots, les remue
> Le vers fait mouvement dans la tête et s'encage
> Quand la rame s'arrête. Un arrêt sur image
> Telle est la poésie au temps de sa venue
>
> Poetry, I've heard, is leaving the page
> She goes on screen, she takes to the streets
> Into the métro Jouet transports his verse-making
> plough: one line per stop on a single trip
>
> The subway starting off takes the words, stirs them up
> The line moves around in the head and cages itself
> When the train stops. Freeze frame
> Such is poetry in Jouet's era   (My approximate translation)

In the tercets, of which one and a half lines are counted *in absentia*, Roubaud reminds us of his view that every poem is double, having a written form plus a spoken one; and he also seems to recall, almost in passing, poetry's association with a fall. Every word awakens, he seems to say, what has surfaced in the black lines placed flat on the page: every word revives what has come up from underneath, that is—or been remembered in— what falls on the page, *there*.

> De la main qui la pose elle ressortira
> Désimmobilisant votre oeil ou votre oreille
> ou les deux (je préfère)
>
>   Tout vocable réveille
> Ce qui s'est souvenu dans ce qui tombe là.

I should add that Roubaud sometimes adopts the poem-a-day rule that I've been describing as characteristically Jouet's. For example, in 2019 he published the complete collection of his "tridents": *Tridents* (Caen: Éditions NOUS). He had been composing one of these three-line poems each day for close to twenty years. The collection contains more than 4,000. He invented the trident form himself: three lines, thirteen syllables (five for the first line, three for the second, five for the third). "C'est une forme mémorisable," he remarks, on the back cover of *Tridents*, "et qui se fait geste quotidien: poèmes de notation, de sensation, de réflexion, de souvenir."

>   avec le 'trident'
> ⊗ j'expérience
>   la vie d'une forme

Further along in this "Interlude," when Roubaud's formal experiments with sonnets comes up, a reader might like to recall this expression, "la vie d'une forme."

9 Jacques Jouet, *Navet, linge, oeil-de-vieux* (Paris: P.O.L, 1998). Michelle Grangaud's essay, translated by Jordan Stump, "A Diary, Some poems (French irregular plural)," *SubStance* 96: 27-36, is particularly interesting on the subject of Jouet's poetry journal. Grangaud is a fellow Oulipian.

10 Jacques Jouet, *107 ames* (Paris: Seghers, 2015). Jouet composed this volume of poems starting from the results of a questionnaire (date and place of birth? marital status? occupation?) mailed to 107 individuals he did not know.

11 See the back cover of *Cantates de proximité*: "If the local cantatas are not destined to be sung at a Sunday service, they nonetheless express a certain reverence for Jean-Sébastien Bach" (my translation). See also the cantate titled "Famille Bach," *Cantates de proximité*, 145-50.

12 See *A supposer . . .* 21, 38, 39.

13 Jouet's words (translated by Jordan Stump), quoted by Michelle Grangaud in *SubStance* 96: 33. I have simplified and no doubt exaggerated this

remark about blankness and its due. It is actually just one of the "characters" in *Navet, linge, oeil-de-vieux*, to whom the comment applies. The turnip, placemat (or dishtowel), and Oeil-de-vieux are the three objects in a still life setup, and also, no doubt, three aspects of a poet, Jouet, and his poetry. It is the oeil-de-vieux (a painter's aid) whose usefulness consists in rendering unto blankness that which is blankness's.

14   On Merrill Moore, see Roubaud, *Poésie*, 425–27. For a fuller discussion of Roubaud and the sonnet form, see my "Jacques Roubaud's 'Sonnetomania,' *Literary Imagination* 12, no. 3 (2010): 344–54.

15   Roubaud devotes the whole of chapter 5 in *Poésie* ("La Tabatière du Notaro") to his apprenticeship as a sonneteer, to his conception of the book of sonnets he eventually published in 1967, and to the gradual construction of this volume. See 145–81. Chapter 13, "Le Livre dont le titre est le signe d'appartenance," discusses the structure and content of the sonnet book in detail. See 447–85.

16   Warren Motte, "Jacques Jouet and the Literature of Exhaustion," in *SubStance* 96: 45–63.

17   Jacques Roubaud, ϵ (Paris: Gallimard, 1967).

18   Raymond Queneau, *Cent mille milliards de Poèmes* (Paris: Gallimard, 1961).

19   For a particularly striking evocation of the company or fellowship of inventor-poets (Roubaud among them) who join each other over the years—sometimes across many generations—as participants in one or another "language game," see Jean-Jacques Poucel, "ChiQuenaude: Vie brève de la morale élémentaire," in *La Morale élémentaire: Aventures d'une Forme poétique* (*La Licorne* 81 (208): 15–54). Poucel emphasizes Roubaud's keen attention to a growing weave of poems, difficult to perceive but slowly materializing through long stretches of time via intersecting poetic forms and the variations, innovations, distortions they continually undergo. Evoking a half-belief on Roubaud's part in a steadily evolving work, or a gradually reemerging poetry world, Poucel writes (54),

> La tâche paléontologique à laquelle nous convie Roubaud est celle de reconnaître et poursuivre, dans les origines les plus lointaines, les plus improbables, le désir d'appartenance—ce drame de s'établir une famille retrouvée et le risque de folie associé à sa perte. [...] C'est l'aventure de rêver d'avant sa naissance, de fonder un mythe, tout en le parodiant, comme pour lier, voire unifier la démystification et la mise en valeur de l'oeuvre même.

In my translation it appears as

> The paleontological task which Roubaud urges us to join is that of recognizing and pursuing, in the most distant, most improbable sources, the desire of belonging—the drama of establishing for oneself a family

found anew, and the risk of madness associated with its loss. [...] This is the adventure of dreaming of the time before one's birth, of founding a myth, all the while parodying it, as if in order to link, indeed unite the demystification of the work itself with its illumination.

For a different perspective on the Oulipo and the idea of a Book comparable to Mallarmé's Livre, see Vincent Kaufmann, *Poétique des groupes littéraires* (Paris: Presses Universitaires de France, 1997), 48-52. Kaufmann stresses—with wit and irony—an Oulipian version of Mallarmé's "pure work," or his Book, having neither author nor reader, developing on its own, or under the direction of a depersonalized or even deceased "operator."

20 For a reflection on the Grail legend in Roubaud and on quests, especially in connection with the mathematical dimension of his work, see Elvira Monika Laskowski-Caujolle, "Jacques Roubaud: Literature, Mathematics and the Quest for Truth," in *SubStance* 96: 71-87.

Chapter Seven

1 Melancholy stems, by definition in Roubaud's *Fleur inverse*, from the loss of an object never possessed. "[L]a mélancolie n'est pas tellement due à la perte d'un object, mais à la douleur insurmontable d'une perte qui anticipe celle de l'objet, qui peut même viser un objet inexistant." Melancholy also has a "phantasmatic capacity," Roubaud continues. This consists in the ability to cause an unattainable object to appear as if lost: " 'la capacité fantasmatique de faire apparaître comme perdu un objet inappropriable' " (*La fleur inverse*, 87). Cardonne-Arlyck develops this thought beautifully, especially at the end of her essay, dwelling on Roubaud's "style mélancolique," and bringing out Giorgio Agamben's notion of melancholy's *strategy*. This strategy grants a kind of existence to unreal beings—to unattainable ones that *appear*, as if lost—and thus it holds off, without ever defeating, the black despair, the "*à quoi bon* généralisé."

Citing Agamben, Cardonne-Arlyck writes: " 'To the extent that it is a form of mourning for an unattainable object, the strategy allows the unreal to accede to existence, defining the scope of a scene or stage where the self can enter into a relation with it [the unreal] and attempt an appropriation which no possession could ever equal, no loss ever compromise.' This scene," she goes on, "would be the whole of *le grand incendie de londres*, as, from branch to branch it evolves. The Project comes into existence here, unreal in itself but actualized by the revelation of its failure." My translation; here is the original: " 'Dans la mesure où elle est le deuil d'un objet insaisissaable, [la] stragégie [de la mélancolie] permet à l'irréel d'accéder à l'existence, délimitant une scène sur laquelle le moi peut entrer en rapport avec lui et tenter une appropriation qu'aucune possession ne pourrait égaler, qu'aucune perte ne pourrait compromettre.' Cette scène, ce serait la totalité du *grand incendie de londres*, tel que, de branche en branche il s'élabore. Le Projet y accède bien à l'existence, en lui-même irréel mais actualisé par la révélation de son échec" (314-15).

For my part, I am suggesting a very similar thought in these pages of *The Play of Light*, similarly indebted to Agamben—a thought that draws together memory, and a "capacity" in us "for deprivation," and our ability to see shadows.

2   Giorgio Agamben, "On Potentiality," in *Potentialities. Collected Essays*, trans. and ed. and with an Introduction by Daniel Heller-Roazen (Stanford, CA: Stanford University Press, 1999), 181.

3   I appear to be assuming the black and the white to be perfectly distinct. But I should acknowledge that ultimately in Roubaud the point, so to speak, is to bear them both in mind, very close together, just without ever allowing either one to exclude or to absorb the other. Cardonne-Arlyck brings out another early memory of Roubaud's, a memory of coal and snow: "Charbon et neige, conjoints en un souvenir unique" ("Jacques Roubaud: 'Je deviens guetteur ...,'" 222). She briefly stresses this "black and white, darkness and light," conjoined.

4   Cardonne-Arlyck discusses this poem at length, very interestingly in "Jacques Roubaud: 'Je deviens guetteur,'" 177-81.

5   *Invent*, from *invenire*: to come upon, to find. Roubaud is not the first to dwell on this ambiguous relation, contained in the words *invent* and *invention*, between discovery and fabrication.

6   See Roubaud's essay "Première digression sur les débuts de la photographie," in *Du Visible a l'invisible*.

For an arresting discussion of photography in Roubaud's work, see Olivier Barbarant, "La Mort photographe," in *Pour Eclairer* Quelque chose noir, 49-63.

7   In *Echanges de la lumière*, 63-64, William H. recites these lines.

> Comment pourrait si grande dame entrer
> Par les yeux miens, puisque si petits sont?
> Et dans mon coeur comment peut-elle tenir
> Qui la porte en lui partout où il va?
>   Le lieu par où elle entre on ne voit pas
> Ce qui un grand étonnement me donne
> Mais je veux à la lumière l'assimiler
> Mes yeux au verre où elle se pose.
>   Le feu inclus ensuite vient dehors
>
> Son illumination mais sans rupture
> Ainsi par les yeux miens vient à mon coeur
>   Non sa personne mais la sienne image

> Renouveler je me veux d'amour
> Qui porte signe d'une telle créature.

8 In "Première Digression sur les débuts de la photographie"—in the section where he stresses Sir John Herschel's having been an astronomer, and the son of another, more famous one—Roubaud recalls Mallarmé's thinking of bright stars on the night sky as a celestial writing ("L'Action restreinte," in *Oeuvres Complètes*, vol. 2 [Paris: Gallimard, 2003], 215). Mallarmé observed that man, for his part, continues God's white on black, but reversed: black on white ("l'homme poursuit noir sur blanc").

Roubaud reflects on Galileo's teaching: God wrote the world in mathematical language, and it is therefore appropriate to decipher it in mathematical language, but he adds it is no less true that God "wrote on the celestial vault with the alphabet of the stars and that man, inspired by this example, continued with letters 'black on white.' And what," he goes on to ask, "was the divine ink, tracing the enigmatic signs of the stars' configurations? Light" (210) (my translation).

So, if Galileo, looking through his telescope, understood the task of science to be to "say the world" ("dire le monde"), as it is written—to say it with a mathematical alphabet, with the signs, black on white, of algebra and calculus—then, if one undertakes to *show* the world ("montrer le monde"), it follows naturally to *name* the instrument that writes the world in the language of light *photography* (210).

Writing with light is a second writing, we read in *Eros mélancolique*: "une deuxième écriture, qui *montre*" (206). Here Roubaud refers, as he often does, to the pair *say* and *show* (Wittgenstein holds that language shows what it does not say). The world that for a short while was his and Alix Roubaud's—their *biipsism*—was one of saying and showing, poetry and photography (and in parallel fashion, French and English). Or again, the prose narratives recounting the adventures of the Grail Knights are said, in *La fleur inverse*, to relate to the poetry of the troubadours as showing relates to saying. And indeed, the "secret" part of young Goodman's Project, his complex assemblage of photographic images would, it seems—had it ever been completed—have "made visible," "*demonstrated*," the truth behind the entire undertaking: the truth that was to be *said* in the Mémoire (the truth that the invention of its name caused photography to be). For my own part, I mainly mean here to underline the black-and-white motif.

9 Anne Portugal, *Le plus simple appareil* (Paris: P.O.L, 1992); trans. Norma Cole as *Nude* (Berkeley, CA: Kelsey Street Press, 2001).

10 See the interview titled "Poésie et méthode" broadcast by France Culture on June 23, 2017, at https://www.franceculture.fr/emissions/poésie-et-ainsi-de-suite.

For a spirited description of Anne Portugal's "fantaxe"—syntaxe and fantasy combined—see Pierre Alferi, "La Poésie et les vieillards," in *Brefs*, 49-56, especially 52-55.

11   Anne Portugal, *et comment nous voilà moins épais* (Paris: P.O.L, 2017); *la formule flirt* (Paris: P.O.L, 2010), trans. Jean-Jacques Poucel as *Flirt formula* (Iowa City and Paris: La Presse, 2012); *définitif bob* (Paris: P.O.L, 2002), trans. Jennifer Moxley as *Absolute bob* (Providence: Burning Deck/Anyart, 2010).

La formule flirt, like the opening section of *et comment nous voilà moins épais*, features pairs of poems. They are always from five to seven lines long, and face each other two by two across the book's central fold. They approach each other flirtatiously: calling out and answering, fancifully imitating, indirectly commenting, and so on, but always parting without quite agreeing, or meeting, without exactly touching. This causes, among many other funny, delicate, virtuoso effects, a small flickering, fluttering agitation just at the book's middle, where a split, about to close, opens again. I may well be overemphasizing this because of the blink or flutter at the center of Hocquard's tautologies, but it is interesting to me to discover in the *Oxford English Dictionary* that *flirt* is a word made up in English to imitate *flick*, and that it can mean open and close quickly—unfold and fold back up the way a fan does, or a bird's wing.

Michael Sheringham's reading of *définitif bob* is especially rewarding: "Dans le quotidien-immersion, résistance, liberté: R. Queneau, A. Portugal," in *Ecritures Contemporaines* 7 (2003): 205-19.

Also interesting to consult, among the few critical texts devoted to Anne Portugal so far, is Peter Consenstein, "Son et perception dans la poésie de D. Fourcade et A. Portugal," *Contemporary French and Francophone Studies* 18, no. 2 (2014): 108-15, as well as John Stout's interview with Portugal in *L'Enigme-poésie: entretiens avec 21 poètes françaises* (Rodopi, 2010). Other interviews are likewise recommended, notably Alain Veinstein's online conversation with Portugal at www.apresvillenoise.free.fr/av/bob/6.html; Sophie L. Thurnberg's, "Translating the Untranslatable: Conversations with Anne Portugal and Pierre Alferi," at https://www.worldlitraturetoday.org/blog/interviews/translating-untranslatable; as well as the interview broadcast by France Culture soon after the publication of *et comment nous voilà*, "Poésie et méthode," to which I have already referred (see note 164). One can find other interviews on YouTube, and those bearing on *la formule flirt* and *et comment nous voilà moins épais* are especially appealing.

12   See "Poésie et méthode."
13   See the back cover of *et comment nous voilà moins épais*.
14   In "Poésie et méthode."

15 John Stout, *L'Enigme-poésie: entretiens avec 21 poètes françaises* (Amsterdam: Rodopi, 2010), 203.

16 Here is the whole poem, followed by Ian Monk's translation, which has not been published yet but was kindly shown me by Anne Portugal.

> amis des plaisirs communs l'attribution d'entrée
> d'un nuage servi de lui par hasard à des usages
> plus étendus ne parvient pas sous la clarté l'apli
> cation dépasse de beaucoup cet étang où l'on nage
> reposé tout en noir d'une facilité de concentration
> sans rigueur on reste indemne on fait les frais dès
> lors il allait se montrer d'un revers recommence

> friends of mutual pleasures the allotting at once
> of a cloud served by itself by chance to broader
> uses fails to reach beneath the clarity the appli
> cation exceeds by far this pond where we swim
> lying back dressed in black an ease of concentration
> with no rigor we remain unharmed foot the bill just
> when it was about to show itself backwards start again

17 Anne Portugal, *De quoi faire un mur* (Paris: P.O.L, 1987), 65.

18 *De quoi faire un mur*, 25. Apollinaire is a favorite of Portugal's: along with Verlaine he is one of the "kind men" in her garden ("The Garden," 42). We will meet him again. The poem by Portugal, which I allude to here, echoes a calligramme of Apollinaire's called "Voyage." In a layout of words suggesting, among other things, train tracks on the page, Apollinaire wrote, "où va donc ce train qui meurt au loin / dans les vals et les beaux bois frais du / tendre été si pâle?" See *Calligrammes* (Paris: Gallimard, collection *Poésie*, 1966), 59–60. Here is the whole of the poem by Portugal.

> de la villégiature
> un sans arrêt qui rêve au loin
> la belle affaire si déposée que je la vois déjà
> servir de lien
> à l'écart   (*De quoi faire un mur*, 50)

19 A furiously pedaling girl whose braids may account for the elastic band in this poem, whose feet on the bike pedals form two mills—this girl with braids riding fast down the sidewalk (like the nonstop train along the Riviera, or the cars that roll sometimes along Portugal's lines, or the billiard balls, or like the lines themselves, "déboulant," or "déroulant" [one thinks of a rabbit streaking out ahead of the dogs, or of a bobbin])—this bicycling girl ends up on the mat. "un sac." Here is the brief poem in its entirety.

> quelquefois nattée descendant le trottoir
> on suit le caniveau
> les deux moulins
> l'isotopie de l'élastique devenu fil
> à rompre entre deux digues
> un sac

20 *Et comment nous voilà*, 95. Here is the whole, fast-moving poem. Notice the Lamborghini. "We want to be like that," the poem starts—at least in my effort at translation, and according to my impression that it takes up where the poem just preceding it left off, evoking stars pasted onto shiny white teeth "the better to call up everything brilliant, precious, like gold, dazzling value, success." "We want to be like that."

> on a envie de faire pareil ce qui est là que
> c'est impossible par conséqent qu'on est
> réels par la reproduction des pare-chocs
> mais rien de concret dans la lamborghini
> qu'un objet roulant un objet roulant bien
> et en bas des pages le volant est réglable a
> justement facile dans le rétro il n'y a rien

Let me call attention swiftly to "ce qui est là" in the first line ("what is there"), followed headlong by "c'est impossible" in the second ("it's impossible"), and in the last by "il n'y a rien" ("there is nothing"). For there is terror in verse, Anne Portugal says. A void. The turn of the line concerns her, but also the cut, "la coupe."

I may be overdramatizing. While underlining one tiny phrase and another, I might also have highlighted "justement facile" ("actually easy") answering to "c'est impossible." And I still might note (rather than the void in verse and the fright) Portugal's stated preference that her poems not settle on the page once their complex and rigorous composition is complete. There should be a trigger mechanism somewhere in them that suddenly discombobulates them completely, so that they finish by having to start over—"recommence." They should never settle. This is because gravity is the enemy of poetry and poems must be light as air in her view. But she did add, having said her work is the lightest thing—and that if ever it touches the ground it must be just to skim, like a skater—that in verse there is an abyss. See "Poésie et méthode." We will return briefly to "la coupe."

21 Another of her garden poems is a very short one in *De quoi faire un mur* which, faintly suggesting the garden of Eden, says, in a startling reversal, "they" entered because what they saw there made them almost frightened. "Then from the garden they saw / that evening could fall / they were

almost afraid / and that is why / they went in" (my translation). Different vowel sounds, each in combination with the consonant *r* whir through this miniature tale—an ill wind?: "*v*irent," "*e*urent," "*e*ntrèrent," and less prominently "*soir*," "p*eur*."

> Alors du jardin ils virent
> que le soir pouvait tomber
> ils eurent presque peur
> et c'est pourqoui
> ils y entrèrent   (*De quoi faire un mur*, 14)

22   One might associate this prohibition (the reflective surface bearing an image and acting as a limit imposed on desire) not only with the conception of desire's object as a fantasy, impossible to capture as if it were real, but also with another invention of the troubadours much studied and admired by Roubaud: *mezura*, the complex art of meter and rhythm that can hold off "le fol amour" and withstand the frenzy of language bent on *saying* love, its black "nien," "gouffre pur." See, for example, *La fleur inverse*, 279.

> La mezura est le seul rempart contre l'anarchie de l'éros, contre le versant destructif d'amors qu'exprime la figure de *l'éros mélancolique*. Et, simultanément, mezura est aussi le concept central de la théorie médiévale du rythme, dans la musique et le vers: la mesure étant ce qui transforme en chant la force désordonnée de la langue voulant dire l'amour." "Mezura is the only rampart against the anarchy of eros, against the destructive aspect of love expressed in the figure of *melancholy eros*. And, at the same time, mezura is also the central concept of the medieval theory of rhyme, in music and verse: measure being that which transforms into song the unruly force of language wanting to say love. (My translation)

23   Jacques Roubaud, *Parc sauvage* (Paris: Seuil, 2008). Among Roubaud's recently published tridents, the reader comes upon vivid fragments of that childhood landscape, its weather, its insects, trees, vines and flowers—wisteria, for example.

> *Glycines*
>
>   Fuji pour Fuji
> ⊗   je préfère
>   revoir les glycines   (*Tridents*, 204)
>
> Fuji for Fugi / I prefer / to see the wisteria again   (My translation)

>   *Fontfroide, 1943*
>
>   passion floribonde
> ⊗   grappes pourpres
>   enfant wisterique   (*Tridents*, 205)
>
> floribunda passion / purple clusters / wisterical child   (My translation)

Chapter Eight

1. Giorgio Agamben, *The Coming Community*, trans. Michael Hardt (Minneapolis, London: University of Minnesota Press, 1993). See pages 28-29, for example.
2. This "suchness" comes up in one of Roubaud's tridents.

    > *suchness*
    >
    >   jamais n'être 'pour'
    > ⊗   ni 'pourquoi?'
    >   mais toujours : 'ainsi'   (*Tridents*, 28)
    >
    > Never be 'for' / or 'for what' / but always 'thus'   (My translation)

3. *La forme d'une ville change plus vite, hélas, que le coeur des humains*, 3.
4. Agamben believes these "exemplary beings" are exemplars of "the coming community."

Chapter Nine

1. "La Poésie et les vieillards," in *Brefs*, 49.
2. These words are the last in the following poem from *Le plus simple appareil*. I suspect that the poem itself is a sort of prologue to the whole book, or at least to the first section ("the bath"), and that it features a vow ("sermon") to "approximate" "aisance" and "charité." This vow seems to be placed on the garden green, as if Portugal were laying all her cards on the table. But this is a surmise.

    > il est mieux de connaître son nom
    > de présenter la scène
    > par son nom
    > ça ouvre sur un pré
    >
    > la valeur d'un serment
    > posé à même le vert
    > et l'approximation de l'aisance
    > et de la charité   (*Le plus simple appareil*, 13)

> it is better to know its name
> to introduce the scene
> by name
> it opens onto a meadow
>
> the value of an oath
> placed next to green
> and the semblance of ease
> and of charity   (*Nude*, 10)

I do not doubt that Norma Cole has her own very good reasons for translating "approximation" as "semblance." Still, I stick with my intuition about "proximity," "drawing into proximity."

3   These are the last lines in a poem from *Le plus simple apppareil*, which I might take as confirmation of my idea that the middle, the "milieu," counts for a lot in Portugal's writing. For the poem features many middles and edges: a cemetery edged with coming-and-going paths in the middle of October nights, the edge of a bathtub, a bisected diagram, or perhaps a cut-in-half ghost.

> le terme vous savez m'évoque un cimetière
> bordé d'allées de va et vient
> et sur le mur de ce jardin une figure s'allume
> coupée par le milieu des nuits d'octobre
> fraîche
>
> il ne se passera pas dix jours
> que cette composition héroïque se tienne en équilibre
> sur le rebord de votre salle de bain
> rachetée par des survivants
> qui disent:
>
> ah l'amour mitoyen
> l'amour mitoyen ah   (*Le plus simple appareil*, 44)
>
> the term for me you know evokes a cemetery
> lined with allées that come and go
> and on the wall of this garden a figure lights up
> cut by the middle of cool October
> nights
>
> not ten days will go by
> that this heroic composition balances
> on the brink of your bathroom
> repurchased by the survivors
> who say:

> oh love in common
> in common love oh (*Nude*, 36)

(I wish there were a way to preserve a hint of "adjoining" for "mitoyen." A "mur mitoyen" is a party wall. "Maisons mitoyennes" are semidetached houses or duplexes.)

4 Maurice Blanchot, *L'attente l'oubli* (Paris: Gallimard, 1962), trans. John Gregg as *Awaiting Oblivion* (Lincoln and London: University of Nebraska Press, 1997), 56.

For the crudeness of secrets, see *L'attente l'oubli*, 111/*Awaiting Oblivion*, 58:

> Parlant, différant de parler.
> Pourquoi, quand elle parlait, différait-elle de parler?
> Le secret—quel mot grossier—n'était rien d'autre que le fait qu'elle parlait et différait de parler.

> Speaking, deferring speaking
> Why, when she spoke, did she defer speaking?
> The secret—what a crude word—was nothing other than the fact that she spoke and deferred speaking.

5 Maurice Blanchot, *Le pas au-delà* (Paris: Gallimard, 1973); trans Lycette. Nelson as *The Step Not Beyond* (Albany: State University of New York Press, 1992), 87.

6 Blanchot, *L'écriture du désastre* (Paris: Gallimard, 1980); trans. Ann Smock as *The Writing of the Disaster* (Lincoln and London: University of Nebraska Press, 1995), 41.

BIBLIOGRAPHY

The works listed here are books and articles that are discussed, or simply mentioned, in *The Play of Light*. I have not provided a *complete* list of works by Roubaud, Hocquard, Collobert, Jouet, or Portugal—only the works that figure (no matter how briefly) in this book.

Primary Materials

Collobert, Danielle. *Oeuvres I*. Paris: P.O.L, 2004.
———. *Oeuvres II*. Paris: P.O.L, 2005.
———. *Dire I, II*. In *Oeuvres I*.
———. *Il Donc*. In *Oeuvres I*.
———. *Meurtre*. In *Oeuvres I*.
———. *Survie*. In *Oeuvres I*.
———. *It Then*. Translated by Norma Cole. Oakland, CA: O Books, 2013.
———. *Murder*. Translated by Nathanaël. Brooklyn, NY: Litmus Press, 2013.
———. "Survival." Translated by Norma Cole, in *Crosscut Universe*, ed. Norma Cole (Providence, RI: Burning Deck, 2000).
Hocquard, Emmanuel. *Aerea dans les forêts de Manhattan*. Paris: P.O.L, 1985.
———. *Aerea in the Forests of Manhattan*. Translated by Lydia Davis. Evanston, IL: Marlboro Press, 1992.
———. *Album d'images de la Villa Harris*. Paris: P.O.L, 1978.
———. *Ce qui n'advint pas*. Marseille: Spectres Familiers, 2016.
———. *Cette histoire est la mienne: Petit dictionnaire autobiographique de l'élégie*. In *ma haie*, 461-89. Paris: P.O.L, 2001.

———. *This Story Is Mine: Little Autobiographical Dictionary of Elegy*. Translated by Norma Cole. Saratoga, CA: Instress, 1999. This translation is based on the 1997 edition (Paris: *Notes*) of *Cette histoire est la mienne*. When Hocquard published *Cette histoire* again, in *ma haie*, he added some pages, which do not appear in Norma Cole's translation. I do not cite any of these additions in my text.

———. *Conditions de lumière*. Paris: P.O.L, 2007.

———. *Conditions of Light*. Translated by Jean-Jacques Poucel. Iowa City and Paris: La Presse, 2012.

———. *Le cours de Pise*. Édition établi par David Lespiau. Paris: P.O.L, 2018.

———. *Les élégies*. Paris: P.O.L, 1990.

———. *L'Invention du verre*. Paris: P.O.L, 2003.

———. *The Invention of Glass*. Translated by Cole Swensen and Rod Smith. Marfa, TX: Canarium Books, 2012.

———. *ma haie. Un privé à Tanger II*. Paris: P.O.L, 2001.

———. *Méditations photographiques sur l'idée simple de nudité*. Paris: P.O.L, 2009.

———. *Un privé à Tanger*. Paris: P.O.L, 1987.

———. *Un test de solitude*. Paris: P.O.L, 1998.

———. *A Test of Solitude*. Translated by Rosemarie Waldrop. Providence, RI: Burning Deck, 2000.

———. *Théorie des tables*. Paris: P.O.L, 1993.

———. *Theory of Tables*. Translated by Michael Palmer. Providence, RI: o-blek editions, 1994.

———. *Tout le monde se ressemble: Une anthologie de poésie contemporaine*. Paris: P.O.L, 1995.

Jouet, Jacques. *A supposer* . . . Caen: Éditions NOUS, 2007.

———. *Cantates de proximité*. Paris: P.O.L, 2005.

———. *Navet, linge, oeil-de-vieux*, tomes I, II, III. Paris: P.O.L, 1998.

———. *Poèmes de métro*. Paris: P.O.L, 2000.

———. *La République de Mek-Oyes*. Paris: P.O.L, 2001.

———. *Ruminations de l'atelier oulipien, de l'improvisation et du potentiel*. Bibliothèque Oulipienne 203 (2014).

———. *107 âmes*. Paris: Seghers, 2015.

Portugal, Anne. *définitif bob*. Paris: P.O.L, 2001.

———. *Absolute Bob*. Translated by Jennifer Moxley. Providence, RI: Burning Deck/Anyart, 2010.

———. *De quoi faire un mur*. Paris: P.O.L, 1987.

———. *et comment nous voilà moins épais*. Paris: P.O.L, 2017.

———. *Fichier*. Paris: Michel Chandaigne, 1992.

———. *La formule flirt*. Paris: P.O.L, 2010.

———. *Flirt Formula*. Translated by Jean-Jacques Poucel. Iowa City and Paris: La Presse, 2012.

———. "The Garden." In *Six Contemporary French Women Poets: Theory, Practice, and Pleasures*, edited by Serge Gavronsky. Carbondale, IL: Southern Illinois University Press, 1997.
———. *Le plus simple appareil*. Paris: P.O.L, 1992.
———. *Nude*. Translated by Norma Cole. Berkeley, CA: Kelsey Street Press, 2001.
Roubaud, Jacques. *La Boucle*. Paris: Seuil 1993.
———. *The Loop*. Translated by Jeff Fort. Champaign and London: Dalkey Archive Press, 2009.
———. *Churchill 40*. Paris: © Éditions Gallimard, 2004.
———. *Ciel et terre et ciel et terre et ciel*. Paris: Argol éditions, 2009.
———. *Description du Projet*. Caen: Éditions NOUS, 2014.
———. *Dors précédé de Dire la poésie*. Paris: © Éditions Gallimard, 1981.
———. *Sleep Preceded by Saying Poetry*. Translated by Matthew B. Smith. Providence, RI and Paris: La Presse, 2019.
———. "Du Visible à l'invisible." In *Pour Max Milner*, Tome II, *La Nuit transparente*, edited by Stéphane Michaud. Paris: José Corti, 1988.
———. ϵ . Paris: Gallimard, 1967.
———. *Echanges de la lumière*. Paris: Éditions A. M. Métailié, 1990.
———. *Exchanges on Light*. Translated by Eleni Sikelianos. Iowa City and Paris: La Presse, 2009.
———. *Eros mélancolique*. With Anne Garétta. Paris: Bernard Grasset, 2009.
———. *La fenêtre veuve*. Courbevoie: Théâtre Typographique, 1996.
———. *La Fleur inverse. L'art des troubadours*. 2d ed. Paris: Les Belles Lettres, 2009.
———. *La Forme d'une ville change, hélas, plus vite que le coeur des humains*. Paris: © Éditions Gallimard, 1999.
———. *The Form of a City Changes, Alas, Faster than the Human Heart*. Translated by Keith Waldrop. Champaign, IL and London: Dalkey Archive Press, 2006.
———. *Graal fiction*. Paris: Gallimard, 1978.
———. *Le Grand incendie de Londres. Récit, avec incises et bifurcations (1985–87)*. Paris: "Fiction & Cie," © Éditions du Seuil 1989, n.e., 2009.
———. *The Great Fire of London*. Translated by Dominic Di Bernardi. Champaign and London: Dalkey Archive Press, 1991.
———. *Parc sauvage*. Paris: Seuil, 2008.
———. *La pluralité des mondes de Lewis*. Paris: © Éditions Gallimard, 1991.
———. *The Plurality of Worlds of Lewis*. Translated by Rosmarie Waldrop. Champaign and London: Dalkey Archive Press, 1995.
———. *Poésie, etcetera: ménage*. Paris: Editions Stock, 1995.
———. *Poetry, etcetera: Housecleaning*. Translated by Guy Bennett. Los Angeles: Green Integer 125, 2006.
———. *Poésie: Récit*. Paris: "Fiction & Compagnie," © Éditions du Seuil, 2000.
———. *Quelque chose noir*. Paris: © Éditions Gallimard, 1989.
———. *Some Thing Black*. Translated by Rosmarie Waldrop. Champaign and London: Dalkey Archive Press, 1990.

———. "*Si Quelque chose noir.*" UFR de Langues et Littératures de l'Universite de Poitiers, 1997.
———. *Sous le soleil: Vanité des vanités*. Paris: Bayard, 2004.
———. *Tridents*. Caen: Éditions NOUS, 2019.
———. *Le voyage d'hier*. In *Le voyage d'hiver/Le voyage d'hier*. Nantes: Le passeur, 1997.

Secondary Materials

POETRY

Albiach, Anne-Marie. ÉTAT. Paris: Mercure de France, 1971.
———. ÉTAT. *Translated by Keith Waldrop*. Windsor, VT: Awede, 1980.
des Forêts, Louis-René. *Les Mégères de la mer*. Paris: Mercure de France, 1995.
Gleize, Jean-Marie. *Le livre des cabanes*. Paris: Seuil, 2011.
Lacoue-Labarthe, Philippe. *Phrase*. Paris: Christian Bourgois, 2000.
———. *Phrase*. Translated by Leslie Hill. SUNY Press, 2018.
Quignard, Pascal. *Inter*. Paris: Argol, 2011.

PROSE

Alferi, Pierre. "Un accent de vérité." In *Brefs* 125-56. Paris: P.O.L, 2016.
Cole, Norma, ed. and trans. *Crosscut Universe: Writing on Writing from France*. Providence, RI: Burning Deck, 2000.
di Mano, Yves and Isabelle Garron. *Un nouveau monde. Poésies en France 1960-2010*. Paris: Editions Flammarion, 2017.

PROSE ON ROUBAUD

Cardonne-Arlyck, Elisabeth. "Jacques Roubaud: 'Je deviens guetteur, guetteur mélancolique.'" In *Véracités: Ponge, Jaccottet, Roubaud, Deguy*, 167-293. Paris: Editions Belin, 2009.
Cosenstein, Peter, ed. *Casebook on Jacques Roubaud's* The Great Fire of London. Champaign, IL and London: Dalkey Archive Press, 2000.
Di Bernardi, Dominic. "Afterward." In *The Great Fire of London*. Champaign, IL and London: Dalkey Archive Press, 1991.
Disson, Agnès, and Véronique Montémort, eds. *Jacques Roubaud, compositeur de mathématique et de poésie*. Paris: Editions Absalon, 2010.
Klebes, Martin. "Jacques Roubaud: Projecting Memory." In *Wittgenstein's Novels*. London and New York: Routledge, 2006.
Marsal, Florence. *Jacques Roubaud. Prose de la mémoire et errance chevaleresque*. Rennes: Presses Universitaires de Rennes, 2010.
Patron, Sylvie, and François Marmande, eds. *Pour éclairer* Quelque chose noir. Paris: Université Paris Diderot, 2008.
Poucel, Jean-Jacques. *Jacques Roubaud and the Invention of Memory*. Chapel Hill: University of North Carolina Press, 2006.

Puff, Jean-François. *Mémoire de la mémoire: Jacques Roubaud et la lyrique médiévale*. Paris: Editions Classiques Garnier, 2009.
——, with Jacques Roubaud. *Rencontre avec Jean-François Puff*. Paris: Argol 2008.
Smock, Ann. "Cloudy Roubaud." *Representations* 86 (Spring 2004): 141-74.

ON HOCQUARD

Fetzer, Glen W. *Emmanuel Hocquard and the Poetics of Negative Modernity*. Birmingham, AL: Summa Publications, 2004.
Maurel, Anne, Olivier Cadiot, Xavier Person, David Lespiau, Pascal Poyet, Gilles A. Tiberghien, Alain Cressan. "Dossier Emmanuel Hocquard," *Hippocampe* 14 (summer 2017): 72-113.
Petterson, James. "Ni frontière, ni limite: *Ma haie* d'Emmanuel Hocquard." *Ecritures Contemporaines* 7 (2003): 91-116.
Smock, Ann. "Geranium Logic: Intensity and Indifference in E. Hocquard." *Qui Parle* 21, no. 2 (2013): 27-59.
Tiberghien, Gilles. *Emmanuel Hocquard*. Paris: Seghers, 2006.

ON COLLOBERT

Daive, Jean, ed. *Danielle Collobert*. Centre international de poésie *Marseille*, 2006.
Stout, John C. "Writing (at) the Limits of Genre: Poetics of Transgression." *Symposium* 53, no. 4 (2000): 299-309.

ON JOUET

Motte, Warren, ed. *Substance* 96 (2001), special issue on Jacques Jouet.
Smock, Ann. "Everyday." *Esprit créateur* 49, no. 2 (Summer 2009): 62-76.

ON PORTUGAL

Alferi, Pierre. "La Poésie et les vieillards." In *Brefs*, 49-56. Paris: P.O.L, 2016.
Cosenstein, Peter. "Son et perception dans la poésie de Dominique Fourcade et Anne Portugal." *Contemporary French and Francophone Studies* 18, no. 2 (2015): 108-16.
Sheringham, Michael. "Dans le quotidien-immersion, résistance, liberté: R. Queneau, A. Portugal." Agnes Disson, Elisabeth Cardonne-Arlyck editors, *Ecritures Contemporaines* 7 (2003): 205-19.

INTERVIEWS WITH ANNE PORTUGAL

John C. Stout. *L'Énigme-poésie: Entretiens avec 21 poètes françaises*. Amsterdam: Rodopi, 2010.
Sophie L.Thurnberg. "Translating the Untranslatable: Conversations with Anne Portugal and Pierre Alferi." https://www.worldliteraturetoday.org/blog/interviews/translating-untranslatable.

Alain Veinstein. "Entretien avec A. Portugal." www.apresvillenoise.free.fr/av/bob/6.html.

"Poésie et méthode, entretien avec Anne Portugal et Marcel Cohen." https://franceculture.fr/emissions/poésie-et-ainsi-de-suite.

OTHER SECONDARY MATERIALS

Agamben, Giorgio. *The Coming Community*. Translated by Michael Hardt. Minneapolis: University of Minnesota Press, 1993.

——. *Potentialities*. Edited and translated (with Introduction) by Daniel Heller-Roazen. Stanford, CA: Stanford University Press, 1999.

——. *Stanzas*. Translated by Ronald L. Martinez. Minneapolis: University of Minnesota Press, 1993.

Lacoue-Labarthe, Philippe. *Agonie terminée, agonie interminable*. Edited by Aristide Bianchi and Leonid Khalamov. Paris: Editions Galilée, 2011.

——. *Ending and Unending Agony: On Maurice Blanchot*. Translated by Hannes Opelz. New York: Fordham University Press, 2015.

Blanchot, Maurice. *L'espace littéraire*. Paris: Gallimard, 1955.

——. *The Space of Literature*. Translated by Ann Smock. Lincoln and London: University of Nebraska Press, 1982.

——. *L'écriture du désastre*. Paris: Gallimard, 1980.

——. *The Writing of the Disaster*. Translated by Ann Smock. Lincoln and London: University of Nebraska Press, 1995.

——. *Le Pas au-delà*. Paris: Gallimard, 1973.

——. *The Step Not Beyond*. Translated by Lycette Nelson. SUNY Press, 1992.

——. *L'Attente l'oubli*. Paris: Gallimard, 1962.

——. *Awaiting Oblivion*. Translated by John Gregg. Lincoln and London: University of Nebraska Press, 1997.

Détienne, Marcel, and Jean-Pierre Vernant. *Les ruses de l'intelligence: la mètis des Grecs*. Paris: Flammarion, 1974.

——. *Cunning Intelligence in Greek Culture and Society*. Translated by Janet Lloyd. Atlantic Highlands, NJ: Humanities Press, 1976.

Lacoue-Labarthe, Philippe. *La Poésie comme expérience*. Paris: Christian Bourgois, 1986.

——. *Poetry as Experience*. Translated by Andrea Tarnowski. Stanford, CA: Stanford University Press, 1999.

Quignard, Pascal. *Le voeu de silence*. Montpellier: fata morgana, 1985.

——. *La Haine de la musique*. Editions Calmann-Lévy, 1996.

——. *The Hatred of Music*. Translated by Matthew Amos and Fredrik Rönnbäck. New Haven, CT and London: Yale University Press, 2016.

Wittgenstein, Ludwig. *Tractatus logico-philosophicus*. Whitefish, MT: Kessinger Publishing, 2011.

——. *Philosophical Investigations*. 4 th ed. West Sussex, UK: Wiley-Blackwell, 2009

INDEX

afterlife/second life, 155, 103, 10. *See also* ghosts/phantoms
Agamben, Giorgio, 5–7, 134, 152–53, 165–71, 173, 181, 187n17, 187n18, 212n1, 213n1, 213n2, n19n4, 228
Albiach, Anne-Marie, 2, 14, 46, 181
Algerian War, 9, 14
attribute, 5, 21–23, 31, 42–43, 50, 62–63, 66, 96, 98, 140–41, 153, 157, 166–68, 180–82. *See also* property

Beckett, Samuel, 49, 52, 55, 58, 68, 77, 121
being, 4, 7, 18, 23, 28, 31, 33, 42–43, 46–47, 49, 51–52, 60, 63–64, 66, 80, 103, 136, 140–41, 155, 164–66, 169, 172, 180–82, 184, 195n16; and not-being, 4, 42, 51, 59–60, 64, 66, 141, 165–66, 169, 196n16. *See also* exemplary being; nothing; whatever being; worldless being
Blanchot, Maurice, 7, 52, 55, 57, 68–70, 180, 182–83
blur, 114, 108, 163–65, 169, 171–72, 176, 184

Collobert, Danielle, 4, 10, 12–15, 43–4, 74–5, 80–82 passim, 87–89, 106, 190n37, 191n47; and birth, 47; and the impersonal, 80; and impossibility, 12, 13, 75, 85, 106; and the present, 82; and private language, 44
commonplace, 35, 43–47 passim, 119. *See also* communication
communication, 4, 34, 64–67 passim, 79, 184

death, 13, 28, 52–59 passim, 66, 69, 70, 72, 81–100 passim, 112, 117, 174. *See also* life
des Forêts, Louis-René, 58, 62, 70

enigma, 2, 12–13, 50, 70, 82–89 passim, 95, 98, 100, 102–4, 109, 160–61, 167, 186n4, 198n30
exemplary being, l69–71 passim, 219n4

gardens, 4, 51, 140–49 passim, 177–84 passim, 217n21, 219n2
ghosts/phantoms, 5, 17, 140, 152, 155

229

guilt, 50–51, 183. *See also* innocence

Heller-Roazen, Daniel, 187n21
Hocquard, Emmanuel, 1–14 passim, 20–23, 31, 34–52, 55–70, 78–80, 122, 124, 140–42, 147, 149–52, 154, 156, 165–69, 175–76, 180–83, 185n1, 192n49, 197n23, 198n30; and attributes/properties, 21, 23, 35, 41, 42, 63; and being/not-being, 23, 31–32, 41–43, 46–52 passim, 60, 63, 64, 66, 140, 141, 166, 169, 181, 182; and birth, 46, 50, 56–70 passim, 183; and communication, 34, 64, 66, 67, 79; and elegy, 47–48, 62, 169; and enigmas, 2, 47, 48, 50, 70; and guilt, 50, 51, 183; and indifference, 21, 23, 62, 66, 67, 141, 175, 176, 183, 184; and innocence, 62, 181, 182; and intonation, 7, 34, 35, 40–47 passim, 55, 62, 65, 183, 188n26; and life, 32, 45, 46, 51, 56–69 passim, 78, 80; and loss, 43, 46–48 passim, 67–68; and memory, 34, 152, 156; on nudity, 140, 141, 149–52 passim, 166–67, 169, 175–76, 199n33; on photography, 140, 151, 152, 185n1; on private language, 34, 36, 41; on secrets, 63–64, 66, 67, 78, 180–81, 183; and simplicity, 67, 80, 140, 144, 150, 181; and tautology, 22–23, 31–32, 40, 64, 66, 79, 166, 181, 199n30, 201n17; and Wittgenstein, 4, 23, 32, 38, 50, 62, 66, 186n3

identity, 4, 17–18, 20, 31, 86–87, 98–103 passim, 164, 165, 168, 171, 184
impossible, 5, 10, 12, 29–33, 37, 43, 85, 87, 92, 93–94, 109, 118, 120–21, 123
impotence, 6, 124, 166, 184. *See also* potentiality
indifference, 6, 7, 23, 62, 63, 67, 91, 141, 150, 173, 176–76, 180–84 passim. *See also* attributes; neutral
innocence, 62, 181–82

Jouet, Jacques, 4, 10, 12, 118, 119–25, 129–31, 177, 205n9, 207n15, 208n5, 209n6, n8, 210n10; on circulation, 122; on everyday poems, 121, 123, 127, 131; and exhaustion, 126; and form, 119–27; and Mallarmé, 127, 209n6; and the Oulipo, 119–20, 205n9; on potentiality, 118–20, 124–25; on quantity v. quality, 122, 125; on words as social animals, 119

Lacoue-Labarthe, Philippe, 52, 56–8 passim, 62, 68, 70, 200n3
life. *See* afterlife/second life; death; secret
Lucey, Michael, 188n26

medium, 66, 131, 167, 175–77 passim, 180. *See also* milieu; mediation
melancholy, 3, 62, 68, 136, 146, 212n1
memory, 3, 9, 25, 27–28, 33–34, 53–54, 77–78, 82, 96, 101, 109, 134–36, 139, 152, 160–61, 170, 184, 196n16, 202n5
milieu, 42, 65, 143–34, 107, 177–80 passim, 220n3
modern, 119–24 passim, 153, 173, 205n3

neutral, 7, 21, 62, 66, 68, 140, 152, 166, 175, 180
nudity, 4, 96, 140–41, 149–53, 166–67, 169, 175–76, 199n33. *See also* neutral; photography
nothing, 2, 5, 6, 11–13, 21, 23, 26, 28–31, 34, 36, 41–43, 47, 50–51, 54, 57–58, 68, 70, 76, 78, 84, 87–91, 97, 117, 118, 127, 129, 131, 133, 152, 165, 184, 217n20

Portugal, Anne, 4, 10, 140–50, 175–84, 215n11, 216n16, n18, n19, 219n2, 220n3; and Apollinaire, 146, 178, 180, 216n18; on approximation, 177–78, 219n2, 220n2; and form, 142–49 passim; on gardens, 4, 140, 143–49 passim, 177, 80, 182, 184, 217n21, n2; and indifference, 150, 180, 182, 184; and Hocquard, 140–41, 149–50, 180; and milieux, 143–44, 167, 177–80 passim, 220n3; and nudity, 4, 140, 149–50; and Roubaud, 141, 142; and secrets,

149, 180; and simplicity, 140, 150, 180, 182, 184; on vigilance, 149, 180, 182
potentiality, 5–7, 18–20, 124–26, 134, 153, 162, 195n14
private language, 5, 33–34, 36, 41, 43–44, 197n18
property, 31, 42–43, 63–64, 141, 171, 181

Quignard, Pascal, 52, 55–56, 58, 62, 27

Raquel, 14, 21, 23, 45, 62, 194n6
Royet-Journoud, Claude, 14, 23, 68, 175–76, 180
Roubaud, Jacques, 2–6, 8–13, 14–15, 17–20, 24–30, 33–36, 52–55, 71–78, 81–106, 109–18, 125–29, 133–42, 151–65, 167–74, 184, 191n42, n44, 193n2, 194n5, 195n16, 202n5, 203n8, 205n9, 207n15, 219n2; and afterlife/second life, 53, 109, 102–3, 155; and black, 2–3, 18–20, 26, 28, 34, 36, 54, 82–85, 87, 89, 92–107 passim, 114, 117, 133–34, 136, 139, 151, 157, 161, 164–65, 167, 184, 191n44, 194n5; and David Lewis, 5, 17, 29, 152; and dream, 28, 53–54, 71–72, 77, 88, 90, 92, 101–5, 109–10, 137–39, 152, 158–61; and enigma, 2, 12–13, 54, 74, 82, 84–89, 95, 98, 100, 102–4, 106, 109, 133, 160–61, 167, 186n4, 189n31; and form, 5, 8–9, 28, 53, 84, 86, 96–97, 100–103, 112–13, 116–17, 125–26, 128–29, 139–40, 153, 155, 157–58, 160, 164–65, 167–70, 172–73, 203n3, 210n8; and grail, 99–101, 104, 129, 206n14; and identity, 4, 18, 20, 32, 86–87, 98–100, 102–3, 164–65, 168, 171, 184; and the impossible, 5, 12, 29–33, 85, 87, 92–94, 109, 118, 162, 167, 173–74, 191n44; and Mallarmé, 25, 129, 172, 214n8; on melancholy, 3, 136, 212n1, 218n22; and memory, 3, 27–28, 33–34, 53–54, 77–78, 82, 101, 109, 134–36, 139, 160–61, 170, 184, 196n16, 202n5, 205n9; and Nicholas of Cusa, 5, 152, 165, 169; and the Oulipo, 14–15, 128, 207n11; and Perec, 72, 84, 100, 102, 155; and potentiality, 5–6, 119, 126, 134, 153, 162; and private language, 8, 33–34; and Pseudo-Dionysius, 2, 17; and quest, 53, 78, 86–89, 98, 100–103, 110, 118, 129, 135, 154, 158, 161; on sonnet, 8–9, 125–26, 128–29; and stateless beings, 5, 195n16; on time, 54, 78, 81–83, 87, 95, 99, 101–6, 109, 115–6, 136, 138, 154–55, 163; and Troubadour poetry, 27, 35–36, 53–54, 90, 96, 128, 137, 139, 174, 124n8, 207n14, 218n22; and Wittgenstein, 4–6, 30, 32–33, 128, 152, 186n3; and worldless beings, 29, 109, 136, 155, 172, 195n16; and World War II, 9, 53, 154–55. *See also* Agamben, exemplary being, whatever being

secret, 4, 7, 63–64, 66–68, 78, 149–50, 168, 180, 181, 183, 221n4
simplicity, 67, 80, 140, 150, 180, 181

vigilance, 149, 180, 182–83

whatever being, 5, 7, 153, 168–69

Index / 231

www.ingramcontent.com/pod-product-compliance
Lightning Source LLC
Chambersburg PA
CBHW020651230426
43665CB00008B/392